# The Talent Thief

Minneapolis

First Edition



Some names have been changed to protect privacy. The events described are based on the author's recollections and observations over fifteen years of coaching.

10 9 8 7 6 5 4 3 2 1
ISBN: 978-1-962834-79-7

Cover design by Ted Kroeten
Book design by Gary Lindberg

# Praise for *The Talent Thief*

"Joy, ownership, self-organization, problem solving, creativity and intrinsic motivation. These are the foundation of building mastery and long-term interest, yet our modern youth sports system often provides the opposite of these essential building blocks. Ted Kroeten and Joy of the People have helped children rediscover childhood free play, and this book will tell you exactly how he did it, and why. It is an essential read for any coach who truly wants to change the game and give sports back to our kids."

John O'Sullivan, Founder of Changing the Game Project

"*The Talent Thief* should be a mandatory read for anyone who truly cares about the player development pipeline within youth soccer. Nobody under 12 should have "elite", or "travel" associated with their level of play, nothing beyond "player". They should play for fun and truly learn the game. Ted's book specifically illustrates through his innovative Joy of the People facility, how the game should be learned."

Skip Gilbert CEO | Consultant | Former CEO of US Youth Soccer

"The book I wish I wrote. *The Talent Thief* is a narrative exploration of athlete development providing real world, long-term examples mixed with sufficient academic rigor to be more than an anecdote. Ted Kroeten has provided the framework to revolutionize our sports development system if we have the sense to pay attention."

Brian McCormick, PhD, International Basketball Coach | Founder, Playmakers League | Author of *20 Hacks for the 24-Hour Athlete*

"I've been a teacher and coach for 25 years, from kindergarten physical education to heading an NCAA lacrosse program. In that time, only a few individuals or ideas have fundamentally shifted my perspective. Ted's work at Joy of the People is one of them—it's forever changed how I view coaching best practices. By defining skill and talent through joyful, play-based approaches and showing how they can be cultivated, Ted lays out a blueprint that could profoundly transform youth sports and address its biggest pitfalls. Drawing from linguistics, neuroscience, evolutionary biology, psychology, and motor learning—interwoven with fascinating case studies and heartwarming anecdotes—Ted has crafted a book that should be required reading for anyone who interacts with young athletes."

Brian Kelly Teacher/Coach | Former pro player Lacrosse

"*The Talent Thief* is a refreshing and much-needed perspective on youth soccer in an era too often dominated by money, politics, and misplaced priorities. Ted Kroeten challenges the conventional path and reminds us of what truly fuels player development—passion, creativity, and the freedom to play. Drawing from both personal experience and a deep understanding of the game, Ted makes a compelling case for returning to environments where young athletes can thrive naturally. This book is an essential read for any parent seeking a more meaningful and effective approach to developing their child's love and talent for soccer."

Jim Froslid, former US Soccer executive and Wisconsin Badgers captain

# The Talent Thief

## Underloading, The Language of Movement and the Search for the Perfect Game

*Ted Kroeten*

Minneapolis

For Colleen, who saw

# Table of Contents


Praise for The Talent Thief . . . . . . . . . . . . . . . . . . . . . . . . . . . i

Foreword . . . . . . . . . . . . . . . . . . . . . . . . . . . . . . . . . . . x

Author's Note . . . . . . . . . . . . . . . . . . . . . . . . . . . . . . .xiii

Chapter 1: The Perfect Crime . . . . . . . . . . . . . . . . . . . . . . . . 1

Interlude: Marco . . . . . . . . . . . . . . . . . . . . . . . . . . . . . . 7

Chapter 2: The Swamp . . . . . . . . . . . . . . . . . . . . . . . . . . . 9

Interlude: What Happened To Play? . . . . . . . . . . . . . . . . . . 25

Chapter 3: The War . . . . . . . . . . . . . . . . . . . . . . . . . . . . 31

Interlude: Emmanuel . . . . . . . . . . . . . . . . . . . . . . . . . . . 43

Chapter 4: The Vote . . . . . . . . . . . . . . . . . . . . . . . . . . . 45

Interlude: Duncan . . . . . . . . . . . . . . . . . . . . . . . . . . . . 59

Chapter 5: The Search . . . . . . . . . . . . . . . . . . . . . . . . . . 61

Interlude: Noah . . . . . . . . . . . . . . . . . . . . . . . . . . . . . 71

Chapter 6: The Landscape . . . . . . . . . . . . . . . . . . . . . . . . 73

Interlude: The Manual . . . . . . . . . . . . . . . . . . . . . . . . . . 83

Chapter 7: The Invasion Of The Body Snatchers . . . . . . . 87

Interlude: Lioul . . . . . . . . . . . . . . . . . . . . . . . . . . . . . 95

Chapter 8: The Spandrels . . . . . . . . . . . . . . . . . . . . . . . . 97

Interlude: Bennett . . . . . . . . . . . . . . . . . . . . . . . . . . . 107

Chapter 9: The Professor . . . . . . . . . . . . . . . . . . . . . . . 109

Interlude: Dare . . . . . . . . . . . . . . . . . . . . . . . . . . . . . 123

Chapter 10: The Confession . . . . . . . . . . . . . . . . . . . . . . . 125
Chapter 11: The Discovery . . . . . . . . . . . . . . . . . . . . . . . . 139
Interlude: Khalid . . . . . . . . . . . . . . . . . . . . . . . . . . . . 153
Chapter 12: The Science . . . . . . . . . . . . . . . . . . . . . . . . . 157
Interlude: Edison . . . . . . . . . . . . . . . . . . . . . . . . . . . . 167
Chapter 13: The Proof . . . . . . . . . . . . . . . . . . . . . . . . . . 171
Interlude: Mika . . . . . . . . . . . . . . . . . . . . . . . . . . . . . 185
Chapter 14: The Underload Index . . . . . . . . . . . . . . . . . . 187
Interlude: The Gift Of Play . . . . . . . . . . . . . . . . . . . . . . 195
Chapter 15: The Monarch Rules . . . . . . . . . . . . . . . . . . . . 197
Interlude: Sean . . . . . . . . . . . . . . . . . . . . . . . . . . . . . 207
Chapter 16: The Environment . . . . . . . . . . . . . . . . . . . . . 211
Interlude: ACE . . . . . . . . . . . . . . . . . . . . . . . . . . . . . . 229
Chapter 17: The Game . . . . . . . . . . . . . . . . . . . . . . . . . . 231
Epilogue: Playing At Life . . . . . . . . . . . . . . . . . . . . . . . 247
The Tuesday Manual . . . . . . . . . . . . . . . . . . . . . . . . . . . 253
Acknowledgments . . . . . . . . . . . . . . . . . . . . . . . . . . . . 255
Questions . . . . . . . . . . . . . . . . . . . . . . . . . . . . . . . . . 259
Glossary . . . . . . . . . . . . . . . . . . . . . . . . . . . . . . . . . . 263
Notes . . . . . . . . . . . . . . . . . . . . . . . . . . . . . . . . . . . . 269
About the Author . . . . . . . . . . . . . . . . . . . . . . . . . . . . 293

# Foreword

Youth sports in the United States is in a state of multiple crises. Participation has become hyper-stratified along socioeconomic lines. The system is increasingly organized in a manner that models professional structures and professional norms—defined by intensity, private commercialization, increased parent labor, heightened rates of injuries, anxieties about securing selective college admission via sport, and more official tournaments, showcases, and "elite" divisions. At the same time, steady reductions of public investment in recreational youth sports coincide with the decline of unstructured, youth-directed pick-up play in parks, gyms, and streets. The consequences include social inequity, burnout, and an erosion of fun in sport, alongside the normalization of coaching practices that separate competitive team success from general athlete welfare and positive social development. Within the world of men's U.S. soccer, frustrations are aimed at why we don't develop players with the right technique, creativity, and vision, and fail to succeed at the highest levels of international competition. Often, these criticisms remain at the level of discourse—a podcast, an op-ed, a long-form video essay. What is less common are the people trying to disrupt these dynamics by creating something new, something vibrant, and something grounded in the foundational reasons why so many people in history have learned to love to dribble a ball, make a pass, run fast, or score a goal.

Joy of the People is a special place where such a needed disruption occurs. It happens through creating a community where creativity and fun are centered and cherished. It happens through trusting young people, a deep belief in the positive power of sport and play, and a motivating purpose that aims to keep the game going for all who participate. And it is rooted in an expansive understanding of talent and development.

I was lucky enough to spend time with Ted, coaches, kids, and parents at Joy of the People as a volunteer, grant-writer, and occasional "coach" for seven years. During this time, there were countless ways to see the efficacy of Joy of the People's approach. The most obvious evidence was through how Joy Kids played the game. Whether it be in free play or an organized game, kids of all ages and ability levels took playful risks on the field, and often with big grins on their faces. This could look like a goalkeeper deciding to dribble out with the ball for thirty yards in an 11v11 match; an 8-year-old experimenting with a rainbow flick during free play; or seeing a high school-aged player move through a game with their own unique artistic soccer style—their own unique movements, ball rolls, feints, and calmness.

In terms of coaching behavior, coaches at Joy of the People do not center themselves and represent a counterbalance to our sports culture that venerates the coach who meticulously directs, strategizes, and organizes all aspects of the sport. In official games, coaches like Ace, Saul, and Jen were always calm and spoke with kids as equals while opposing coaches constantly barked out directions or loudly responded to nearly every action on the field. In free play sessions and camps, coaches were facilitators of energetic and exciting play. They actively embraced being resources for the kids, mentors, and fellow play collaborators.

One moment will always stick with me. A group of Joy of the People families did a group trip to the 2015 Women's World Cup in Canada. Prior to a double-header match, thousands of soccer fans, including many youth clubs, were hanging out and tailgating outside of the stadium. The only kids in the entire venue who decided to get their own pick-up game going were the boys and girls at JOTP. Coaches and parents joined in this mixed-age, co-ed game, and we all played for around thirty minutes before entering the stadium. I did not see any other young person or adult outside the stadium playing with a soccer ball. This little pick-up game matters because it's an example of how JOTP's play-forward and kid-centered model encourages an active lifelong love of the sport that is not dependent on adults to organize the game.

*The Talent Thief* is a gift to all of us who are trying to figure out how to participate in and create social environments where fun and creativity are crucial, and intertwined with the opportunity to learn and develop skill. Ted has combined practice and theory for decades, and as such he can draw bold and needed links between a five-year-old Hula-Hooping next to other kids blasting a soft volleyball at a goal, the importance of music and timing to keeping pick-up games lively for a group of twenty, and the need for eighteen-year-olds spending afternoons playing pick-up soccer with twelve-year-olds. Ted's passion for learning, love of play, and desire to support young people has been channeled into decades of everyday action. Through humility, diligence, and fun, he has become fluent in the language of play and facilitated a community where youth of all ability can be artistic, athletically inspiring, make deep social bonds, and develop a love of the game that can be transmitted to others in their life. Striving for a utopian play and sport environment through soccer and an emphasis on pick-up play may seem like naïve nostalgia given the current state of youth sports and our collective assumptions about competitive success. But its lessons and practices can be applied to any sport, and more importantly help anyone who is trying to enjoy learning, master the language of play, and build healthy, meaningful, and fun communities.

—Alex Manning
Lecturer and Research Scholar in Sociology
Yale University

# Author's Note

Some names in this book have been changed. The kids who appear in these pages were children when I started watching them, and they didn't sign up to be used as evidence. The ones who wanted to be here—Z, Dare, and a few others—you'll recognize. The rest I've protected. The events are real. The outcomes are real.

I didn't set out to write a book about science. I set out to understand something I kept seeing—kids who learned more from an hour of unsupervised play with their friends than from a month of organized training. Not sometimes. Every time. There's something happening in those games that we've spent fifty years trying to coach around, and the more we've coached around it, the more we've lost.

That observation sent me searching—into linguistics, evolutionary biology, game theory, neuroscience—not because I was looking for a theory, but because I was looking for an answer. And that answer kept pointing the same direction. Back to the street. Back to the sandlot. Back to the frozen pond with no adults and no whistles and the kind of freedom that turns out to be the most powerful learning environment ever invented.

I believe underloading and kinetic linguistics are real. Not as metaphors, not as useful fictions, but as mechanisms that explain things the current frameworks can't—and that, if taken seriously, could change how we develop players at every level. The Underload Index is a testable hypothesis. The acquisition model is a testable hypothesis. I'd rather be wrong and specific than right and vague.

This book is written for anyone who has ever watched a child play and felt something the coaches couldn't measure. You don't need a background in the science to follow the argument. But if you have one, I hope the framework gives you something worth testing.

The truest development isn't the fastest path to the top. It's the one that leaves the player more themselves than when they started.

The purpose of this book is to make a compelling case for that—compelling enough that someone opens up the dead-end street, organizes the neighborhood, finds the empty lot, turns off the screen. The kids are waiting. They have always been waiting. They just need a story. And what do we say when we hear a good story? We say that story really moved me. In this book, that's not a metaphor. It's the whole argument.

# Chapter 1:

# The Perfect Crime

## Belgrade, 1976

A stadium holds its breath.

The European Championship final has gone to penalties. Czechoslovakia and West Germany, deadlocked after one hundred and twenty minutes, now stand at four to three. One kick left. Antonín Panenka walks toward the spot.

In goal waits Sepp Maier—one of the greatest keepers of his generation. Cat-quick reflexes, arms that seem to span the entire net, a wall built from ten thousand repetitions. Panenka is slight, mustachioed, more Inspector Clouseau than hero. He has none of Maier's physical gifts. Everyone knows this. Maier knows this.

The referee blows his whistle.

Panenka's run-up screams power—hips opening left, eyes flicking to the corner. Maier reads the story and dives. Panenka, gently, chips the ball straight down the middle. It floats into the empty space as Maier sprawls helpless in the wrong corner.

Czechoslovakia are champions.

## The Martian

Here is the question no one asked that night in Belgrade:

What team was Sepp Maier playing for?

Think about it. A Martian, visiting Earth for the first time, lands in that stadium. It has never seen soccer. It doesn't know the rules. It simply watches what happens.

The Martian sees a man approach a ball. It sees another man standing in front of a net. It watches the first man move his body in a particular way—and then it watches the second man throw himself out of the goal. At first, the Martian is baffled. Why would the defender evacuate the space he's supposed to protect? Why would he clear a path for the ball? It looks like Maier is playing for the other team.

But this Martian has visited many planets. It speaks three thousand languages—some with words, some with colors, some with magnetic pulses, some with movement. On every planet where creatures must coordinate and deceive, they develop ways to author movement and a response in each other. And as it watches the replay, something clicks.

*Oh*, the Martian thinks. *I know what this is.*

*This is a language.* Panenka wasn't just kicking a ball. He was speaking. His hips, his eyes, his run-up formed a sentence. And Maier, fluent in the same grammar, had no choice but to obey.

## Belgrade, 2016

The Euro qualifiers. Portugal versus Serbia. I had come to watch a player named Ricardinho, a tiny man from Gondomar who had been named Best Player in the World a record six times. They called him *O Mágico*.

I sat close to the court. Futsal is played in a phone booth—forty meters by twenty, tight spaces, ball moving fast as light. No space to hide.

And then it happened.

Ricardinho received the ball with a defender in front of him. He lifted the ball, pushed it outside, flicked it behind the defender's back, ran around him, and volleyed into the corner. The defender froze. The crowd erupted.

I had seen it before—forty years earlier, on video, in this same city. Different sport. Different decade. Same language.

## Underloading

Here's the disturbing truth I finally understood in that Belgrade arena: in the moment of the goal, the defender helped Ricardinho score.

Not consciously. His own body decided for him. Ricardinho told the defender's muscles a story, and they obeyed. The better he was at reacting, the more completely he was fooled.

Like a matador with a cape and a bull compelled to charge: the attacker authors the movement, the defender answers.

This is what the Martian recognized. This is what connects Panenka to Ricardinho to a kid nutmegging his friend in a favela, a hockey player deking on a frozen pond, my own son slotting home the winner against the undefeated giants.

There's a word for it: underloading.

Overloading is doing more work—run faster, hit harder, try harder. Underloading is the opposite: make others do the work for you. Panenka let Maier's own reflexes score the goal. Ricardinho told the defender to pick a card—any card—then vanished behind him. The opponent moves. The ball finds its own path. When it's over, no one's quite sure what happened. The underloader leaves no trace.

This book is about underloading. How it works. Why it wins. And why the system that's supposed to develop talent keeps coaching it out of kids before they ever learn to speak.

## Free Play

I wasn't in a lab. I was at a rec center in St. Paul.

For fifteen years I watched the same kids from age six through college. That longitudinal view gave me something no controlled study has: the complete arc. Darwin had his boat. I had a gym.

A small soccer program the establishment considered a backwater—or worse, a threat. No prestigious academy. No federation support. Just kids playing, year after year, mopping floors, moving goals, sweeping the gym, cleaning bathrooms, clearing roof drains. They may not have needed instruction—but they did need the water fountain to work.

I saw who washed out and who emerged. I saw what the system predicted—and what it missed. What I saw was not simply a collection of talented individuals. It was a language. Spoken by bodies. Acquired through play. Invisible to anyone looking for skill instead of conversation.

## The Cult of Overload

I didn't always believe this.

For years I was a true believer in what I now call the Cult of Overload. I thought talent was manufactured through deliberate practice: more hours, more intensity, more structure, early specialization. I ran youth soccer programs, preached the gospel of development, and built player sheets with ten thousand checkboxes. I sent kids through the machine.

Then I started noticing the cracks.

They looked like Zlatan Ibrahimović, who came from the concrete courts of Rosengård, not an academy. They looked like the data from Dinamo Zagreb, where nearly all of the club's ten best players in history joined after age fourteen—products of street soccer. They looked like Ricardinho, too small for the eleven-a-side machine, left to invent himself in school gyms. They looked like my own son Z, written off at eight for wandering behind the action, yet learning something in free play that drills could never teach.

The cracks became a chasm. When I fell through, I found myself in a different world—one where the science of language acquisition, evolutionary biology, and game theory all pointed to the same heretical conclusion: the way we train young athletes is backward.

The search took me from futsal courts in Belgrade and Cali to coaching courses in São Paulo and Amsterdam, from academies in Porto and Jundiaí to research conferences in Finland and Manchester, from the St. Paul gym to street soccer all over the world. Everywhere I looked, I found the same thing. And it took me through something harder than any of that: the years of not knowing if I was right. The demotion. The sleepless nights. The parents who pulled their kids. Watching Z and the others grow up in that gym, carrying something I couldn't yet prove.

And it took me, finally, to a mezzanine in Kansas City, watching a laptop screen from five hundred miles away, as my son and his buddies faced the undefeated giants.

"C'mon, Z," I whispered to no one.

Would he speak?

# Interlude:

# Marco

From the age of nine, Marco was my right hand. Not because I appointed him. Because he simply was. The way certain kids arrive already knowing their role—not the leader, but the leader all the same.

He was the accountant of our chaos. The risk manager. The kid who, when someone floated the idea of raiding the tournament kitchen, would offer that quiet smile and a single raised eyebrow that said: let's think about this. You didn't need a lecture. You just needed Marco.

On road trips he ran the headcounts. He found suitable places for everyone's towels. He kept track of the rabble with the calm efficiency of a man who had been keeping track of things his whole life—because he had.

He lived at the same complex as Lioul and Emmanuel, and later his family moved to a trailer park up north, where Danielson lived too. I would drop them off in a Suburban full of kids and get pulled over regularly by police who couldn't figure out what we were doing coming in and out of there. I tried to explain it once.

"Free play," I said.

The officer looked at me. "Free play? What's that?"

A pause.

"Oh—you mean soccer."

Yes. I meant soccer.

Marco could have explained it. He could have explained most things.

When he played, it was entirely for the team. No flourish, no appetite for glory. Just that smile—the one that told you the risk management was handled, the midfield was covered, and everyone's back was being watched simultaneously. He played with a kind of devotion that most people spend their whole careers trying to coach into kids and never quite get there.

He took care of the midfield. He took care of his parents. He took care of Joy and the other kids and his siblings—all of it running through him like current through a wire, quiet and constant.

He's a man now. He still stops by the office sometimes. And when he does, the room feels slightly more organized than it did before he walked in.

He knows he always did his best. He's right.

# Chapter 2:

# The Swamp

## Haunted

All my life I have been haunted by play.

From as early as I can remember, I played.

Boxing with my mom and dad in our Lowry Avenue kitchen—heavy brown leather gloves we could barely lift. Dad stood over a stool with my older brother Bill, whispering in his corner, the black-and-white linoleum our second-story "ring." I could see Dad giving instruction: jab, duck, move. I felt robbed. Mom just laughed. Where was my advice?

She rang a wooden spoon off a pan, and the four- and five-year-old heavyweights touched gloves and went at it.

Baseball in the backyard. Tennis with Mom and Dad in a converted roller rink, steel racquets catching light from the disco ball. Pool and ping-pong in the basement. With seven kids, there was never a shortage of competition.

One winter I took on a singular mission: build a luge run.

Six-foot-high banks of pure ice. Hours hauling snow, filling buckets, shaping curves like Michelangelo in the below-zero dark. When it was finished, it was too scary to send anyone down. So we sent a forty-pound bag of silica sand. It flew twenty feet in the air off one of the lower banks, exploding against a giant elm.

And then there were the neighborhood games. Football in the fall, hockey in the winter, basketball in the spring, baseball and tennis in the summer. When it got dark, kick the can or capture the flag. Always different numbers, ages, and abilities. We played in vacant lots, and when a house went up, we moved—sliding to the next patch of rough ground with the ease of Zoilo Versalles fielding a grounder. During an improbable Minnesota Twins run one summer, we tramped down a patch of wetland behind the neighborhood. We carved out a stadium—eight-foot cattails lining the "walls" of our own private world. Pre-*Field of Dreams*, we built it ourselves.

"It's like a crop circle," said my brother Bill. "What's that?" we all asked. "A coordinate system for aliens." We were all staring skyward when Rob shrugged, "I hope they bring some good balls."

We called it the Swamp.

We played there morning till night. The cattails swayed like a crowd. The ground was soft in spring, hard-packed by August. When it rained, we played in the mud. When "Sugar, Sugar" played on the transistor radio, we danced. When mosquitoes swarmed, we played faster. When our mothers called for dinner, we negotiated: five more minutes, ten more minutes, next score wins.

"What's that smell?" my mom would say when I came through the door.

"Go hose yourself down."

The neighbors complained so much—kids disappearing into "the swamp," as if the earth had swallowed us—that the next summer, the city built a park there.

A proper park. Flat grass. Fenced backstops. Clean lines.

I don't remember ever playing on that field.

## The Best Athlete

My best friend was Debbie.

She was the best athlete in the neighborhood. Not the best girl athlete—the best, period. Faster than most of the boys. Tougher than all of us.

The local Little League wouldn't let her play. I brought her to practices anyway. Sometimes the head coach wasn't there and the assistant—a former Yankees catcher; we knew because Debbie had his card—would run things.

"I have your card!" she'd say, and he'd toss her a bat.

One day she hit three home runs in batting practice.

One fall she broke her leg jumping off a garage roof to retrieve a baseball stuck in the gutter.

That cast turned out to be perfect for ice hockey. She'd plant that plaster leg in front of the net like a wall, daring anyone to shoot high. We played on the frozen pond at the park. Debbie stopped everything.

We were a tight, trusting group. We didn't think in those terms; we just showed up, played, figured out teams, and went home when it got dark. Community by accident.

But all good things end.

I remember running home crying when Debbie told me her family was moving. I was twelve. She was my best friend, and she was leaving. The world I knew was starting to crack.

As I moved into high school, and even when I came home from college, I always visited the park—the proper park they'd built where our swamp used to be. Each year there were fewer kids.

The cattails were gone. The magic was gone. The kids were somewhere else—or nowhere.

## Polyathletes

I played five sports in high school. I was offered both tennis and soccer scholarships. I didn't play organized hockey until college, when some Canadians found out I was from Minnesota and insisted I try out. I made the team. Eventually I captained it. First-team all-region.

In soccer I captained the Minnesota select team for eight years. Went to two regional camps, one national camp. Played for the Minnesota Thunder, the highest level in the state. Kept playing as long as my body let me.

All this with no formal coaching until high school.

But I wasn't unusual. When I first played with a soccer ball—as a high-school sophomore—it was the first time for many of us. We were multi-sport athletes. Polyathletes.

Like a polyglot enjoys the subtleties of new languages, we were fascinated by this new sport, this new grammar of movement.

Our right back was a track star and state champion sailor. Our center forward was the baseball shortstop who ended up kicking for Oklahoma football. Our best player was an English tennis ace whose favorite sport was something called field hockey. Two Colombian brothers were competitive bikers.

They were also the ones who showed me you don't kick the ball with your toe—you use your laces.

"Wait," I said. "That's impossible."

It wasn't impossible. It was just a different language. And they spoke it because they'd grown up speaking it—in the streets and parks of Colombia, in games that looked a lot like our swamp.

## The Internationals

I arrived on the Minnesota amateur scene at the right time.

The Kicks—Minnesota's brief NASL professional phenomenon—had folded as quickly as they'd appeared. With the pro path gone, everyone just played because they loved it.

The Minnesota Soccer Association blossomed into one of the best amateur leagues in the country. Teams built on cultural connections—Germans, Mexican-Americans, college kids, Brits, Iranians—each with its own system and flavor. Every game felt like the highlight of the week.

I played for the Internationals—named for what we were. Players from Brazil, Mexico, Honduras, Cameroon, Morocco, Nigeria, Denmark, Germany. Our Scottish goalkeeper had the foulest mouth on the team, but it didn't matter—with that accent, no one could understand his English anyway.

These players hadn't come out of American academies. They'd been grown in streets and parks and dirt lots around the world. They had acquired fluency through play, not drills.

When they took the field against American kids who had done everything "right"—travel teams, showcases, professional coaching—the difference was obvious.

The Americans could execute.

The Internationals could play.

Franklin, our Cameroonian coach whose favorite movie was *Patton,* saw this before anyone.

"You can't form a team from just anywhere!" people said. "They'll never be a team."

Franklin brushed that idea aside. "A good player is a good player, no matter where he's from."

Victor—a Brazilian who would become my best friend and co-conspirator in everything that followed—was his first recruit. I stayed with the Harlequins. In their first First Division game, the Internationals beat us four to one and almost never lost again. I joined a year later.

That group became the backbone of the first Minnesota Thunder, and the foundation of the state select team that dominated regional play and eventually national play. In 1990, at Tampa Stadium—the "Big Sombrero"—the Minnesota Select team won the Donaldson Cup. With no pro leagues in the US at the time, this was the top prize in American soccer. In our first game we beat Maryland three to one. Maryland had eight players with US Men's National team caps.

"Ted," Victor said before kickoff, "I've never played under the lights before."

He was, as usual, the best player on the field.

Those players were byproducts of vibrant local leagues in Minnesota in the '70s and '80s.

## The Triple Crown

In 2005, we won the Triple Crown. We all chased the two big prizes. There was the League and the Minnesota Cup. But there was also a third prize: the Thunder Bay Tournament, up in Canada, against the best amateur teams on the continent.

No Minnesota team had ever won all three. The Triple Crown.

I remember Buzz Lagos, legendary coach of the Minnesota Thunder, tracking the amateur scene like any good soccer junkie.

"You guys haven't lost a game all year," he said, "and your midfield is forty-seven and forty-six."

My midfield partner was Sergei Gotsmanov—one of the supersonic Soviets who finished second to Holland in the 1988 Euros. His sons Sasha and Andrei played with us too—immense fluent talents who moved with grace and care.

I played every minute of every game that year. I was forty-seven. The local paper did a story on me. The reporter asked, "Do you have any hobbies?"

"No," I said. "Just soccer—and how to get better."

When I read it later, I was embarrassed. But it was true.

## Thunder Bay

Thunder Bay was a whole other country—which, of course, it was. But it felt like something rarer than that. It felt like a place that hadn't decided yet to be complicated.

The beer store was called "the Beer Store." A man with a microphone called out your order—case of Molson, case of Labatt's—and it came rolling out of a slot in the warehouse wall. Those were your two choices. Nobody seemed to find this strange.

Getting there was half the magic: north on Highway 61, along the pine cliffs of Lake Superior, one of the great American road trips. That drive always came at the end of a long summer season, and for me it felt like redemption and possibility in equal measure—and some of the best soccer in North America waiting at the other end. From 1981 to 2005 I was there every Labor Day.

One year we drove up in a van singing "The Wreck of the Edmund Fitzgerald" the whole way, twenty-plus nationalities packed in together, and somehow every single one of them knew the words. Customs at the border was always an adventure. Canada just took us in.

That's what I mean about innocence. It wasn't naivety. It was generosity. A willingness to let things be simple.

The final that year was against the Canadian national amateur champions. Regulation ended level. Extra time solved nothing. Penalties.

We traded kicks. Made, made, made, made.

Their fifth shooter hit the post.

If I scored, we were champions.

A young winger named Fru—powerful, fast—walked over.

"Are you going to do what you did at practice?" he asked.

I knew exactly what he meant.

The week before, fooling around after training, I'd done something ridiculous. I'd made the keeper dive early—my body shape screaming hard and right—then rolled the ball as slow as I could toward the opposite corner. The keeper realized his mistake. He scrambled back across goal on all fours, desperate. The ball rolled so slowly it almost stopped on the line. But it crossed.

He gathered it up, held it to his belly—a normal save, except the ball had already gone in.

Our team weren't just laughing. They were on the ground.

When the keeper protested—that "What? I made the save!" face—it triggered a second wave of laughter and finger-pointing.

Then something better happened. The keeper started laughing too.

That's true play. Everyone goes home happy.

"Make the goalie laugh," Fru said.

The two shooters before me—Moroccan brothers—had both gone right and scored. Maybe this Canadian keeper was sensitive to that side. Maybe he'd want to prove he could stop one there.

Victor was on the bench. His girlfriend sat next to him. Later he told me what she said:

"If Teddy misses, he'll be devastated."

The referee blew his whistle.

I approached with my whole body screaming one message: hard, right, top corner. Everything in my run and shape said power.

At the last second, I only brushed the ball.

With that spin, it rode every divot in the pristine grass—soft, slow, inevitable—toward the opposite side.

The keeper dove hard right, fully committed.

The ball rolled left.

Over the line.

A national champion keeper, beaten clean by a player twice his age. But really, not by the player—by play.

I tell you that story because it matters for what comes next.

I believed in play before I could explain it. The swamp had taught me something drills never could. Brazil and the Internationals confirmed it every season. In one of the biggest moments of my amateur career, with everything on the line, I reached back not for a rehearsed pattern, but for something born in the chaos of unstructured games:

The art of making the goalkeeper do my work for me.

And smile.

I knew the secret. I just didn't know the theory.

## RHS

I started coaching shortly after college, assisting Rudy Martignacco at Richfield High School. Rudy was an Austrian immigrant, a beloved German teacher who also coached the ski team. He'd won two boys' state titles in soccer, then quit when parent pressure sucked the joy out of it.

He saw the next opportunity: start the girls' program.

"All kids do better when they just play," he'd say. "Practices should be about play. So should games."

But his fuse was short. "Take her out!" he'd demand, and then go sit on the end of the bench, disappointed with himself that the girls were too uptight to play.

For nine years I assisted him. He never once asked me to run a session or a game. I was just there—watching, learning, absorbing.

Nine years of observation before I stood in front of a team as the one in charge.

I didn't know it then, but Rudy was teaching me the most important lesson: How to acquire.

## Brazil

In 1989, I was a bit lost.

I worked at a video store. Played soccer on weekends—or broomball, or basketball, or tennis, or hockey, whatever was in season. I didn't know what to do with it or with myself. I had just turned thirty and had little direction.

Victor was the one who suggested we go to Brazil. He loved playing even more than I did. Born in the U.S. but raised in Brazil and Paraguay, he became my teammate on the Internationals. He always wanted to play; he loved American sports and wanted to try them all—and surprisingly, he was great at them.

His favorite was touch football in the tree-lined traffic triangle at Knox and Lake Street. As cars waited at the busy Lake Calhoun intersection, their lights would catch a streaking Victor picking out a ball from the darkness of the fall night. The only sport he couldn't master was hockey; his ankles would flop, and he'd try to blame equipment, "My cheap skates are broken." Still, throughout all my travel teams and national camps he remains the best soccer player I ever knew—a man who once marked U.S. National Team strikers out of a game simply for the joy of it.

How did he get so good? I was always asking him questions he could not answer. "How did you grow up? What kind of training? Where was your academy? Futebol de Salão? What is that?"

I think he gave up and decided to show and not tell. *Let's go to Brazil.*

Carnaval season. Summer there, winter here. Victor had connections—old teammates, a place to stay. We could play every day. See where the beautiful game came from.

We stayed in Jundiaí, a working-class city about an hour outside São Paulo. Victor's place was a four-story brick building his grandfather had built—warehouse-style, solid, with a rooftop deck overlooking the city. You could feel the love in every beam. The town was concrete and factories, not glamour.

But Jundiaí is one of the birthplaces of Futebol de Salão—the original indoor game, popularized on the docks of Santos and Rio in the 1930s, played with a small dead ball that stayed at your feet. FIFA eventually absorbed it, renamed it Futsal, standardized the rules. But in Jundiaí the old courts are still there. The culture is still there.

And right outside Victor's bedroom window—close enough to touch—were two of them.

For two months I played there every night.

From my journal:

> *Friday, February 17, 1989, Jundiaí, Brazil.*
>
> The Brazilians are very touchy about their soccer. They deeply want to hold on to the claim as world's best. But can such a claim be made? Brazil has not won the World Cup since '70. Since Pelé.

Let's start on ground level. Here, on the streets, on the *campinhos*, everyone is good. Many are great. They play more than we do and they enjoy playing more than we do—perhaps more than anyone.

They laugh. They tease. They joke. They play hard. They play for fun. They play to look good more than to win.

I remember the score. They remember who they dribbled.

Zé, the calmest, nicest guy off the field, was a trash-talking loudmouth on it. Afterward it was always the same. In his limited English, he'd recap all his best moves, forgetting everything else.

"Did you like my show?"

The first days, Victor was the junior mayor of Jundiaí. Friends and family paraded through the living room and patio to see him, home after six years, and to meet "the American."

I pestered Victor: "What did he say? Translate." He did—then he stopped.

I was frustrated. The world seemed to rotate without me. But I realized what he was doing. If he translated everything, I'd never actually learn. I had to listen, enjoy, and make mistakes if I was going to pick up Portuguese.

Meanwhile, Zé was always there to help.

Tied up as I was in how good I was at soccer, it bothered me when Zé kept saying, "Did you like my show?" But he was so lovable and fun.

On weekends, we went to the sítio—a sort of Brazilian cabin in the jungle. A perfect grass field ringed by three-foot concrete blocks that were perfect for spectating, and futsal goals. There was a small pool, a massive barbecue pit, and fifteen bunk beds in the middle of the jungle.

Here was the rhythm: Play soccer until everyone got hot. Jump in the pool. Fire up the churrasco for Brazilian BBQ. Play again. Intersperse card games of truco and Brazilian beer at just the right moments.

At night, under the southern sky, we played hide-and-seek. Fifty-year-olds and toddlers. Grandparents and kids. Almost complete darkness. Zillions of stars.

Always play.

As the weeks went by—on the futsal courts, at the beach, at the sítio, on the *campinho*—I started to let go of the score. Of the win.

I started to embrace the joy.

By then I could tease Zé back. He'd fire something in Portuguese, and I could catch enough to hit him with a comeback. That's when I saw him smile in a different way. He was Victor's best friend. I could see why.

I started to recall the great play of my childhood: the swamp and kick the can; winter pickup on our backyard rink; spring touch-football games at USC; pickup at Trinity; Internationals scrimmages.

Those games had something in common.

They were always fun. Really fun.

Was this the key?

Were these "meaningless" games Brazil's secret? Their key to development?

Could this kind of environment be cultivated in the U.S.?

Maybe.

I wrote in my journal. I asked questions. I was determined to bring it home.

## Play and Work

Over the next decade, I became a coach on a mission—obsessed. I wanted to split the atom of development. Kids were receiving more instruction than any generation before them. Surely this made them better. But something kept nagging at me: what was the role of play? Was there a difference between acquiring a skill through play and learning it through formal instruction?

I already knew the answer. I just didn't know I knew it yet.

In college, I'd been on the hockey team for two weeks—the first real organized hockey of my life. First home game. I found a seam and split the defense, a defender swung his stick, caught my skates, sent me to my knees.

Chaos. Speed. Noise. Ice rushing up at me.

I didn't think. Something older than thought took over.

Sliding on my knees, I choked up on my stick, kept the puck on my blade. And suddenly I wasn't in an arena—I was in our basement, playing knee hockey with my brother on linoleum floors. I pulled the puck forward like I was shooting, then slid it to my backhand and tucked it in.

The crowd sang happy birthday. It happened to be my birthday.

I stood up and thought: what just happened?

I had played at hockey.

I had to work at soccer.

Meanwhile, youth soccer around me was obsessed with winning now—selecting the best kids, stacking teams, using trophies as proof of concept.

They needed their select group. "Iron sharpens iron. Best with the best."

"We have whiteboards with the best eight-year-olds" one Director of Coaching told me.

I put it bluntly in my interview to become a Director of Coaching:

"Whatever you do to win the game hurts the development of the player."

I thought that sentence would kill my chances.

They hired me.

## Orchard

For eight years, I tried to build something different. A club based on play, not pressure. Development over trophies. Community over comparison.

Keep them together. Let them play. Let their competitive drive build slowly.

The winter gyms became my lab. Sixty kids in a high school gym. Small-sided games on every bit of floor. Chaos that somehow produced learning.

I watched. I took notes. I ran experiments.

The summer teams became my tests. Would what I saw in the gym translate? I'd sprint down the hallway after sessions, babbling with excitement: Deliberate practice vs. free play. Implicit learning vs. explicit instruction. Fun vs. work.

I thought I had cracked it.

The kids were clearly improving. The club was growing. Energy was building. We started winning state cups at the younger ages.

The board designed a new crest and asked if they could use the words from my personal motto.

I was humbled and said yes.

Person. Player. Team.

My three-word coaching compass became the club's.

Some ideas arrive as whispers. This one arrived as a key to an empty building and the sudden certainty that I knew exactly what to do with it.

In my moment of hubris—hiring two new assistants, more excited than ever—I reached far. We partnered with the city of St. Paul and took over the Orchard Rec Center, a building that had been empty for two years, with the idea of turning it into a sanctuary for play.

A soccer club running a rec center? Impossible.

The ten-year-olds who came through the doors—little futbolistas with big dreams—didn't know they were part of an experiment. They just knew they were having fun.

My idea was to use play as a developmental vitamin—balance it with smart, focused hard work, and you'd see world beaters.

But something was wrong.

The play at Orchard wasn't producing what I expected. The results were inconsistent. Some kids flourished. Most seemed stuck.

My assistant directors of coaching started asking questions I couldn't answer.

"Why isn't it working?" they asked. "Why is it so slow?" "Why so much goofing around?" "Where is the wow?"

I didn't know. It wasn't in my wheelhouse yet—the idea that play does its work precisely by not trying so hard that the magic happens in spaces you can't control.

I was still looking for proof that fit my timeline, my metrics, my need to show the board this was "working."

I kept rushing down the hallway. I kept believing.

Around me, doubt grew.

That summer our teams didn't do as well. We won no state cups. I noticed.

The kids were having fun.

They just weren't winning as much.

That's when they came.

The super club. The youth sports industrial complex. The coaches who believed in selecting the best and grinding them into "winners."

They walked into our board meeting with a PowerPoint and an ultimatum.

"Give us your players," they said, "or we'll take them from you."

And they did.

# Interlude:

# What Happened To Play?

In March 1969, a school bus carrying seventeen kids, two coaches, a student manager, and a pile of hockey bags rolled out of Warroad, Minnesota, for a seven-and-a-half-hour drive to the state tournament.

The senior class had thirty-eight students. The hockey team had two seniors. There were no tryouts. When the season started they simply took every boy who showed up.

It was the twenty-fifth anniversary of the Minnesota High School State Hockey Tournament—the most iconic high-school sporting event in America. Games were now televised from the new sixteen thousand seat Metropolitan Sports Center. Families gathered around black-and-white TVs.

The people of Warroad—fewer than a thousand souls—didn't know what to expect. They only knew this: their kids played. Always had.

Play was the cultural fabric. In paper-mill and iron-range towns across northern Minnesota, parents worked shifts in the mills and mines. Kids were left to their own choices. What they chose, day after day and winter after winter, was hockey.

On that bus rode their traditions, their values, their friendships—kids built in a community of play. Through the frosty bus windows on the way out of town, they could see those same parks where tiny kids backlit under floodlights raised their sticks at the passing bus. Cut-out shadows from their past. Floodlights weren't needed in Edina.

There, a different community was forming—a western suburb with more students than Warroad had residents. They had varsity, junior varsity, B and C squads, a thousand-kid association, and a new secret weapon: indoor artificial ice.

For years the question had been simple: How do you beat play?

Since 1945 the state tournament had been dominated not by programs but by environments. Small northern towns built outdoor rinks for fun, not titles. Thief River Falls, Eveleth, Hibbing, International Falls, Roseau, Warroad—those were the names on the banners. The thing about fun is that it is very hard to beat.

One city school had managed it: St. Paul Johnson. Pond hockey and creek hockey on Phalen Creek created the "Grand Army of Phalen Creek"—kids who shoveled their own ice and played from lake to river. Johnson won four state titles and posted twelve top-four finishes in twenty-one years. A number of Grand Army kids skated on the 1960 Olympic gold-medal team. Cut from that roster was another Johnson kid, Herb Brooks.

From 1945 to 1968 the championship bounced between Johnson and the small-town rink rats. Environments that let kids play.

Meanwhile the growing suburbs—crawling with hockey players and money—kept losing. So they asked the question again, this time with urgency: How do you beat play?

The answer they came up with was simple: You organize it. You schedule it. You control it.

Indoor ice was the ticket. In 1960 Minnesota had four indoor sheets. By 1970 it had twenty-five. Edina saw it not as comfort but as a training method. They built the association, filled the coaching slots, and aimed the whole machine at one target: achievement.

In Edina the game stopped being community-based. It became performance-based.

As the Warroad boys slept on hockey bags and the north plains slid past, they might have remembered the long nights on outdoor rinks:

floodlights stretching shadows across rough ice, charcoal heaters glowing in warming houses, the slap of pucks and whoosh of skates leaking through cracked walls. Inside it was quiet as a church. But if you listened closely, you could almost hear the deity of play whispering: listen to me. This is important. You don't know it, but you are about to play for the very soul of the sport.

## The Assassin

One day my mom found me slumped on the stairs.

"What is it?" she asked.

From my bedroom window I would sit still as an assassin. Through the bare birch and maple trees I could see the park rink had been flooded overnight—shimmering, perfect ice. Movement. A game was on. I would run through the house, for my hat, choppers, jacket, stick… Oh no.

I didn't have a stick.

Mom went to work. She found my broken one and hammered a piece of wood onto the blade. I thought, well, that would never work, but that wasn't the point. The point was that she wanted me to play.

I thanked her, laced up my dull skates, and went.

Debbie was there, of course—in goal with a catcher's mitt and a hockey stick, her lower leg in a cast. I had signed it, Gump Worsley.

Then the Wesley Park kids arrived, dropped off by their parents.

Wesley Park was just over General Mills Mountain—a hill really, but a natural border that was generally respected. Wesley had a full-size rink with boards, a heated warming house and a concession stand with hot chocolate and Chuckwagon infrared sandwiches. Three of them wore matching bantam jerseys. They were slinging perfect saucer slap shots—something I had only seen on TV. We had come to play. They turned it into park against park.

But I knew the real reason they were there. They wanted to see Rob. Parents and kids alike had heard the stories: "He plays every day," "He floats on the ice." So they made the trip over the mountain to see for themselves.

Rob was a ninth-grader, a high-school football linebacker who had blocked a record four punts. Neighborhood legend—wise, gentle, fearsome. Once, the whole neighborhood was on edge—police had stopped at the swamp—a rabid dog was on the loose. Debbie drove a ball to the edge of the cattails, and an unknown dog appeared and grabbed it. We all ran. Not Rob. He chased the dog into the cattails and came back parting the reeds with the only good ball we had.

He skated in total silence, never making a sound as he spun and twisted. Never spray, no stopping and starting, just beautiful cursive writing on the ice. He wore a golden leather helmet his dad had given him. From my window, a gold streak meant Rob was there.

Years before he had invited Debbie and me into the game when we were eight, barely able to skate. We hadn't known each other before that. Debbie and I became fast friends, and if the pond was clear, the three of us could be found there.

Some of his friends left for Golden Valley travel, yet when he tried out for high school he was the only ninth-grader to make varsity. He chose not to play. His dad was sick. The high-school coach came to the house to talk him back. Rob stayed at the park.

Never sharpen your skates, I heard him say once. Whether it was true or not, it was what I was going to do.

"Wesley against Swamp," they said. "Let's play to five."

One of the Wesley kids smirked at my mom's stick. Rob looked at it, then at me. "Nice stick. Let's trade." He handed me his.

As we started to play you could see the travel kids and their parents looking at each other: What? These kids? This pond? This guy with the homemade stick?

Early in the game someone slashed the makeshift blade, and it snapped at the nub. Rob skated to the stick can—nothing usable. So he kept playing. Nub of a stick. Never stopped moving, no sound at all.

He spun and cut through the Wesley boys with that cursive grace. They triple-teamed him. That's where I came in.

He skated past me with the puck and nodded. Get forward. When I did, the puck arrived on my stick as if placed there. I put it in.

What I noticed in the Wesley kids was a kind of silence. Their slapshots and toe drags suddenly meant nothing against a man they could not catch with a stick that had no blade.

The parents who had driven their kids over went quiet.

We played to five. And when it reached four to four, something shifted in Rob.

He dropped back. Stopped attacking. Started moving the puck to me—every time, deliberately, patiently—as if the game were no longer about the score. As if he had decided something. He could have gone end to end. He had been doing it all afternoon. Instead he kept finding me, setting me up, steering the play toward the moment he wanted me to have.

When I scored the winner, I turned around and he nodded, still moving, never stopping.

He already knew what I didn't: that he was almost done. That his dad was sick and his friends had left and the park was changing and one day soon it would be Debbie and me and whoever we could find to keep the game going.

He was passing something on.

Swampies won, five to four. Championship of the swamp, the neighborhood, Golden Valley, and the world.

Rob played less and less. One by one the Golden Valley kids disappeared into travel hockey. They didn't vanish overnight. But one day they were just gone.

Debbie moved away that winter.

I remember our last afternoon on the ice. No ceremony. Just skates and cold and then she was gone.

Take away the people and you take away the language.

So when my friend's dad pulled up the next winter and shouted, "Who wants to go to Golden Valley tryouts?" my friends left. When they came back they brought their fancy saucer slap shots.

I stayed at the pond.

He looked like a dad who wanted good things for his kid. He had a station wagon and a schedule, artificial ice, coaches with clipboards, and ice time scheduled to the minute.

He had a plan.

The pond had February and a shoveled-off rectangle and kids who showed up because there was nowhere else they wanted to be.

The pond had Rob.

And the station wagon was going to kill it.

The pond is still there. Rob is gone. The Grand Army is gone.

Somewhere right now, a parent is loading hockey bags into an SUV.

# Chapter 3:

# The War

## The Super Club

Across the country, clubs started to get serious. They merged. They rebranded. They made promises.

They came for the kids.

Minnesota was no exception.

I thought I could manage the youth industrial sports complex. I thought I could build something different from inside the machine. And for a while, it looked like I was right.

Over eight years as Director of Coaching, I had steered the club away from the rat race of competition toward play. Let them play. Keep them together. Prioritize fun over work. Let the competitive drive build slowly. We grew from twenty-eight to sixty-six teams and organized futsal, dome training, and technical sessions. Our kids weren't just players—they were a family, evolving alongside one another.

I looked at what we'd built—top-tier teams, a loyal staff, pristine facilities, even a sanctuary for free play—and thought: Who would ever leave?

They walked into the boardroom not as enemies, but as men who believed they had seen the future. These were the same players who had once dominated the state, who had carried the flag for Minnesota soccer when few others cared. Now, in their mid-thirties, with pro careers behind them, they carried a different kind of urgency.

"We've watched kids with real talent get left behind," the lead speaker said, voice steady. "We've seen them plateau because no one pushed them early enough, no one gave them the structure, the competition, the edge. We can change that. We can build something that actually prepares them for the next level—not just keeps them happy."

The PowerPoint clicked forward: best players, best coaching, best environment. A metro-wide club. Tryouts. Selection. Intensity.

Then, an unexpected turn.

A board member spoke up. "This is an amazing, well-thought-out plan, but I have a question. How did you do it? Tell us how you grew up."

For the first time, their polished facade cracked.

"We'd call each other—'Meet at the park.'"

"There was a basketball court ... we'd make goals out of whatever we had."

"We played every day. Even in winter."

The room shifted. Nostalgia thickened the air.

Then that same board member said something that got to them.

"It seems like you grew up under our model."

Catching on, they answered back. "We respect what you've built here. The play, the skills, the community—but it's too soft. Not tough enough. The real world is harsh. Play alone doesn't get kids to the next level. It doesn't get them ready for D1 colleges and beyond."

I felt the room shift. Several board members nodded; the logic was clean, measurable, reassuring. Parents want certainty. They want to know their child is on the fastest track.

The ultimatum came last, delivered quietly: "Join us and be part of the future. Or we'll build it without you—I hate to be blunt, but give us your players or we'll take them from you."

When the door closed, the silence lasted a long time. Here's what I didn't say in that room. I agreed with them more than they knew. I was not some gentle idealist who didn't care about winning. I had the competitive drive they were selling—I wanted to build the best environment. But I had a technical eye—I could see something missing in the kids that grew up in our program. The difference wasn't ambition. It was direction. They wanted to climb. I wanted to explore. They looked at the landscape and saw one peak. I looked at the same landscape and saw a valley nobody was searching.

## The Coffee Shop

We met in the coffee shop on Nicollet because it was neutral ground. The attorney—father of three boys who had grown up in our program—wanted what every parent wants: the best possible path for his sons. Sitting beside him was a coach I had once hired, a man whose talent on the field had been undeniable, and whose belief in structure had only deepened over time.

The pitch was polished. The super club had resources, a pathway, and a plan. The attorney nodded along. I sat there like a man watching his furniture get loaded into a moving truck.

Then the attorney stepped away for a call.

The coach leaned forward, earnest.

"Ted, what have you accomplished in eight years?"

I wanted to say something back. Nothing came out.

"You can't take them any further. We can."

Then he glanced toward the door where the attorney had stepped out, and his voice dropped—not to a whisper, but to the register men use when they're letting you in on something.

"Too bad about Rich."

Rich was the middle son. Twelve years old. The most talented of the three—and that was the point. Every super club needs a keystone player, the best kid in the age group, the one whose name alone pulls the rest. Parents don't leave their friends and their clubs for a brochure. They leave because the best kid left first. Sign Rich, and the other families follow. The whole age group tips. I knew it and so did the coach.

"Why is that?" I asked.

"Just look at the parents."

Five months. They had spent five months courting this family. Phone calls, emails, the whole choreography. Rich wasn't just a player to them. He was the domino.

Before he had even laced up for a single session, the coach had already written him off—not because of anything Rich had done on a ball, but because of the two people who drove him to practice.

We parted. He shook my hand. The boys would leave. Others would follow.

## The Fall

The tryouts that fall were a disaster. We decided not to join the super club, but everyone noticed who wasn't there. The faces that should have been on the field. The families that had quietly slipped away.

I held the fall coaches meeting. Afterward, I was outside showing the coaches my vision for the rec center—a sand court here, a nine-v-nine field there, converting the tennis courts to outdoor futsal. I refused to give up on the idea.

Then I received a phone call.

An emergency meeting of the board was held. There was a vote.

I was out. Just like that.

Eight years of building. The winter gyms. The summer teams. The rec center. The philosophy I had staked my career on. Gone in an afternoon.

## My Bosses

I sat in what felt like the ruins of my career, across from the new co-directors of coaching. Yesterday they were my assistants. Today they were my bosses.

The club was losing too many players to the super club. They had given Ted the space and time to try out this "play" idea—and what had it gotten them? Teams—even whole age groups—were devastated. Teams that were last year among the state's best were now seen as leftovers, without ever playing a game. The super club gathered all the stars. Parents lost their lawn chair coffee-drinking partners. Everything broke down.

Play had failed.

The new directors made it clear: from now on, the club would refocus on being the best. No more free play nonsense.

The logo that said "Person, Player, Team"—my personal contribution, the motto the club had asked me if they could adopt—was removed from the website.

A board member asked me what I wanted. My reply came fast.

"To never run another tryout again."

"How in the world would that even be possible?"

But still, they wanted me around.

"You'll work directly with the kids," one of the co-directors said. "It's what you're great at."

Plain English translation: they still needed me running the club's immensely popular skills clinics and futsal sessions. The ones I'd built from scratch. But now I'd be paid hourly. Only paid for coaching. Half the money, twice the work. No more salary, no more security, no more influence—just hauling equipment up and down school stairs.

Oh, and they'd scheduled me seven days a week.

Seven. Days.

## The Nights

I tried to prove I was still important. My wife Colleen said, "Hold your head high."

I worked like a man possessed. Every clinic, every session, every gym. I hauled my two kids there (Don't forget the dinosaur books and the dolls). I was there early, stayed late, hauled the equipment, ran the drills. If they wanted seven days, I'd give them seven days. I'd show them they couldn't run this without me. I'd make myself indispensable.

It didn't work.

The more I ground, the less anyone noticed. The super club kept growing. The families kept leaving. The board had moved on. I was just the guy who set up the cones.

I was getting nowhere.

## The Mission

One Sunday, Victor showed up with his team on schedule. We would always leave together at five p.m. I had been there since ten a.m.

Victor found me in the parking lot after the session. I was loading equipment into my car, tired and defeated. He leaned against the hood and watched me work.

"You don't look so good," he said.

"Thanks."

"I'm serious. You need to stop feeling sorry for yourself."

I slammed the trunk closed. "Easy for you to say. You didn't just lose everything."

Victor shook his head. "You didn't lose anything. You just got rid of the people who didn't believe."

I stared at him.

"Think about it," he said. "Did they ever really understand what you were doing? The parents who left—were they ever going to trust the process? The super clubs took the people who wanted shortcuts. Let them leave."

"And what am I supposed to do? Start over with nothing?"

Victor smiled. "You're supposed to do what you've always done. Build something."

"Build what? I have no club. No salary. No support."

"You have Dare and Z. Others will come."

"They barely like soccer."

He pushed off the hood and started walking to his car.

"No clubs to compete with. Just play."

He got in his car and rolled down the window.

"Call it Joy of the People," he said. "If you build it, they will come."

## The Remembering

I stood in that parking lot for a long time after Victor drove away.

Joy of the People. The words hung in the cold air. I knew he was sending me somewhere—back to Brazil, back to Garrincha, back to something I'd felt but never named.

But I didn't know how to get there.

Victor had given me the mission.

He sent me back to that first trip to Brazil—the language, the customs, the soccer. It was all overwhelming at first.

After almost two months, something shifted. A calmness overtook me. I stopped asking the questions. I stopped measuring.

Brazil got into me somehow. The rhythm of the days—play until you're hot, swim until you're cool, eat until you're full, play again under the southern stars. The way Zé would ask "Did you like my show?" and mean it as pure joy, not competition. The way nobody seemed to be keeping score of their lives.

I fell in love with a place that loved play as much as I did. But more than that, I fell in love with the permission Brazil gave me: It's okay to be you. It's okay to not know. It's okay to just play.

Just before we flew home, Victor got sick. So Zé picked me up that last night to rent a movie.

In the sports section of the video store, I saw a title I didn't recognize: *Alegria do Povo.*

"What is that?" I asked Zé.

"A documentary," he said. "On Garrincha." And then, of course: "Did you like my show?" And the laugh that always came after.

I knew who Garrincha was. Everyone who loved soccer knew Garrincha. But the nickname—*Alegria do Povo*, Joy of the People—I had never heard it before.

Garrincha.

The greatest dribbler in Brazilian history. In a country where superlatives take on a life of their own, "Joy of the People" was reserved for him alone.

He was poor, from the favelas of Rio. Born with one leg shorter than the other, his spine curved, his body a medical impossibility. Smallish and tricky—Garrincha means "little bird." To practice, he took a ball to the local schoolyard and challenged the kids to take it from him. That was his training. Just him and a ball and anyone brave enough to try.

He won two World Cups—1958 and 1962. Before the critical group-stage match in Gothenburg, 1958, all of Brazil was nervous. The Soviets had just sent a rocket into space. It was rumored that they were using scientific training techniques and their players could cover twenty kilometers per game. The first three minutes of that game are often considered the best football ever played. Brazil won two to zero. The Swedish newspaper headline the next day read: "Soviets can put a satellite in space, can't stop Garrincha."

Garrincha carried Brazil on his crooked legs, dancing past defenders, making goalkeepers look foolish, playing with such pure joy that crowds came to feel it too.

He didn't play to win. But he won. He played to make people smile. He gave them joy. He played to hear the crowd gasp. He played because the field was his home and the game was the most beautiful thing in the world.

Zé had been telling me about Garrincha all along. Every time he said, "Did you like my show?"—that was Garrincha. That was the Brazilian way.

## Raffi

On Wednesdays, I sat with Raffi. Raffi was my kind of soccer guy: stubborn, visionary, maybe a little crazy. An Armenian who grew up in Lebanon, he lost his father early and spent his youth playing street soccer in the bombed-out streets of Beirut. He immigrated to Minnesota as a fourteen-year-old. He got his divinity degree at the University of St. Thomas. We became friends coaching together at Richfield High School.

Whether it was his belief or whether he wanted to back me up, he decided to give play another try. The two co-directors were firm. "U11, this is the very best age group in the club, we are not going to waste it with play."

Raffi stood his ground. They relinquished.

He had dedicated Wednesday nights to pure, uncut free play. No whistles. No coaching. No analytics. Just kids running three-v-three games on two tiny courts, swapping onto random teams every so often. Winner stays up, loser moves down. No instruction, no parents—at least until the last twenty minutes, when they could quietly observe.

For two hours each week all winter Raffi and I sat on the rolled-up wrestling mat, watching the kids figure it all out for themselves.

"Play invents everything," Raffi said one night, leaning back like some mad prophet.

I suggested keeping score each night and posting the results. Who was the best three-v-three player?

Raffi shook his head. "The street doesn't have a whiteboard."

"Kids will show us," he continued. "Kids in play are never wrong."

The guy would not stop talking. But I was finally ready to listen.

At first, I saw only chaos. Little bursts of brilliance—a nutmeg here, an unexpected skip pass there. Kids trying things they wouldn't dare try if we'd been shouting patterns and diagrams.

But over time, I started to see something else: actions and movements I couldn't have taught. Solutions I wouldn't even think to drill. It wasn't perfect, but there was life coursing through that gym.

One parent—a former Costa Rican pro—pulled me aside after a session.

"Raffi," he said, "is ahead of his time."

## The Vision

In the margins, I read.

On the bench between sessions, in the parking lot before clinics, late at night when the house was quiet—I read.

Two books found me that year.

The first was Michael Lewis's *Moneyball.* I wasn't reading it as a baseball fan. I was reading it as a man who had just watched the machine devour everything he'd built.

The Oakland A's had found the arbitrage: the market misprices talent. The scouts overvalued what looked right and missed what actually worked. They built a winner out of players everyone else had discarded.

I sat in my car after a Sunday session, engine off, reading by the dome light. The parking lot was empty. Everyone else had gone home.

I thought about Rich. Twelve years old. The most talented of three brothers. Five months of courtship—not because of what he could become, but because his name on a roster would tip an entire age group. And before he'd played a single session, written off in a coffee shop because of what his parents looked like.

The machine wasn't evaluating talent. It was evaluating conformity. Selecting for kids who looked the part, who fit the template, who made the scouts feel smart.

What if the real talent was hiding in the kids they cut? The dandelion-pickers and the Hula-Hoopers and the ones who followed fifteen yards behind the ball?

Lewis had found the arbitrage in baseball. Maybe there was one in soccer too.

The second was Jonathan Wilson's *Inverting the Pyramid*. A quote from Jorge Valdano—Argentine World Cup winner turned philosopher of the game—stopped me cold.

Valdano's argument was that results aren't what endure. Sacchi's AC Milan is remembered more than Capello's, even though Capello won more. The Dutch total football teams of the seventies are legendary; the Germans and Argentines who beat them in World Cup finals are footnotes. "It's about the search for perfection. We know it doesn't exist, but it's our obligation towards football and maybe, towards humanity to strive towards it. That's what we remember, that's what's special."

What survives is the search for perfection—not its achievement.

I sat with that for a long time.

The machine had won. The super clubs had taken my players. The board had fired me. By every measure that mattered to them, I had lost.

But Valdano was saying the measure itself was wrong. What endures is the search.

Holland lost those finals. They're still legendary.

Maybe losing wasn't the end. Maybe it was the beginning.

## Glenn

My brother had quit the club after my demotion, pulled his daughter, never went back. Now he was helping me chase something new.

"You showed them how successful Orchard was," he said, talking about the Rec Center partnership. "Do it again."

Glenn saw the opportunity of Orchard. And he understood the lay of the land. While I sat on wrestling mats talking philosophy with Raffi, Glenn was seeing the picture and how to paint it.

"It's like a game of *Survivor.* You have to play or you'll get voted off the island."

He got busy setting up meetings. The booster club. The deputy mayor of St. Paul. Our city council rep. District 12. Parks and Rec.

Every meeting, every open forum, every community event—we showed up. "Here comes the guys who won't stop talking about free play," I could see them thinking. Some rolled their eyes. Some nodded politely and moved on. A few leaned in.

I was still hauling equipment. Still running clinics. But every spare hour went into the pitch: play works. Give us a building and we'll prove it.

## JOTP

Lewis told me the market was wrong.

Valdano told me why it didn't matter.

Raffi showed me what play could produce when you got out of the way.

Glenn kept opening doors.

The machine can't manufacture what Valdano was describing. It can't drill the search for perfection into a kid's body.

That has to be acquired. Through play. Through joy. Through the obligation toward the game that has nothing to do with trophies.

Victor had said: Call it Joy of the People.

Now I was starting to understand what he meant.

## The Flight

I remembered that flight home from Brazil so long ago. I couldn't stop talking about it.

"Joy of the People," I kept saying to Victor. Garrincha this, Garrincha that. The notion that a nation would extend that nickname to a player—not "the greatest" or "the champion" but "the joy of the people"—that was everything. That was what I wanted. Not for myself. For the kids. For Dare and Z. Happiness. Joy. Standing in that parking lot twenty years later, I finally understood. Victor hadn't just given me a name. He had given me a commission.

Then the city announced it was putting six recreation centers up for partnership.

# Interlude:

# Emmanuel

Nobody would have guessed that a kid told he lacked "killer instinct" would score in his first German game.

Emmanuel—Eman—played U10s for Coach Dan with Z, Marco, and Lioul. Fast, fearless, reckless in the best way, he'd come from Nigeria at four and made Joy his home. When his family moved to Arizona at twelve, the team threw him a giant going-away party. He kept coming back each summer, sharing a room with Dare and Z.

Coaches noticed early: ODP, regional pools, national camps. At an open combine for Minnesota United FC he went from walk-on to a second-team contract, then to the first team. Then minutes dried up. The team panicked toward playoffs. Eman sat.

The club once brought shelter puppies to a training session. Eman was the only player to adopt one. A Belgian Malinois pup—said to be the acrobat of dogs. He named him Iggy.

We walked our dogs every morning. Eman watched Iggy trip and tumble and worried he might never be graceful. I said maybe thousands of clumsy falls were the raw material of acrobatic skill.

He listened. He talked about how toxic the first-team culture felt: negative, harsh, exhausting.

When the coach changed and the old guard returned, Eman was let go. "You don't have a killer instinct," they said.

His agent lined up trials in Germany—six months away. Everyone had advice: personal trainers, private drills, more speed, more intensity. "Train with us!" they urged.

Eman ignored them. "I'm trusting Joy," he told me.

So we made a different plan: find the next chance, and be ready by playing. All winter he underloaded—futsal with teenagers, six-a-side with adults, mixed games with the girls, low-stakes pickup at Joy. He played fast and slow, tried things, talked on the field, coaxed teammates into the play. He wasn't chasing measurable metrics. He was rebuilding his football language.

In May, he trialed in Germany, made SV Sandhausen, and scored in his first match.

Victor visited him there. "He stands out."

Victor doesn't use hyperbole.

# Chapter 4:

# The Vote

## The Gym

I slipped through the heavy doors, late, my heart hammering. The room was a time capsule from 1978—psychedelic green and brown waves on the walls, four giant roof windows black mirrors in the winter dark.

It had been a difficult year.

The eight years I had put into building the club—the long, hard work of creating something formidable—had been reduced to a single sentence on the website: "We wish Ted well and thank him for his service to the club."

A year since my demotion. A year of humbling winter nights in dark gyms around St. Paul.

But the idea—the stubborn, foolish idea that play could still win—wouldn't let me go.

For me, everything depended on tonight.

I found my brother Glenn in the bleachers, his face tight with the same tension. The seats were packed, a sea of unfamiliar faces from the neighborhood.

"Huge turnout," he whispered, not taking his eyes off the crowd. His voice was tight. "This is it."

"It's just an informational meeting," I whispered back, clinging to a naive hope.

Glenn shook his head slowly. "Nah, Kathy wants this done. She's going to call for a vote tonight."

The air went out of me.

A vote? Tonight? We weren't ready. We were a phantom organization—no nonprofit, no name, just a desperate idea scribbled on a proposal. We were bringing a dream to a knife fight.

## The Prize

When my old club took over Orchard Rec Center two years before, Mayor Chris Coleman praised the partnership in his State of the City address. It became a model for what the city could do with its thirty aging rec centers—facilities built in another era, now underutilized, expensive to maintain, serving neighborhoods that had changed.

Inspired by the partnership success, the city decided to put six more centers up for partnership. Nonprofit organizations could propose to take over operations, bring their own programming, revitalize these forgotten spaces.

Of the six, South St. Anthony was the prize.

It was the only center with a real gymnasium—a wood floor gym with natural lighting from four massive roof windows. It sat on the soon-to-be light rail line, centered almost dead in the middle of the Twin Cities, on the far western edge of St. Paul. The neighborhood had aged and the center was rarely used anymore. But to me, it was a gold mine: a huge space, lots of grass, a beautiful gym, a kitchen, offices, a lounge, a warming room. Two tennis courts, a playground, and a half-court basketball play area. Everything we would need.

The city tried to guide me elsewhere.

I wanted South St. Anthony. So did everyone else.

Glenn understood the lay of the land. "That's a big ask."

## The Presentations

The other presenters took the floor first, and with each word, the hole we were in grew deeper. The YMCA representative unveiled glossy renderings: an expansion, a state-of-the-art fitness club with locker rooms and a shimmering new swimming pool. A few appreciative murmurs rippled through the crowd.

Then Urban Tennis followed with a sleek flyover video animation, promising six pristine indoor courts—the park outside glistening in digitally rendered sunshine.

Then I heard my name.

"Ted Kroeten and his ... organization."

"Just be you," whispered Glenn.

The walk to the front felt miles long. Every eye was on me. I had no placards, no videos, just the echo of my own footsteps on the gym floor.

"Thanks, Kathy." My voice sounded thin in the vast space. I cleared my throat.

"Hello everyone. My name is Ted Kroeten. I've coached in this city for a long time. And I've watched something disappear."

I paused, letting the silence hang for a beat.

"Kids don't play anymore. Not real play. Not the kind that happens when adults aren't drawing up practice plans. The system out there—it's built to chew kids up. I believe in the possibility of kids at play. My friends and I ... we just want to give them back a place. A sanctuary. Inside, in the winter, we'll play futsal. Outside, soccer. No tryouts. No selection. Just ... play."

Dead silence.

None of the applause given to the YMCA or Urban Tennis. I saw a few skeptical glances, but also a few slow, considering nods from people who remembered a different time.

I sat down, my hands trembling.

## The Hands

Before the room could fully process our ramshackle vision, Kathy from Parks and Rec stood up.

"Thank you all. I think we've heard enough. Given the strong turnout tonight, I propose we move to a vote."

My blood ran cold. Glenn was right. This is happening now.

This was the culmination of every meeting, every rejected proposal, every door slammed in my face. The system that had chewed me up and spit me out was about to finish the job.

Kathy looked out at the community members.

"All in favor of the Y?"

A smattering of hands.

"Urban Tennis?"

A few more.

Then, almost as an afterthought, she said, "And Ted's ... Free Play group?"

More than half the hands in the room went up.

Glenn slugged me in the shoulder.

## Alegria do Povo

Two weeks later, the city handed us the keys to the South St. Anthony Rec Center.

We were excited, scared, hopeful, determined, and idealistic to a fault. We named our new nonprofit after you-know-who. Garrincha. *Alegria do Povo:* Joy of the People.

JOTP was born.

Our goal was to create a ground zero of free play. But we had a real problem: we didn't really know what we wanted.

We had been good at selling the ideal. It made a good story. But when it came to implementing it—that was different.

Which is why, at our first board meeting in the rec center, I slid a piece of paper across the table to Victor—who had agreed to be our president.

Printed on the paper was the weekly schedule for the gym. It was packed with clinics, structured practices, and coached sessions—the very system I knew how to run.

Victor's face, usually alive with charm, was clouded.

"What is it?" I asked.

"Where is the free play?" he said, his voice quiet but firm.

"It's there," I said, pointing defensively. "7 a.m. here, 11 p.m. there."

I had tucked it into the margins, an inconvenient afterthought. I wanted to develop the small number of kids we had quickly. I thought that required my training, my coaching, to fast-track them. After all, look at the old club—so many good players. Victor and the rest of the board wanted the free play. I felt it was important, but not as important as my coaching.

Victor looked at me, thoughtful and deliberate.

"You're hiding it," he said. "If you believe in it, you need to dedicate the space to it."

He was right.

We engaged long and hard on how to implement it. What is free play? Are coaches allowed? Should the goals be small or big? Do we keep score?

In the end, we defined it: self-directed, no coaching, everyone invited, everyone plays. Coaches and older players could participate, but they were not allowed to coach. They could only say what they needed to try to win that game—nothing more. Victor asked me to give it a chance.

## The Originals

So that winter, we set loose what few kids we had.

There were seven regulars in those early days. My kids—Z and Dare. Franklin's two kids—Joey and Emmy. And the kids from St. Louis Park—Lioul, Emmanuel, and Marco.

I would pick them up after school, drive them to St. Paul, and open the gym. And they played. Some did cartwheels in the corner. Some Hula-Hooped. And sometimes they would play soccer.

Dare was the goof-off. She would always disappear when soccer started. She loved Hula-Hooping. Once I made a video of her Hula-Hooping and pulling off soccer moves as a six-year-old—missing teeth, dead serious: “Hi, my name is Dare and we are about to do some Hula-Hooping and some tricks with a soccer ball.” Play soccer? No chance. Make a video Hula-Hooping? Now you’re talking. She was often in the rubber room stacking dolls on the ping pong table.

Lioul was the kid who would not stop calling, “I’m ready to go, coach!” He never forgot what time training started. He was never late. He took care of Emmanuel, who lived in the next apartment building. While Emmanuel was ungodly fluid, could sprint up a wall and do a backflip, Lioul was the opposite. He struggled to shoot a volleyball across the gym.

Z was the quiet player who really took to free play. He loved scoring goals. If he stayed with the old club he would never have made his age group team. But now—with no stakes—he was playing, inventing, enjoying. It was good to see.

One day, kids dug up some plastic bats in one of the back storage rooms and spent the next two days chasing each other around the building—they called the game Beggar’s Canyon. They played it to exhaustion.

I bit my tongue, fighting every instinct to organize them, to drill them, to coach them. I just asked them to be productive and play.

It was messy. It was chaotic. It was everything those glossy presentations in that gymnasium weren’t.

And I couldn’t see what it was building.

## The Doubt

Watching the dismantling of my free play dream in real time, the question kept nagging at me. What is talent? Where does it come from? How do you build it?

I had spent my whole career believing I knew. Structured training. Deliberate practice. Coaching.

Watching these kids loiter and Hula-Hoop and chase each other with plastic bats, I felt the ground shifting. The activities were slow, disorderly, almost unwatchable. Kids loitering. Some not participating. What seemed to be bad habits everywhere. Still, they were smiling and laughing. They were dancing to the music, doing almost everything except playing those intense, fast-paced games I wanted to see.

But Victor's words echoed in my head: If you believe in it, you need to dedicate the space to it.

So I let them play.

## Goalie Wars

One day I was called into a Parks and Rec meeting.

"Ted, as you know, we have two nights a week of volleyball."

I nodded.

"The coaches are complaining that their volleyballs are ... well, splitting. They think you may know what's happening?"

I did know.

The kids had invented a game. They were shooting across the gym at futsal goals using a special lightweight volleyball they'd found in the equipment closet. They called it Goalie Wars.

Z and Emmanuel had figured out that if you pumped up the balls, they flew faster. The balls were hitting the corners of the backboard and splitting open.

"Oh, I'm sorry. I think you're right. We will pay for the broken ball."

"Balls."

"Balls? How many?"

"Nine."

"Nine?"

Volley-Lites are thirty dollars apiece—about as much money as we had in the bank.

I paid for the split Volley-Lites and purchased some more out of my own pocket.

"Use ours," I told the kids. "Don't over-inflate them."

## The Ball

I watched the nine- and ten-year-olds take their shots. With the smaller, seven-ounce ball—less than half the weight of a soccer ball—their swings looked more like adult shooting motions. With a regular ball, they were often forced to muscle it—all arms, no technique. But with the Volley-Lite, they could focus on form, on timing, and on placement. They invented complex rules that equalized the game. They made each other "prove" their shot. They came up with the High Ball Rule—three shots above the psychedelic green arch and you were out. And the Redemption Shot—when all was lost, a player could call redemption and take a risky last-chance shot to get back in the game.

All done with a Volley-Lite that doesn't destroy the building—and kids aren't afraid to save.

I was impressed that the kids had discovered and governed this game on their own. But surely shooting with a volleyball wasn't "real," was it? No way would this be as good as practicing with a full-size ball.

I almost stopped them. I almost pulled out the "real" balls and ran a proper shooting drill.

But I remembered Victor. I sat down and watched.

My Brazilian mentor once said: "You Americans are crazy spending millions on speed training equipment. Change the ball. Change the surface." So there was some theory behind the experiment.

So I let it be. It felt right. It's what Victor wanted.

Goalie Wars became and still is the most popular game at Joy—so popular I had to put limits on it. I still had no proof it worked. I worried the light ball would teach bad habits, train them for something the real game would punish.

But Z, Emmanuel, and Joey became three of the best ball strikers I have ever seen, able to shape, dip, knuckle, and drive balls past keepers at all levels, high school, college, and beyond. Not because I taught them. Because they taught themselves one Goalie Wars game at a time. Even today, Eman and Z argue over their fifteen-year running score.

I was very good at teaching shooting technique. I could break down and rebuild every piece of a shooting motion.

But since Goalie Wars, my coaching was no longer required.

## The Tournament

Later that winter, I received a phone call from a director of a small futsal tournament wondering if we could fill a spot.

I wasn't expecting much. But I entered a team.

I should have known better.

I asked my friend Coach Dan to coach the team. As the kids progressed through the tournament, they seemingly recognized the situations in front of them as if they were just another of the thousand games they had played at the center.

The JOTP kids played with absolutely no fear. They enjoyed themselves as they moved through the tournament, winning their group. They played with lightness and calmness and took lots of risks. They qualified for the final.

## Two Teams

The other finalist was the super club that came for our kids a couple years before. They had grown quickly and had a fresh batch of eleven-year-olds, including some from my old club.

U11 boys soccer is an intense age group. Clubs race to create top teams at this age, enticing young families with promises of elite development, top leagues, professional coaches. The super club had taken this to another level—they set up multi-tiered age groups, gathered players early, and coached them as hard as they could. They came with real purpose and dominated tournaments like this.

They were coached by a friend of mine—we had played on Minnesota Thunder together. The packed gymnasium got the message: Best uniforms, best warm ups, best organization—wanna join us?

The JOTP kids showed up in spray-painted t-shirts we had made the night before.

They could not have been prouder.

But there was a bigger difference between the two teams than their kits and gear.

It was their defending.

## Flat Feet

When first introduced to free play, the kids at Joy of the People played no defense. All they wanted to do was score. They were uninterested in everything else.

Often they would stand flat-footed on the floor as an attacker moved near. They rarely even moved to the ball. And when they did engage, the youngsters—mostly eight and nine years old—would take big, huge swipes at the ball, as if they were going to break the leg of the attacker.

Generally, the attacker saw it coming and would skip by, leaving our kid with a big whiff.

I desperately wanted to correct the situation. But it was free play. It was not my role. So I left it.

This continued throughout the winter. I watched. I bit my tongue. I let them fail.

But then they somehow made it work for them.

## First Defender

In the final, the opposition played impeccable first defender—get low, deny the ball carrier forward, buy time for teammates. It's one of the earliest things coaches teach, and these kids had it down cold.

Meanwhile, the JOTP kids were charging right at the ball.

I understood this came from the free play. They meant well—they just wanted the ball. Seeing our kids flying at them, the kids from the big club just sidestepped the action.

I thought: Yeah, I probably should have taught them first defender.

But if you step back, you can understand why those JOTP kids ran at the ball. It could be that they were poorly coached—that's true. Or it could be that they were just being kids, following their own curriculum. The kid curriculum.

Is there power in allowing kids to be kids?

As the game went on, we were about to find out.

## Ball Thieves

Somewhere along the winter—in those hundreds of hours of unstructured play, those frozen lazy feet, those crazy swipes at the ball—something had transformed.

The wild lunges had evolved into occasional smart, darting movements. The feet of children who once stood flat had become the feet of pickpockets.

The big swipes at the ball were still there. Sometimes they got beat by the dribble. Sometimes there was a foul. But also, some of the time, the JOTP kids were stealing the ball—tapping it behind the surprised, dispossessed attacker, then moving deftly around to pick it up and attack as if they had done it thousands of times before.

Well, they had.

The kids had spent the winter wanting the ball and going after it. And somehow, they had figured out a way. Luckily, they figured it out before it was coached out of them.

Those many hours of free play had not developed classic first defenders.

They had created ball thieves.

## The Strip

It was like street basketball—when a player strips you of the ball as you drive to the basket, and you're left wondering where it went.

The JOTP kids had nurtured the fun before the optimal. First defender in basketball or soccer is important, but it's hard, sometimes thankless work. It's way more fun to let the player go by and try the trick of reaching around to tap the ball away.

And that's what the kids did during those "mindless" hours: accumulating thousands of repetitions of stripping the ball off dribblers.

As the final went on, the big club kids started to glance at their coach, looking perplexed. Hey, where is their first defender? Can they come that close?

They had never seen kids come for the ball like this. They looked like they had never practiced against anything but proper first defenders who stayed low and didn't dive in.

They lost the ball as they tried to penetrate. They became tentative.

Meanwhile, the JOTP kids were not swayed. They attacked whether they had the ball or not.

## Emmanuel

Toward the end of the game, the score was tied.

One of our young attackers—Emmanuel—pressured their ball carrier near midfield. The ball carrier attempted to skip by the same move that had worked against proper defenders all game.

But Emmanuel saw it coming.

He tapped the ball behind the attacker, spun around him, picked it up, and was gone.

Emmanuel was off. He scored.

We won the game three to two.

## The Question

I could see that if I had followed the prescribed curriculum, I would have taught these kids proper first defender—and I would have robbed them of the chance to discover something greater.

If I was making a mistake on something so basic as first defender, where else was I making mistakes?

The psychologist Jean Piaget once said: "Each time one prematurely teaches a child something he could have discovered himself, that child is kept from inventing it and consequently from understanding it completely."

I had almost intervened.

But I didn't.

Victor was right. Raffi was right. The kids were right.

## Why

Standing in that gym after the final whistle, watching our kids in their spray-painted shirts celebrate like they had won the World Cup, I understood something I had been circling for twenty years.

Play was not just a good skill-developer.

It was a better skill-developer.

But why? How?

The question that had haunted me since Belgrade—What is talent?—was getting louder, not quieter. Something was happening in that gym. Something was working. These kids were doing things no one had taught them. They were inventing solutions that coaches with decades of experience hadn't considered.

I didn't have the language yet. I didn't have the theory. All I had was the evidence of my own eyes: a bunch of kids in spray-painted shirts who had just beaten a club with professional coaches, matching warm-ups, and a curriculum endorsed by every expert in the sport.

Play was right.

Now I needed to understand why.

If play were just fun—just kids wasting time—I couldn't see how natural selection would have kept it. Every calorie a lion cub spends wrestling is a calorie not spent growing. Evolution is ruthless. It doesn't preserve what doesn't work.

Yet play persists. In every culture. Across millions of years.

Which told me evolution kept it for a reason.

The question was, what reason?

# Interlude:

# Duncan

The kid with glasses. His mom came to me concerned that Duncan was struggling with school. In those early years, he was skinny, a little uncoordinated. He settled in at goalkeeper—placed himself there as much as he could. He was always in the middle of the group. Summer camps, talent shows, wet court, futsal, street ball. A real part of the friendship glue, but not the strongest player. His skills did fine in pickup games. In goal, he was strong. Then one day, I was asked to attend a meeting with three parents of the very best kids we had. The play in the gym was humming at an incredible level. I expected this to be a positive meeting. Everything seemed to be going so well. Too well. "We don't want to cut anyone," they said, "but we feel like certain kids are holding our kids back." They named three kids. Including Lioul. Including Duncan. "They can still be part of free play. But if you want your program to grow, you need to focus on building the very best." I said thank you. They never came back. Neither did their kids.

***

Later that year, those same parents put a team in our futsal tournament. They designed jerseys, called themselves Joga Bonito—they saw themselves as the proper mix of free play and elite—the beautiful game meets the beautiful people. In the semis, they played against a Joy team with Duncan in goal.

The Joy kids understood the dynamic. A mini super club in the making, ready to take down Joy. At that moment, they were all behind Duncan. Save after save, always followed by a finger pushing the glasses back up. I noticed it was the middle finger. The kids never knew this. Duncan never knew. They just felt it. All those hours in goal had made Duncan positionally fluent. He swept out on balls. He stood up attackers. The gym was packed three deep. Duncan was the best player on the court that day. The game went to penalty kicks. Eight shooters. Then Endolo—one of three girls on the team—missed the goal. They lost. But the Joy kids swarmed the court. They swarmed Duncan. They swarmed Endolo.

***

JOTP was never going to be about only the best. When you try to be the best, you eliminate the Duncans and Liouls of the world. And most diabolically—you lose your chance of being the best. Duncan decided who belongs. Not me. Not those parents. Not any tryout. He decided by showing up. By playing. By pushing his glasses back up and making another save. That's who decides.

# Chapter 5:

# The Search

## Growth

Years two and three passed, and I still didn't know exactly what I was looking for. But I kept an open mind.

Every single day, I watched. Raffi had suggested the space itself needed to call kids in—compelling, inviting—so I took a chance and had two inflatables made, emptying our yearly budget. The kids loved them and we grew. The kids grew too.

Lioul had developed a thunderous toe-ball power shot. Dare was still completely absorbed in doll stacking. Z and Emmanuel facing off in epic Goalie Wars battles. The set of regulars kept growing—Noah, Nick, Phil, Bennett, Duncan, and many others. The gym was becoming famous. Players and coaches from around the metro would show up to see what all the fuss was about.

That super club leader even showed up. He sat in the stands, silently watching his kids get lost in the middle of the play. I could see it in his face: This gym? These kids? This messing around? This was supposed to be development?

I was asking myself the same thing. Teach them. Correct them. This is chaos.

But Victor's voice was louder: "If you believe in it, you need to dedicate the space to it."

Then the tournament ended with a mystery. The Ball Thieves had beaten the First Defenders. Emmanuel's steal had won it. A group of kids in spray-painted shirts had outplayed a well-organized club with professional coaches and matching bags.

The super club coach came looking for answers and left convinced it was a mirage. I understood—it was almost impossible to see past the chaos.

I was not so sure either.

Something real was happening in that gym. I just couldn't name it yet.

## Play Knows the Way

Watching our kids play soccer that first couple of years was both fascinating and deeply confusing. At a tournament in Iowa, we entered our U10 and U11 teams into three matches. Over the course of those games, our kids, under Colleen's coaching, didn't pass the ball a single time. Not once. They dribbled furiously up and down the field, ignoring wide-open teammates, taking ill-advised shots, and losing possession over and over.

The kids didn't notice. They loved every second of it. But the parents on the sidelines? They squirmed in frustration. By the end of the tournament, some were outright mortified. They had paid for travel, hotel rooms, and meals. They had heard me preach over and over that play was going to deliver higher level skills—not this chaos. It was a long car ride home. The parents called for a meeting shortly after we got home.

"Will our kids ever learn to pass?"

"For our family, teamwork is really important. This feels like—we're missing something."

"Can't we teach them movement off the ball? They're all just bunched together!"

"Some of the kids aren't even defending. They're just waiting for the ball so they can cherry-pick!"

And, of course, the inevitable comparison:

"At Barcelona, they start training kids to pass at age eight. Are you saying you know more than Barcelona?"

The parents loved the fact that their kids enjoyed soccer in this new setting where they just played. But deep down, many were worried we were leading them down the wrong path.

Honestly, I understood. I spent many sleepless nights asking myself similar questions: Were we doing the right thing? Was this approach going to work? There is no blueprint. Was letting them figure it out on their own a mistake?

But then, in that same parents' meeting, Victor stood up and said something unexpected.

"When my younger brother was little, instead of saying 'green tree,' he would say 'gween twee.' Nobody panicked. No one assumed he'd talk like that forever. We knew he'd figure it out eventually—and he did. It's the same concept here.

"In theory—and in practice—the kids will learn how to pass. But they need to exhaust their own instincts first: dribble until there's nowhere to go and every path is blocked. That's how they'll discover passing. The kids bunched together? They just want to touch the ball. The ones cherry-picking? They just want to score. These early instincts aren't wrong—they're developmentally essential."

It was a defining moment for our club. The parents stayed and gave us a chance.

## The First Clue

Then an interesting thing happened one day.

It was hot—mid-nineties and humid. Outside, we had placed a large sheet of canvas on the ground, set up goals at each end, and kept the hose running. The kids cooled down on our makeshift splash court, sliding and laughing in the spray.

As they filtered back inside the gym, they stayed barefoot. The game going on was a pickup game of seven-v-seven to futsal goals with a soft play volleyball—one of those light, squishy balls that couldn't hurt anyone. The kids had discovered it weeks ago, and I'd let them keep using it.

First a Volley-Lite and now a play volleyball? This wasn't "real." No way would this transfer to the actual game.

What happened next was perhaps the most surprising moment of my coaching career.

Emmanuel—faster than a jungle cat, one of the best players in the gym—broke free and nailed that play volleyball right into the smiling face of a six-year-old.

For a second, I was worried.

But the six-year-old was smiling even larger now. He had just made a save against the best shooter in the gym.

Then Emmanuel turned the corner again. This time he took something off the shot, but he still pinged it. The little six-year-old stayed active and went for it, deflecting it away at the last second.

The gym went crazy. This six-year-old goalie was hot.

Now Eman comes again. But this time he saw the keeper cutting off the angle. A very soft chip. The six-year-old, slow to recognize the vector, backpedaled late. The ball dropped just over both outstretched arms—no chance to jump. The six-year-old picked up the ball, still smiling.

He knew it took a great finish to beat him.

I was stunned.

What just happened?

## What I Thought I Knew

"Finishing can't be taught."

I had heard this my whole career. It was coach-speak for "I have no idea how to teach it."

I had tried everything. Drills. Repetitions. Breaking down the motion. "Low to the far post, high to the near post." Functional training, conditional training, training with pressure.

None of it worked. The highest level of skill in the game—putting the ball in the net—remained a mystery.

And here, in a chaotic pickup game with a ball that wasn't even a soccer ball, I was watching kids solve the problem and find the solution I couldn't teach.

Why?

I started to replay what I'd seen:

The six-year-old stayed active. He didn't flinch. He didn't turn his back. He didn't duck. The ball couldn't hurt him, so he was fully present at the most important moment—the moment of the finish.

And that changed everything for the shooter.

With a regular ball, keepers at this age protect themselves. They half-step away. They turn. They shrink. They're too smart to stand in front of a size-five ball from five meters.

But this kid? With this ball? He was fearless. He made saves that required great finishes to beat.

And so in this little game on a forgotten day of a long summer—if he was to win this game, Eman had to become a great finisher. Not because I taught him. Because the six-year-old demanded it.

The environment had asked a question I never thought to ask.

And the kids had answered it.

## The Theories

Over the next few months, I dug in—reading books, taking courses, talking to other coaches—trying to understand what play actually does. Five explanations kept surfacing. None of them felt right.

**Practice Light:** Play is just informal practice—kids messing around with rainbows and nutmegs before we teach the real skills in training. But that gets it backward. My structured sessions were pale copies of what I'd just seen happen naturally in that gym.

**Ecological Dynamics:** Modern coaches love rich, variable environments and "self-organizing exploration of affordances." They're right that chaos helps. But play already includes the variability EcoD wants to engineer. The design layer is sometimes the thing that gets in the way.

**Fun Play:** Play matters because it's fun. Kids enjoy it, then eventually outgrow it and get serious. This felt dismissive. The six-year-old wasn't having fun instead of learning—the fun was the learning.

**Dog Eat Dog:** Play builds toughness. You remember the super club leader—he once told me, "My favorite player is Suárez, and he is willing to bite an opponent to win." Only the strongest survive. But that didn't hold up. Bullying drives people away; the game dies. Real play has competition, but it also needs mutual dependence. Cruelty kills what makes the game worth playing.

**Motivational Flow:** Play feels good, so kids rack up hours without noticing. Closest to the truth. But coaches still try to fake it—gamification, points, rewards slapped onto controlled, high-pressure environments. You can't manufacture intrinsic joy that way. It's either alive or it isn't.

These ideas circled the truth but never landed. I kept coming back to the same question: if play produces something so powerful, why do we spend so much effort replacing it?

## The Sixth Theory

Each of these theories orbits around play, trying to describe its gravity. Each captures a fragment. None explain why play is so stubbornly powerful, across every culture, every era, and every sport.

To find that answer, you have to zoom out—past sport, past childhood, past humans.

Many people think of Darwin as being only about reproduction—genes passing from parent to child, species branching over millions of years. But Darwin's insight is far more general than that.

Everything evolves.

Soccer players evolve. Literature students evolve. Businesses evolve.

Languages evolve. Your finishing technique evolves.

Things change. Things are selected. Better versions persist.

Evolution runs on three ingredients:

- *Variation*—There have to be differences. Different moves, different ideas, different attempts. No variation, no raw material.
- *Replication*—The successful variations have to be repeated. No repetition, no learning.
- *Differential Survival*—Some variations have to "win" over others. No pressure, no direction.

When all three ingredients are present, something improves. Anything. A startup. A free throw. A first touch. A joke.

Fun is nature's Pavlov's bell.

The feeling of fun is evolution's signal that all three ingredients are present. When you're having fun—real fun, not manufactured fun, not "gamified" fun—your nervous system is telling you:

- You are varying.
- You are repeating what works.
- You are being selected.
- You are evolving.

That's why you can't fake it with slogans. That's why "make it fun" doesn't work when shouted over suicides and cone drills.

The feeling of fun isn't the cause of learning.

It's the effect of a learning engine that is already running hot.

It is feedback.

Keep going. This matters. You are adapting.

## The Soft Volleyball, Revisited

Now we can understand what happened that day in the gym.

The barefoot kids. The soft volleyball. The six-year-old keeper who couldn't be hurt.

**Variation:** Eman tried different solutions—power, placement, chip, feint, delay. The keeper tried different saves—reaction, positioning, reading the angle, holding his line, charging out.

Nobody told them to vary. The game demanded it.

**Replication:** They did it again. And again. And again. Hundreds of times in a single session. No coach organizing lines. No whistle resetting the drill. No water-break lecture on "coaching points."

They simply wanted to keep going. The bell of fun kept ringing, so the repetitions kept coming.

**Differential Survival:** Bad finishes died. No problem for the six-year-old.

Decent finishes died too. He got a hand to them.

Only great finishes scored.

The environment turned this smiling six-year-old into a ruthless selection pressure. He never flinched, never turned his back, never ducked. The ball couldn't hurt him, so he stayed fully present in the most important moment.

You will not get that from a full-size ball at five meters. No matter how "competitive" the kid is, his lizard brain will make him protect himself. He'll half-step away. He'll turn. He'll shrink.

Our soft ball didn't make the game safer. It made the game truer.

The missing ingredient in most finishing drills is not more reps. It's real selection pressure on the solution.

In that gym, every shot was a little hypothesis: From this touch, at this angle, with this keeper in this spot, this finish will score.

Sometimes it did.

Often it didn't.

Watch what happens after a huge miss in front of goal. You see it on every continent, in every league, from U9s behind a strip mall to the Champions League: the same little ritual.

The striker fluffs the sitter … and their hands fly straight to their head. They grab their hair, cover their face, squeeze their skull as if they're trying to physically staple the moment to their brain.

It looks like melodrama. It's closer to science.

Every miss is expensive information.

Don't forget this one.

Don't repeat that version again.

In our gym, that process was happening in fast-forward. No coach was "teaching finishing." The kids were evolving it.

They couldn't have explained any of this. But they could feel it.

They felt the fun.

## The Question

Play works. We've seen it. A ball hitting a six-year-old in the face and turning him into the most valuable teacher in the gym.

The barefoot kids with the soft volleyball.

The ball thieves who beat the first defenders.

Emmanuel's steal that won the tournament.

They are evidence, I believe, of an evolutionary process at work.

The obvious question is:

Why does this "inefficient" wandering of play so often beat the "efficient" climbing of deliberate practice?

Why does our carefully planned training so often produce players who struggle in the chaos that play thrives in?

I had seen the evidence. I had felt the fun. I knew play was building something that coaching couldn't.

But I still couldn't explain why.

Why does "work harder" sometimes make you worse? Why does the kid who looks lost at twelve suddenly explode at sixteen? Why do the early stars so often flame out, while the wanderers find their way to the top?

The answer, I would learn, has to do with the shape of the problem itself—not a single mountain to climb, but a landscape of peaks and valleys. A landscape where there is one rule: "Only step up."

The most successful college soccer coach in American history built his entire philosophy on "only up." Twenty-two national championships.

A method called the Competitive Cauldron.
It looked like the answer.
It was a local maximum.

# Interlude:

# Noah

Noah showed up early, every summer, long before Joy became anything official. Small and quiet as a kid—easy, unhurried—he was the kind who gets missed in tryouts because he doesn't demand attention. Coaches read him as low intensity. I read him as presence.

He never rushed. Never panicked. He just showed up in the right place, over and over, like he'd been there waiting all along.

When he shot up to six-foot three, most kids lose coordination. The body changes faster than the brain can adapt. Suddenly they're tripping over feet that used to know where to go. Not Noah. He'd already logged so many hours moving in real games with friends that the new body arrived with the software installed. The growth spurt didn't break his fluency—it extended it.

The clearest image I have: his shirt was never dirty.

Defending often looks like collision and panic—slides, desperate clears, fouls born from arriving late. Noah rarely needed any of that. He anticipated. He neutralized danger before it existed. Attackers came at him expecting a battle and found air. He'd show them a lane, let them commit, take the ball, and play out calmly.

Never rushed. Shirt still clean.

He went on to be indispensable, subtle, secure, reliable. U19 national champion. Joy AC's all-time leader in minutes. The game couldn't happen without him. He was the opposite of a highlight reel. A forward would break free, a highlight ready to happen. Noah swept it away. The crowd letting out a soft groan. If you looked closely, very closely at that point, Noah would show that short little smile. That steady presence is another form of underloading. It isn't spectacle. It's efficiency.

Fluency isn't only what you do with the ball.

It's everything you don't have to do without it.

# Chapter 6:

# The Landscape

## The Hidden Parking Lot

Danielson arrived at Joy as a skinny, street-smart eleven-year-old, already one of the strongest players on the field. He told me he played with his dad a lot. I pictured backyard drills, the kind of father-son bonding that builds fundamentals through repetition and sweat.

I was wrong.

One Saturday a few years later, we drove twenty miles north to Forest Lake and found a hidden parking-lot league: four-on-four under floodlights on asphalt and gravel, goals improvised from traffic cones and rope, tacos sizzling on a grill, music blaring, a hundred dollars on the line per game, and beer flowing on the sidelines. Legend had it that even future MLS pros showed up for easy cash. Whatever the truth, the place was real—and raw.

And Danielson belonged there.

He played like no one I'd ever seen. He'd slow defenders simply by leaning back, take on a keeper with calm eyes, and somehow the keeper would dive the wrong way. For years I couldn't figure out how he did it. Most kids I coached were climbing one hill: faster feet, quicker reactions, more power. Danielson had found a different hill entirely. He wasn't working harder—he was exploring smarter.

It would take me years, and a geneticist, and a Brazilian hurdle, to understand what he already knew.

## The Shape of the Problem

Anson Dorrance built twenty-two national championships on one simple philosophy: "The only practice environment in which you truly develop a player is a competitive arena."

The legendary coach of the University of North Carolina women's soccer team did it through a system he called the Competitive Cauldron—a data-driven, hyper-competitive environment where every action in practice is tracked, ranked, and published. Every sprint, every small-sided game win, every tackle recorded. Players ranked from one to thirty on a whiteboard for everyone to see. Your rank determines your playing time.

More, better, faster. The summit of overload. Twenty-two national championships.

The methods spread everywhere. Teams put up field banners: Seek Discomfort. Embrace the Suck. Total buy-in was the ask. I watched a top-ten Division I women's team recently. One of the new recruits beamed as she zipped past the sidelines: "I wasn't sure I wanted to play here, but when the coach said this will be the hardest thing you ever do, I was sold."

In the highlight reel, four players cheered from crutches.

The Cauldron and other overload methods are magnificent machines. Overload works. The problem is not that overload is wrong; the problem is that everyone who uses it believes it is the only way.

But nature rarely allows one strategy to dominate. To understand where the strategies lie, we need a different picture. A landscape.

## The Fitness Landscape

Geneticist Sewall Wright needed a way to visualize how evolution works—how different designs compete over time. So he imagined a map. The horizontal axes hold every possible version of a system. In biology, that is gene combinations and traits. For a soccer player, it is technique, tactics, decision-making, physical capacity. For a club, it is structure, culture, style of play.

The vertical axis is fitness—how well each design works. In soccer, contribution to winning and long-term development.

Plot everything and you do not get one smooth hill with a single peak. You get many hills and valleys. Some peaks are tall. Some are short. Some look tall from where you are standing but are dwarfed by mountains you cannot see yet.

The goal is to get to Everest.

Overload understands this well. To get to the top, it lives by one rule: only step up. It prescribes work, rest, recovery, supercompensation, and repeat. It assumes up is always good. But it also—though this is not in the overload manual—assumes only one hill. It never asks the dangerous question: what if this is the wrong hill?

Wright saw the problem too. He created the concept of a local maximum—a peak higher than everything immediately around it, but not the highest overall. In doing so he created a counterintuitive yet elegant way to visualize the problem. If you are standing on a local maximum and your only rule is always go uphill, you are stuck. Every direction looks like down. The only way to reach a higher peak is to descend first—to get worse before you get better. As any mountain climber worth his salt knows: it's the going down that gets you.

## Up and Down

In this landscape, up is what the system knows: overload, conscious effort, deliberate practice, the grind that coaches can measure and parents can see. Every drill, every rep, every sprint repeat is a step up the hill you are already on. The body works. The mind monitors. The effort is visible and therefore valued.

Down is what the system cannot see: play, unconscious acquisition, the wandering exploration that looks like nothing but is building vocabulary the grind could never reach. It does not feel like progress. It does not look like progress. You cannot put it on a whiteboard or rank it one to thirty. But it is how you find the higher hill.

The Competitive Cauldron keeps you moving up. It just cannot show you when you have reached the top of the wrong mountain.

Danielson was not climbing the Cauldron's hill. He was playing in a parking lot in Forest Lake, under floodlights, for a hundred dollars, with his dad. He was going down—exploring the valleys, building a vocabulary no drill could install—and finding his way to a peak the system could not see from where it was standing.

## The Brazilian Hurdle

In 1970, Brazil eviscerated the competition at the World Cup in Mexico. Every federation wanted to know how they had done it. The only standout element anyone could point to was something called circuit training—players running through stations, sprinting, shooting, heading balls hanging from ropes.

And then there were the hurdles.

Spaced out over forty yards, six hurdles alternated tall and short. Three or four feet, then six inches. High, then low, then high, then low.

I understood the tall hurdles. Maximum effort, maximum explosion—the kind of demand that shows up in GPS data and makes sense to a federation committee.

But the six-inch hurdle? They must have run out of hurdles. This had to be a mistake. But then when we look closer, maybe it was pure genius.

In 2004 and 2008, I studied in Brazil with Thadeu Goncalves at the Instituto Brasileiro de Futebol. He mentored under Julio Mazzei and Telê Santana. Thadeu had a wonderful way of grounding Brazil's sometimes elusive aesthetic. Brazilians sometimes call their skill "magic." Their systems, "art." On the Brazilian definition of skill he was clear: an action completed successfully in the least amount of time with the least amount of effort. Least time. Least effort. Same result.

## Orgel's First Rule

Another scientist helps us see how we move on this landscape. Leslie Orgel, a chemist at the Salk Institute, spent his life on one of the nastiest questions in biology: How does lifeless chemistry bootstrap itself into living systems?

You don't answer that by imagining a coach in the sky with a master plan. You answer it by looking at millions of tiny reactions in a messy environment, where some patterns run quicker, some require less energy, some waste fewer resources—and those are the ones that stick.

Orgel captured this pattern in what became known as his First Rule: "Whenever a spontaneous process is too slow or too inefficient, a protein will evolve to speed it up or make it more efficient." In plain terms, the reactions that survived were the ones that either ran faster or required less energy for the same result. He reduced this to a simple rule of thumb: improvement tends to survive along two paths—faster or easier.

On our fitness landscape, those are just two different ways of going uphill. You can climb by getting to the result sooner. Or you can explore the valleys and look for the best way up—little adventures up, little movements down. That's the near-perfect play system Danielson's dad set up for him. Each game, you'd see Danielson roaming, scanning, and discovering easier paths.

We've industrialized "faster": overload, volume, hypertrophy, sprint times, reaction drills, GPS metrics. All visible, countable, easy to sell to anxious parents. The Competitive Cauldron is a faster machine. Most academies optimize for faster.

We've neglected Danielson's "easier." In evolutionary terms, "easier" is underloading: same result, less cost. That's what survives. "Easier" is discovered through underloading—smart constraints that reward economy and information, not just exertion. It doesn't announce itself with grunting effort or complicated drills. It masquerades as intuition, as a clever trick, as sheer luck.

The tall hurdle trains faster. The six-inch hurdle trains easier.

Easier is not simpler. The most talented player clears the six-inch hurdle by the smallest possible margin without touching it. Maximum precision. Minimum expenditure. The body doing exactly what is needed and nothing more. The athlete who clears it by two feet is wasting energy. The athlete who clears it by a quarter inch has found the line between possible and not possible with surgical accuracy.

Brazil was training both axes. Most federations watching went home and built more tall hurdles. They measured the effort they could see and missed the precision they couldn't.

Easier doesn't grunt. It doesn't show up on a whiteboard. It is Panenka chipping when he could have blasted. It is the six-inch hurdle that looked like a mistake.

Deliberate practice selects for faster. Play discovers easier. We need both. We have forgotten one almost entirely.

## The Western Roll

I learned about local optima long before I had the language for it.

I was a middle school high jumper, obsessed with the Western Roll—the dominant technique of the era. I studied Valery Brumel, the Soviet world record holder. The library had two track and field books; one had grainy stop-motion photos of Brumel's approach. Debbie and I built a neighborhood jump station: coat racks as uprights, a bamboo pole as the bar, an old mattress for landing.

I spent hours refining. Hundreds of jumps. I won gold at the sixth-grade city-wide Olympics. I was the best Western Roll jumper in my little city—a perfect local maximum.

The next year, aiming for a personal record of five feet, an untrained 880-yard runner asked for a try. He backed up and shouted, "Here comes the Fosbury Flop!" We laughed.

Before 1968, high jumpers went over the bar face-down. Coaches drilled it. Athletes optimized it. Then Dick Fosbury showed up at the Olympics and went over backward. He looked ridiculous. Commentators laughed. But he won gold—and within a decade, every elite high jumper had abandoned the straddle.

The Fosbury Flop was a higher peak. But no amount of perfecting the Western Roll would get you there. You had to abandon what you knew, descend into awkwardness, and climb a completely different hill.

Fosbury wasn't trained into the flop. He played his way into it—experimenting as a kid, finding what felt easier, ignoring coaches who told him he was doing it wrong.

The 880 runner cleared five feet easily. Then five feet six.

The coach stared, then turned to me: "Kroeten, you're moving to hurdles."

Years of practice, obsolete in an afternoon. I had maximized the wrong hill. No harder work on the Western Roll would have gotten me there. And years later, setting up those dome training sessions with nothing but tall hurdles, I was doing the same thing again—optimizing the wrong axis, not knowing the six-inch hurdle existed.

## Kauffman: When Up Gets You Stuck

Stuart Kauffman asked a simple question: What happens when everything affects everything else?

In a simple system, improvement is straightforward—work harder, get better. One path up. But in a complex system, where your move changes my options and my response changes yours, the landscape becomes rugged. Hundreds of peaks and valleys. Many decent solutions, few great ones.

Kauffman showed that on a rugged landscape, the better you optimize locally, the more stuck you become. Hill-climbing works on smooth terrain. On rugged terrain, it guarantees getting trapped on the first decent bump you find.

Think of it this way. A player who only drills never discovers the move that makes defenders dive the wrong way. A coach who only measures never sees what Danielson was building in that parking lot. On rugged landscapes, refusing to descend is mathematically equivalent to refusing to improve.

You can tattoo that across the gates of every over-coaching, early-selection program in youth sports.

Danielson's parking-lot wanderings weren't grind sessions. They were explorations. He roamed the field, meeting the valley folk, discovering easier paths—and somewhere in those wanderings he found his backbend move, the one no mountain summiter had ever seen.

I'm pretty sure he won more than he lost.

## The Intentional Descent

Jannik Sinner, the Italian tennis player who rose to world number one, said it out loud after a defeat to Carlos Alcaraz at the 2025 US Open final. To reach the next level, he realized he had to get more creative—accepting short-term losses while his game reorganized.

"I was very predictable," Sinner admitted. He had cruised through earlier rounds using baseline power, but that same linear strategy failed against Alcaraz's variety. He had avoided serve-and-volleys and drop shots, leaving him trapped in his comfort zone when it mattered most.

"I'm going to aim to maybe even lose some matches from now on, but trying to do some changes."

The valley allows a temporary dip to build a more complete toolkit. Moving away from a pure baseline game to embrace easier paths—using touch and angles to make opponents do the work. Most development systems punish exactly this kind of descent. Coaches panic at the drops. Parents pull their kids. But Sinner understood the fitness landscape: his current peak was blocking his path to higher mountains.

## The Dan Plan

Sinner understood the landscape. Dan McLaughlin didn't get the chance to.

In 2010, photographer Dan McLaughlin quit his job to test Anders Ericsson's theory of deliberate practice. He launched the Dan Plan to see if 10,000 hours of rigorous training could take a novice to the PGA Tour.

I met Dan at a skills acquisition conference in Finland in 2015. He was compelling. Precise. Hopeful. Completely committed to the climb.

Starting with just a putter, Dan followed a strict incremental path, spending months mastering shots from just one foot away before moving back. By 2014, after 5,100 hours, he reached a 3.3 handicap—top four and a half percent of US golfers. Ericsson held him up as proof that expertise is available to anyone willing to work, rather than a gift for the talented few.

At just over six thousand hours, Dan's back gave out from the constant physical overload.

The Dan Plan was the ultimate experiment in linear hill-climbing. As Kauff man discovered, up is only a good direction if you are on a smooth, simple hill. On the rugged landscape of a sport like golf, the very discipline that brought Dan to a 3.3 handicap was exactly what kept him from going further—and eventually what stopped him cold.

## Two Paths Through the Landscape

Imagine two kids at age eight, both standing at the bottom of a mountain range.

Kid A gets a coach. The coach points to a nearby peak: There. That's the goal. Here's the path. Kid A climbs. By twelve he is at the top. He is better than everyone his age. The system rewards him—select team, premier league, academy invitation.

But it is a local peak. There is a higher mountain in the distance, but Kid A cannot see it from where he is standing. And to get there he would have to climb down first—back into the valley, back to looking bad, back to the bottom of a ranking. No one does that. The system will not let him.

Kid B has no coach. She wanders. She explores. At twelve she is still in the foothills, and hasn't committed to any peak. She looks lost. The system ignores her.

But by then she has seen more of the landscape. And at sixteen she finds a path to the highest peak—one Kid A never knew existed.

Play keeps kids in the foothills longer. The system rushes them up the nearest peak. That is the trap.

Danielson was Kid B—wandering parking lots, reading faces, discovering easier paths while everyone else polished their Western Rolls. The U10 phenom who dominates at twelve is Kid A. Done by sixteen, stuck on a peak he didn't know was small.

Danielson bloomed late. But he bloomed higher.

## Grow or Squeeze

Gérard Houllier knew something about lemons. I saw him present at SoccerEx London in 2008. He was the architect of Clairefontaine—the academy built to replace (guess what?) the street football culture that was disappearing from French cities. An institution designed to replicate what play had once provided for free. Under his leadership Clairefontaine produced Thierry Henry, David Trezeguet, and a generation of French players who redefined the game. But Houllier didn't try to maximize fourteen-year-olds. He gave them time, space, and freedom. A deliberately lowered pressure. A protected environment where young players could explore without the landscape crushing them.

"You can grow the lemon, or squeeze the lemon. You can't do both."

Overload methodologies like the Competitive Cauldron squeeze. Twenty-two championships, a hill climbed all the way to the top. Houllier grew. And produced players who kept producing for decades.

Danielson grew in a parking lot in Forest Lake. Same principle, different soil.

The choice is always the same: grow or squeeze. Underload or overload. Easier or faster. One peak now, or the highest peak later.

The question that haunted me was simpler than all of that: when does the climb begin? When does work start to matter?

Before I found the science, I found the symptom. A diagnostic marker that my wife noticed before I did.

# Interlude:

# The Manual

## How to Get Kids to Quit Video Games

Video game companies used to provide manuals with their games in hopes kids would delve into the arcana, become experts, and dive even further into the game. Companies built levels on levels. Their theory was simple: the deeper you got into the game, the more you would love it. The manual said: "By pushing the B button and the thumb toggle at the same time, your avatar can kick off the head of the ninja."

But kids weren't reading the manuals. What they did was just press lots of buttons until they slowly discovered what those buttons and combinations did. They learned themselves how to kick the head off the ninja. Soon the companies stopped producing the manuals. And then a funny thing happened. Video games took off. Kids enjoyed them more than ever. The companies observed that the discovery process was totally addictive. Kids would spend hours and hours to find a new skill, method, or tactic. Could it be that the discovery of what the buttons did WAS the fun part? That the level of the game you achieved was secondary? Video game companies have bet billions on it. Piaget tried to warn us: teach a child something he could have discovered himself, and you've stolen the understanding. The game companies learned. Youth sports hasn't. Now, I have nothing against video games. But I have seen the following deprogramming techniques work in other fields to devastating effect. Remember: level of play is secondary to discovery. So it's very simple. Attack the discovery. Attack the fun.

## Deprogramming

- **Step 1**: Actively get involved. Demand that your kids learn it the way the manual says. (If there is no manual, pretend there is one.)
- **Step 2**: Park yourself over or behind your kid and watch. Beach chairs work great. Watch EVERYTHING.
- **Step 3**: Comment on mistakes and be more demanding. Say general things like "Let's really want it!" or "Be aggressive!" or "Let's show a little hustle." This sends a friendly message that you would like to see some improvement from their video play.
- **Step 4**: Make use of the captive audience. When they are riding in the car, really drill down. Try to use specific examples of mistakes and of course stick to the manual. Say things like: "It says here that if you press the B button and the thumb toggle at the same time you kick the head off the ninja! DON'T YOU REALLY WANT TO KICK THE HEAD OFF THAT NINJA?" (It's OK to add a little emphasis.) At this point your child, hoping to continue playing video games, might say something like: "But I really do want it!" Refer to the manual to back up your argument: "Well, you must not, because if you REALLY wanted it you would kick the head off the ninja. You're not pressing the B button and the thumb toggle. I don't think you really want it."
- **Step 5**: Repeat steps 1 through 4.

***

It won't be long before your son or daughter takes up some other activity—usually one with no manual—like skateboarding or playing in a garage band. Your child's days of playing video games are over.

# Chapter 7:

# The Invasion Of The Body Snatchers

## Alien Spotting

It was Colleen who pointed it out first.

"Why does she always do that?" she asked, nodding toward a girl on the field during a high-level match.

"Do what?"

"That thing with her arms… watch."

The player, a left-back, received a simple pass. As the ball arrived, her hands abruptly shot up above her shoulders in a frantic, bird-like flutter before settling back down. It was a split-second spasm, a hiccup in the flow.

"That's just her thing," I said, brushing it off.

But then I started seeing them everywhere. The Noisy Arms.

It wasn't every player—just specific ones. My daughter and the girls from Joy had arms that were quiet, natural, tied to their balance and to what their partners were doing. But for certain kids—the ones who seemed to be carrying something heavy—the arms were a consistent tic. A brief, unnecessary seizure of movement during receiving, dribbling, or passing.

I had watched millions of skill actions. Why had I never noticed this?

## The Tell

In the 1956 sci-fi classic *Invasion of the Body Snatchers*, the Pod People look exactly like their victims. What gives them away is the language—not the words, but the lack of emotion, the uncanny delivery, the failure to truly connect. "Hello. How. Are. You. Today?"

The Noisy Arms are the tell. They are the halted speech of someone trying to speak a language alone, without a conversation partner. Movement that has been isolated, decontextualized, practiced in a vacuum.

And they don't appear out of nowhere. They are manufactured.

## The Temple of Hard Work

A coaching friend opened a training center focused on individual skill improvement. A thirty thousand square foot soccer facility. Instagram paradise.

I visited and saw the Pod People being made.

Kids navigating Ninja Warrior obstacle courses with a ball. "Bounce here, flip there, spin around this pole." Sharp, fast, decontextualized. No partners. No interaction. Just individual performance.

I saw eight-year-olds and pros alike flailing. One pro player had developed a bizarre "swimming motion" with his left arm every time he shot with his right foot. The kids were running through five to fifteen seconds of high-octane movement patterns—faster, cleaner, harder. Everything overstimulating: encouraging coaches, bright cones, pristine turf, giant mannequins, goals with bells, blinking lights.

For years, I thought this was the source. The facility. The isolated training.

I was only seeing half the picture.

## Colorless Green Ideas

The linguist Noam Chomsky composed a famous sentence in 1957: "Colorless green ideas sleep furiously."

It follows every rule of English grammar. Adjective, adjective, noun, verb, adverb. Your brain accepts it as a sentence. But it means absolutely nothing. Ideas cannot have color. Something colorless cannot be green. Sleeping cannot be done furiously.

Grammatically perfect. Semantically dead.

That's what the Temple was building. Kids assembling technically correct movements that said nothing. Syntax without semantics. Sentences uttered into a void.

The arms were the tell. They were reaching for a conversation partner who wasn't there.

## The Weight They Carry

The Noisy Arms don't just appear in kids who train alone against cones. They appear in kids who are overloaded—overwhelmed by demands that exceed their capacity to respond naturally.

I started noticing the same flutter in kids who had never set foot in a training facility. Kids on high-level teams with demanding coaches. Kids in systems that required constant conscious attention to positioning, shape, and role. Kids whose parents had ambitions that preceded their own.

The arms weren't a symptom of isolated training specifically. They were a symptom of overload generally. A warning sign that the system—whatever system—was asking more than the nervous system could give.

Wolfgang Schöllhorn, the developer of Differential Learning, gives us a dire warning: "Too much repetition along with too much ambition leads to a sort of disease of the prefrontal cortex. It wants to take over control."

And then it gets scary: "This ambition and repetition together creates something similar to Parkinson's."

What I think we are seeing is a nervous system hijacked by conscious control and deprived of the ability to respond naturally, going into revolt. The "coach in the head" is micromanaging movements that should be fluent responses to living, breathing partners. The body fights back with uncontrolled tics.

## What My Father Taught Me

I saw this mechanism play out in my own father, who battled Parkinson's for the last years of his life.

The automatic, unconscious movements we take for granted—grasping, reaching, turning—became conscious negotiations. Every action required deliberate effort. The body trembles and freezes because the brain is trying too hard to manage what should flow naturally. I watched my father as simple tasks became exhausting puzzles. He drank coffee from a straw.

But hand him a tennis racquet, and something remarkable happened.

His Jack Kramer-inspired serve was silky as ever. The tremors quieted. The hesitation vanished. For those few seconds of motion, the disease seemed to release its grip.

Why? Because he had learned that serve decades earlier, through countless hours of mindless play with partners. It wasn't installed through conscious, deliberate practice in isolation. It was absorbed through the conversational flow of the game.

That serve was embedded so deeply in his procedural memory that it was safe from the prefrontal takeover. The disease couldn't touch it because it had never been consciously controlled in the first place.

## The Un-Snatched: Leo and the Harvest Moon

It was senior night at Minneapolis Edison High School under a giant harvest moon. With fifty-three seconds left, the game was tied. Leo stood over a free kick.

Just seconds before, St. Paul Harding had countered with a chip over the Edison keeper. Heads went down; quiet filled the stadium. After the kickoff, Leo took the ball and drove at the Harding backline. At about twenty-five yards from goal he was taken down with a foul. Sitting on the bench I heard the kids cheer—the senior captain had scored four times this season on free kicks. Could this be another moment?

The opposing team set up a wall, and—having scouted Leo—they put a player on the near and far post as well. I understood this was a big ask. But this was Leo, and his teammates hugged each other—they believed magic was about to happen.

I recognized the Leo free-kick pattern: same stance, quiet, still, a little closer than you might think. A sudden acceleration to the ball. He strikes with the side of his foot and the ball barrels away—up and over the leaping wall, then down and under the crossbar. Two inches over the head of the near-post protector, an inch under the bar.

A perfect goal. Then bedlam.

Leo would score seven free-kick goals that season in fifteen games on twenty-one total attempts—a thirty-three percent conversion rate. Cristiano Ronaldo converts around 6.7 percent. Lionel Messi about 9.1 percent.

As his high school coach, I never saw Leo practice a free kick—not once—nor did I ask him to train it. He didn't stay late to grind. I never told him how to hit the ball.

Leo grew up at Joy of the People. From age five, he just played. He lived nearby; when he was old enough, he and his friends biked the short distance—fall, winter, spring, summer. His "practice" was thousands of hours of goalie wars with a volleyball and make it, take it with a futsal ball. His feedback was his own, his acquisition unconscious. There's a video on our website—seven-year-old Leo slip-sliding on a wet court, grinning. In more than ten years with Leo, including high school, I never gave him a coaching instruction.

When Leo stood over that free kick on senior night, his arms were quiet. His body was calm. The movement that followed—the strike, the curve, the ball settling under the crossbar—emerged from a brain that wasn't fighting itself.

## The Candle and the Fire

In *Antifragile,* Nassim Taleb gives us the perfect metaphor: "The wind extinguishes a candle but energizes a fire. You want to be the fire and hope for the wind."

The Candle is the skill built under too much pressure, too much demand, too much conscious control. It requires a windless environment to survive. When it encounters the wind of real-game pressure—the screaming fans, the harvest moon, the living, breathing conversation partners—it flickers and dies. This, I believe, is one origin of the Noisy Arms.

The Fire is Leo. Fluency forged in constant conversation. The wind is not the enemy—it is fuel. The pressure of the final seconds, the presence of teammates and opponents, the shared stakes don't break the fluency; they make it burn brighter.

Leo's thirty-three percent conversion rate isn't a statistic about individual practice. It is proof of conversational fluency energized by the social, high-stakes environment it was created for.

## A Different Path

Leo never showed the Noisy Arms. Neither did my daughter, nor the kids who grew up at Joy of the People.

Their development wasn't less rigorous—it was differently rigorous. They faced competition, pressure, high-stakes moments under harvest moons. Score against their sister, then their friend, then the oldest kid at the park. Their nervous systems developed through conversation, variation, and play.

Not overload.

This isn't an argument against coaching. It's an argument against coaching that suppresses the conversation play was already having.

## What Colleen Saw

Colleen is an overload spotter. She didn't need me to walk her through fifteen years of theory. She just watched.

I remember that first spray-painted jersey futsal tournament. I had to coach in St. Paul and couldn't be there for the first few games. I called her, nervous. "How are they doing?"

"You would not believe it," she said. "The score is thirteen to twelve. They score and then they just let the other team score so they can get the ball back sooner."

I could see it in my head—the smiles, the chaos, the joy of kids who understood that the point was the play, not the scoreboard.

In fifteen years, she never once told me the Joy kids failed to display that art and warmth.

So when she pointed at that girl's arms and asked, "Why does she always do that?" I should have listened sooner. Colleen had been watching the whole time. She knew what fluency looked like.

She could see when it was missing.

I finally understood the mechanism. But understanding play isn't the same as using it. For years, I tried to harness play—to direct it, schedule it, make it serve my goals.

I was missing the point entirely. Play doesn't walk in through the front door of improvement. It sneaks in through the side door of fun.

The architects had a word for what I was missing. They called it a spandrel.

# Interlude:

# Lioul

Lioul was eight when he started calling for rides. He was the most in love with the game. He struggled to move fluidly. Emmanuel could sprint up a wall and do a backflip. Lioul struggled to shoot a volleyball across the gym. But he called. Every day. "I'm ready to go, coach!" He was temperamental, yes. Naughty hallway visits. Storms to ride out. He could erupt over a bad call, a missed pass, a look he didn't like. More than once I nearly gave up on him. But he always came back. When everyone else drifted away—Eman moved away, Marco moved up north, Z to high school ball—Lioul still called. Still showed up. Still played. He was the last one in the gym and the first one asking when the next session was.

When Coach Dan subbed him in during the serious minutes of that spray-painted jersey futsal final I shook my head. We were down, the clock was dying, and we had more athletic options on the bench. But something told me to trust. A scramble. Bodies everywhere. The ball ricocheted off his knee and in. The tying goal. He didn't score it with skill. He scored it with presence. His skills did not ignore the profits of that presence. He turned himself into a national champion, a key part of the 2019 Futsal team. He kept showing up through every trip, every summer, every odd practice nobody else attended. When the other kids left for college and moved on with their lives, Lioul asked a different question: "Can I coach?"

Now he's the Technical Director at Joy. Beloved High School Assistant Coach. Running sessions, working on his badges, building the next generation. "Lioul!"—a hundred kids shout it when he walks into the gym. We tend to classify kids early—this one has it, that one doesn't. Joy showed me otherwise. Lioul helped prove it. Every kid has a native language. Every kid can play. I used to think I was looking for the next great player. I was actually looking for something rarer: the person who would keep the game alive when I'm gone. Lioul is the oldest kid at the park now. The one who opens the gym brings the balls, gathers the kids, and says: play. The game doesn't select for the best players. It selects for the people who love it enough to keep it going.

# Chapter 8:

# The Spandrels

## The Trivela

When I began playing soccer, I was never formally instructed on technique. Being pigeon-toed, I found it natural and easy—and maybe even a little lazy—to use the outside of my right foot for shots and long passes.

Later, a British coach at a training session told me to stop those "sloppy" outside-of-the-foot passes.

He was trying to remove an architectural quirk. My feet didn't match his blueprint.

But I was simply using the architecture of my own body to solve the problem. By the time I played in college, that "sloppy" pass had been refined into a sixty-yard weapon.

My pigeon-toed gait was the spandrel.

The *trivela* move was the mosaic that ended up painted there.

## What Is a Spandrel?

In architecture, a spandrel is the triangular space between two arches.

When medieval builders constructed cathedral ceilings with rounded arches meeting at angles, they created these accidental spaces—areas that weren't designed for anything. Structural byproducts. Geometric inevitabilities.

But look at any great cathedral, and you'll see what happened to those accidental spaces.

They became canvases.

Artists filled them with mosaics, paintings, sculptures. The most beautiful decorations in the building often occupy the spaces that were never meant to exist.

The spandrel wasn't the goal. It became the masterpiece.

In evolutionary biology, Stephen Jay Gould and Richard Lewontin borrowed this concept to describe exaptation—traits that evolved for one purpose but got co-opted for something completely different. Feathers almost certainly evolved for temperature regulation. Flight came later. Much later.

The feather wasn't designed for flying. It was co-opted for it.

Play creates spandrels. It fills accidental spaces with things no one ordered, no one scheduled, no one wrote into the curriculum—until suddenly, those decorations turn out to be the most powerful tools a player has.

## Silly Shots

Consider John McEnroe, who spent countless hours messing around on the tennis court with his friend Mary Carillo. In those long days of relaxed, fun tennis, freed from formal instruction, they explored every quirky shot they could imagine. McEnroe would hit loose, "silly" volleys at the net—wristy, unconventional, nothing like textbook form.

One coach who witnessed this told him pointedly to "stop hitting those 'girly' shots."

From the coach's point of view, those shots didn't match the model.

From McEnroe's point of view, there was no model—just a ball, a net, and a thousand possible answers.

Those "silly" shots became the wristy, soft-handed volleys that defined his genius at the net. McEnroe and Carillo went on to win the 1977 French Open mixed doubles title. They remain lifelong friends.

## The Ball Thieves, Revisited

Remember the JOTP kids in that futsal tournament? The ones who couldn't play proper "first defender"? Let me tell you what was really happening.

**Phase 1: Escape.** When the kids first started playing, their defensive behavior looked like a glaring deficit. Frozen, lazy feet. Crazy swipes at the ball. Huge lunges. They didn't perform the coached skill of "first defender"—staying low, moving feet, containing the attacker.

Any coach watching would have identified this as a mistake. Something to be drilled out.

**Phase 2: Exaptation.** But we didn't drill it out. We let them play.

Through hundreds of hours of unstructured play, a transformation occurred. The chaotic swipes were tested thousands of times. A wild swipe usually resulted in a whiff, but a well-timed swipe could steal the ball.

The frozen, lazy feet became occasional, smart, darting movements—the feet of pickpockets. The big swipes became precise taps behind the attacker.

They weren't learning "first defender." They were inventing ball thievery.

**Phase 3: Underload.** The futsal final was the unveiling.

The big club kids were trained to face first defenders who stayed low and didn't dive in. They had no framework for this frenetic, swarming, almost anarchic style of pressure. They glanced at their coach, perplexed.

The winning goal came from this exact spandrelized skill. Emmanuel pressured the ball carrier, saw the skip coming, used the refined tap to steal the ball, and scored.

A "weakness" had become a championship-winning strength.

## The Rosengård Factory

Nowhere is this clearer than in the story of Zlatan Ibrahimović.

In 1999, my club team was spending the week training with the Malmö FF academy in Sweden, where a young Zlatan was emerging.

A coach pointed him out as someone who had "put in his ten thousand hours." I wrote down his name, skeptical. This tall, skinny seventeen-year-old didn't move like an athlete. He wobbled when he ran.

Then in 2004, now with Ajax, he dribbled half of the NAC Breda team in a swerving, underloaded symphony—defenders lurching, grasping, looking like they were trying a bit too hard. Our Martian would have been impressed. FIFA named it Goal of the Year. I said to myself: well, that Swedish coach must have been right. There is something to those ten thousand hours.

He turned out to be one of the greatest players in the history of the game.

But here's what the Malmö coaches didn't tell me: Zlatan only joined their academy at fifteen, just three years before I saw him. There was no way he had accumulated ten thousand hours of deliberate practice. If something separated him, it had to be what he was doing before that.

From Zlatan himself: "Just outside my mother's house, on the dusty playing fields of the infamous Rosengård projects, I taught myself to play. When we played football in Rosengård, it was all about putting the ball between people's legs, doing different things. After every trick, people were like 'oohhh,' 'eeeyy.' It was all about who had the best trick, the craziest move. I loved it."

Read that carefully.

"It was all about putting the ball between people's legs." It's the nutmeg. You thread the ball through the defender's own legs and collect it on the other side. Their legs become the gate of their own defeat.

The wonder isn't about effort. It's about ease. You made it easy.

"It was all about who had the best trick, the craziest move." The selection pressure of the street wasn't about who worked hardest. It was about who could produce easy magic.

And then the most important words: "I loved it."

That's the key. That's the back door. The love came first. The skills followed.

Rosengård was a spandrel factory. The kids weren't trying to become professional soccer players. They were trying to make their friends gasp. And in solving those problems—the problems of style, of panache, of "oohhh" and "eeeyy"—they accidentally built skills that transferred to problems they'd never imagined.

The tricks were spandrels. They weren't designed for professional competition. They were exapted for it.

## Javi's Eyeball

Javi was a disaster. He came to Joy with his sister as a four-year-old. For fun, he would panic the staff by hiding somewhere on the complex. In boxes in the storage room. On top of the equipment shed. In the park tunnel. "You seen Javi?" was the slogan.

He could not have cared less about soccer. If he was forced to play goalie wars, it was toe ball or bust—kicking the ball to show his rage at being pulled away from hide and seek.

I remember early on being involved in the search for Javi. What happened? Where was he? Was he lost? Could he have wandered off?

Then I saw, in the crack of a closed box in the kitchen storage locker—an eyeball looking right at me.

I snapped a picture. But I didn't say "got you."

I understood.

One day Javi decided he was going to play. But he kept hiding—on the field. He never calls for the ball. He understands the value of silence. Years of hiding taught him that: never speak, often tiptoe, compress yourself into nothing until the moment comes. And when he appears with the ball close to goal—that "just let me play" power shot—the keeper has no chance.

Javi wasn't developing soccer skills in those storage lockers and park tunnels. He was developing explosive movement, spatial awareness, the ability to disappear and then materialize exactly where no one expected him. Looking back, hide and seek was his Rosengård. The skills he built escaping detection were exapted for the most dangerous thing in soccer: arriving unseen.

Remember Orgel's Second Rule: "Evolution is cleverer than you are."

## Stefan Holm vs. Donald Thomas

In his book *The Sports Gene*, David Epstein covers a case study that haunted me for years.

Stefan Holm was a Swedish high jumper with about as much deliberate practice as any human could accumulate—twenty-five years' worth. Everything he did was focused on capturing the next micro-inch.

Donald Thomas was a virtual nobody. He had only been introduced to high jumping eighteen months before he beat Holm at the World Championships.

A year and a half.

Epstein's point was that genes play an important role—Thomas had unusually long Achilles tendons. Nature matters.

But Epstein missed something.

Thomas wasn't "not jumping" before those eighteen months. He just wasn't high-jumping.

He was a basketball player at Lindenwood, a small NAIA school in Missouri. What Thomas was really known for was show dunking. He posted YouTube videos of himself jumping over various obstacles—like three standing classmates—to dunk at the rim to the cheers of half the school.

Think about that.

Holm consciously worked at jumping. Training. Technique. Coaching. Planning. Difficult. Not inherently fun.

Thomas played at jumping. Unconscious. Joyful. He had no idea how he became good at jumping—but he did know how many likes he got on YouTube.

Thomas's jumping ability was a spandrel. He wasn't trying to become a world-class high jumper. He was trying to be the coolest guy on campus.

Holm spent decades climbing the same hill on purpose.

Thomas spent years running around the valley chasing cheers.

The valley won that day.

## Danger

We think of fun and games as mindless. Safe. Easy. But under this theory, play is the opposite. Play is the descent into the unknown. Play is the exploration of valleys where you might get lost.

When Z was six years old, I dressed him up as a pirate for Halloween, equipped with a two-foot tinfoil and cardboard saber.

"Dad, is this sword dangerous?" he asked.

Before I could answer, he answered himself: "'Cause I need danger."

That's the expert opinion. That's the six-year-old's intuition about what play is for.

Play should be dangerous—not physically, but dangerous in the sense that matters: uncertain, risky, unpredictable. The possibility of failure. The thrill of trying something that might not work.

Danger is just another word for real stakes.

No stakes, no spandrels.

## The Backdoor of Fun

In 2003, researchers at Queen's University interviewed four elite hockey players who had signed NHL contracts as undrafted free agents—making their path to expertise even more remarkable.

One of them put it simply: "I never went out to play street hockey to polish my skills or whatever, we played to play. We'd never go out and set pylons up and practice because we wanted to get better—we'd just go out and have fun."

These players had spent fifty-five percent of their childhood hours in deliberate play versus only ten percent in deliberate practice. They accumulated more hours playing street hockey than they ever spent in organized training. And none of it was aimed at improvement. They were just playing.

You can't aim play at a target. The moment you do, it stops being play. It becomes training with a playful veneer. The kids feel the difference.

Viktor Frankl said it plainly: "Don't aim at success—the more you aim at it and make it a target, the more you are going to miss it."

This isn't a rule against structure. It's a rule about what structure can and can't do. Coaches can build the arches. They cannot paint the spandrels.

Play only works through the backdoor of fun. The kids have to be chasing something they actually want—the "oohhh," the nutmeg, the trick that makes their friends laugh. They have to be solving problems that matter to them.

And in solving their problems, they accidentally build skills that solve your problems too.

That's the spandrel. That's exaptation. That's the hidden trail to the higher peak.

But you can't see the trail while you're walking it. You can't plan the spandrel. You can only create the conditions—the arches—and trust that the accidental spaces will fill with something beautiful.

## The Cathedral

After everything fell apart—after the demotion, the coffee shop betrayal, the year of hauling equipment in dark gyms—I finally understood what Victor had been trying to tell me.

Play isn't a tool you use. It's a space you create.

You build the arches. You create the conditions for fun. You let the kids chase what they actually want to chase.

The spandrels will emerge. The accidental spaces will fill with something you never planned, never imagined, never could have designed.

Our Martian from Belgrade would recognize what's happening. It has seen this on many planets—creatures playing, failing, adapting, and accidentally building fluencies that no curriculum could teach. The Martian knows: you don't design the masterpiece. You build the arches and let it appear.

That's where the Ball Thieves come from. That's where Zlatan's tricks were born. That's where McEnroe's volleys took shape. That's where

Donald Thomas built the explosiveness that beat twenty-five years of deliberate practice.

Not in the arches themselves. In the spaces between.

I had the image now. But I still couldn't explain how.

The answer had been waiting for me since 1977, in a linguistics classroom at USC.

# Interlude:

# Bennett

If you wanted to design a perfect soccer player, you would produce Bennett. Tall, charismatic, left-footed—able to defend, attack, even play keeper. Half Korean, half Ivorian—built like an athlete, moved like a dancer. He walks into a room and the room rearranges itself around him. Every club wanted him. Every sport wanted him. His mom—one of the strongest people I know—fielded dozens of calls and offers. She trusted what she saw instead. Since he was eight he was the social center: playing keeper, wing, pivot, sitting on the bench so others could play, gluing teams together. At the 2021 Nationals our keeper was red-carded and Bennett stepped in. With the clock bleeding out he made the patented Joy Run, a JOTP rite of passage—Bennett caught, baited a defender, sprinted, and played the ball outside to Diego who crossed in the air. Instead of heading it at goal he nudged the ball back into space because he trusted a friend would arrive. Mika did, volleyed it in, and the clock expired.

At seventeen, playing against adults, Bennett won the National Premier Futsal League player-of-the-year award. He leads not by solo brilliance but by building the conditions for everyone else to shine. He underloads through friendship: he organizes movement, calls teammates into play, and makes others better. He built relationships first, and the skills followed. The Ecuadorian league in Minneapolis saw it week after week: Bennett inviting a thousand voices into a party where the party was the point. Every week massive crowds packed Edison High, kids followed him around, dads and uncles placed friendly bets, families dance. Who was this Yankee who played with such beautiful sorcery? Bennett showed me you can't acquire fluency in a game without people to play with—friends come before skills.

# Chapter 9:

# The Professor

## The Mystery

My daughter never wanted to play soccer.

She was six when we opened Joy of the People. The gym became her second home—but not for the reasons I'd hoped. While other kids chased the ball, Dare hung out in the kitchen with her grandmother, played Legos in the lounge, faked injuries so she could quiz the team doctor about whether her taped wrist was "serious."

"Go play," I'd tell her.

She'd wander off to the playground instead.

I stopped pushing. Some kids aren't soccer kids. That's fine. She was happy.

But here's what I couldn't explain: when she did play—once in a while, when the mood struck her—there was something there that shouldn't have been.

She'd receive a pass and turn backward, inviting a defender to commit, then spin away. She did the Maradona—a move the older kids loved—but she did it spinning the opposite direction. Technically wrong. Except it worked.

Where did that come from?

She barely touched a ball. She spent most of her time watching from the sidelines or stacking dolls in the rubber room. The other kids were getting thousands of touches. She was getting dozens.

And yet.

I didn't have a framework for what I was seeing. The traditional youth soccer world runs on a simple equation: touches equal development. More reps, more improvement. The kids who touch the ball most become the best players.

By that logic, Dare should have been hopeless. She wasn't.

Something was being installed in her that had nothing to do with reps.

## The Drowning Freshman

In my freshman year, I almost flunked out of college.

USC, the late 1970s. I was drowning in English 101. My friend Lindy played on the volleyball team. "Just drop English and pick up Linguistics," she said. "It's easy and the credits are the same. And the professor is … different."

I didn't know what linguistics was. I didn't care. I just needed to pass something.

The classroom was smaller than I expected. Maybe fifteen students. Old building, worn wooden desks, the history of learning baked into the walls. I sat back for the show.

At the front, a man who was thin, quick, and never stopped moving. Energetic, informal, pacing. I wondered: how could someone be this interested in such a boring topic?

His name was Stephen Krashen.

He didn't lecture the way other professors lectured. He told stories. He'd start with something that seemed irrelevant—a kid he'd seen at a playground, a phrase he'd overheard at a restaurant—and he'd unspool it slowly, weaving back and forth, building toward something. You didn't know where it was going. You just followed. And then, at the end, the lesson would land.

One day he wanted to show us how we really learn. He made us read Dutch phrases aloud: "*Dit is mijn oor... dit is mijn neus.*" This is my ear. This is my nose. We stumbled through the words, understanding nothing.

Then he did it differently. He touched his nose and said "*Dit is mijn neus*" in a vibrant, commanding voice, dramatically moving his finger. Then touched his ear: "*Dit is mijn oor.*" Suddenly we understood. The meaning was in the action.

"Input," he said, "needs to be comprehensible. But it also needs to be compelling."

I don't remember much of the specific content. I remember the feeling. This man understood something about how people actually learn—something the English 101 grad assistant with a trigger finger and a red marker had completely missed.

I passed the class. I made it through school. I became a soccer coach.

Then I forgot Stephen Krashen's name for thirty years.

## The Ghost

In 2013, I was researching how video game designers teach players to navigate complex worlds without tutorials. The best designers don't explain the rules. They build environments where the rules become obvious through play. They let players acquire the game instead of learning it.

The designers kept citing a linguist. A professor at USC who had figured out, back in the 1970s, that this was how humans learn language.

The name hit me like a ghost: Stephen Krashen.

The same professor. The same storyteller from that classroom forty years earlier. While I was barely passing his intro course, he was developing a theory that would blow up the entire field of language education—and that would, decades later, explain my own daughter to me.

I started reading everything he'd written.

## The Braid

The discovery wasn't clean. For years I'd been collecting mysteries I couldn't solve. Dare's hidden fluency. Z's transformation. The Noisy Arms appearing on academy players but never on ours. The way our kids seemed to have something to say while other kids—more drilled, more corrected, more coached—seemed to recite it.

Krashen gave me the lens. But even after I started reading his work, I kept testing his framework against what I was seeing in the gym. Where did it fit? Where did it break?

Discovery isn't a lightning bolt. It's a slow braid—watching and reading and watching again, until one day the pattern clicks.

The theory floated over me. The true evidence came from the gym.

## The Playground

Krashen's own breakthrough came at a playground.

He was tutoring a young Japanese girl in English, working through the standard lessons—vocabulary, grammar, pronunciation. Progress was slow. Across the park, a group of Japanese children were climbing, swinging, laughing alongside American kids. No one was teaching them anything. They were just playing.

He watched them for an hour.

By the end, those kids—the ones with no tutor, no curriculum, no grammar drills—were speaking more English than his student. Not perfect English. But functional English. English that let them stay in the game.

The rigid methods miss the magic, he realized.

He went home and started writing.

## The Heresy

What Krashen proposed was heresy—but not for the reasons people think.

The real revolution wasn't "input matters" or "drills are bad." The real revolution was direction.

For centuries, language teaching assumed a simple progression: conscious to unconscious. Learn the rules, then practice until they become automatic. Knowledge first, fluency later.

Krashen said: the direction is backward.

Acquisition doesn't flow from conscious to unconscious. It flows from unconscious to conscious. You absorb the language first—without knowing it, without studying it, without being able to explain it. The rules install themselves through meaningful exposure. Only later, if at all, can the conscious mind step in to edit, refine, polish.

Children don't learn grammar and then speak. They speak—clumsily, imperfectly, fluently—and then maybe, years later, someone teaches them what a gerund is.

And here's the proof—so large and obvious that everyone ignores it:

High school Spanish.

Millions of American students. Four years of instruction. Vocabulary quizzes. Conjugation tables. Grammar worksheets. Conscious, deliberate, structured learning—exactly what the traditional model prescribes.

How many of them graduate speaking Spanish?

Almost none.

The failure rate isn't fifty percent. It's closer to ninety-five percent.

That's not a pedagogical accident. That's evidence.

Meanwhile, a three-year-old immigrant kid, dropped into an American preschool with no instruction whatsoever, is fluent in six months.

The kid didn't *learn* the rules. The kid *acquired* the language. Unconscious first. Conscious later—or never.

Krashen didn't just offer a different method. He reversed the arrow.

## Youth Sports

Now look at youth sports. An entire industry built on the same assumption: conscious instruction produces unconscious skill. The same direction. The same arrow.

Most corrections interrupt the input. Krashen called the anxiety barrier the affective filter—the emotional gate that slams shut when a learner feels judged. Most "do it this way" moments raise the affective filter and block the installation. In many cases we're actively interfering with the process that would make them fluent if we'd just get out of the way.

Krashen figured this out for language in 1977.

Youth sports still hasn't heard the news.

## The Critics

They came for him in the journals.

His terms were "vague and unfalsifiable." When does learning become acquisition? Can you measure it? You can't acquire what you don't notice.

The most important challenge came from Merrill Swain. Her data came from Canada's French immersion programs—Anglophone kids learning math, science, and history entirely in French. Hours of meaningful, content-rich input every day. Low anxiety. Real communication with real stakes. If Krashen's strong version were going to win anywhere, it should have been here.

The results were fascinating. Listening and reading comprehension? Excellent. Everyday fluency? Solid. But grammatical accuracy? They made the same basic verb agreement errors after five years that they'd made after one. The errors fossilized.

This became the ammunition for those who argued that early correction and formal instruction were vital—that without explicit teaching, bad habits would calcify and the window for proper development would close. The immersion kids' mistakes were held up as proof that Krashen was dangerous, that letting children figure it out on their own was a recipe for permanent mediocrity.

## Bumper Cars

The skeptic's favorite analogy is driving. You learn the rules consciously—mirrors, signals, hands at ten and two. You practice the techniques. Eventually they become automatic. Conscious to unconscious. Proof that deliberate instruction works.

But driving is not play. The road isn't trying to deceive you.

Now imagine driving where you get extra points for hitting red cars—and you drive a red car.

Everything changes. Your blinker becomes a lie. Your lane position becomes a feint. Your brake lights become Panenka's hips. The other drivers are reading your car-body language and trying to fool you while protecting themselves. You're not automating a procedure anymore. You're in a conversation—and the other speaker keeps changing the question.

That's sport. That's why the driving analogy proves the opposite of what its advocates think. Automation works when nobody is trying to fool you. The moment deception enters—the moment you're in a language—conscious to unconscious breaks down. You can't drill a response to a question that hasn't been asked yet.

Now imagine two driving schools. The first is traditional: a manual, hands at ten and two, look over your shoulder while backing up, top-down instruction. The second is bumper cars. Go-karts with extra points for tagging. Kids chasing each other around a parking lot, learning to read intention and hide their own—not because someone explained the theory of deception, but because the game demanded it.

Which school produces the driver who survives the red-car world?

That's what play is. Bumper cars for the nervous system.

## Gween Twee

I thought about the parents who had sat across from us at the "gween twee" meeting, arms crossed, voices tight. "Teach them movement." "At Barca they teach passing at eight." They weren't wrong to sense the problem. Swain's immersion kids were proof that without selection pressure, errors lock in. The window closes. Miss it and optimal performance never comes. They were worried that perceived bad habits like over-dribbling and head-down play would persist without correction.

What the parents got wrong wasn't the urgency. It was the cure. More instruction wasn't the answer to fossilization. The right interaction was.

The question was never whether to demand precision. It was how to build a game that demanded it for you.

## The Paris Thought Experiment

The problem wasn't input. The problem was the environment's indifference to precision.

Take those same immersion kids and drop them into Paris for a weekend every month. No English escape hatch. No patient bilingual teacher who understands their broken French anyway. Just shopkeepers, teammates, kids on a playground—all of whom go blank if your grammar mangles the message.

Suddenly, accuracy isn't academic. It's the price of being included.

That's natural selection pressure: the world quietly saying, "Say this better or it doesn't work."

The Canadian classrooms were missing what Paris would have provided—not more instruction, not grammar drills, but an environment that cared about precision.

And here's where sport has an advantage that language doesn't: there is no second language.

In a French immersion classroom, the kid can coast on broken grammar because everyone shares a secret escape hatch—they all speak English. The system is forgiving because it has a backup running underneath.

On the street, playing soccer, you don't get to switch to badminton when the game gets hard. The only way to stay in the conversation is to solve soccer problems in real time—with your body, your timing, your deception.

The game itself applies the pressure.

Bad first touch? You lose the ball. Poor scan? You get stripped. Predictable pass? It gets jumped. No coach has to explain it. The environment edits you.

In most organized youth systems, adults accidentally remove that pressure. They script decisions, freeze play, explain solutions, protect kids from the very failures that would have taught them. They create the soccer equivalent of Canadian immersion—lots of input, no selection.

In Paris, French sharpens itself. On the street, soccer does too.

## The Synthesis

You don't get geniuses by yelling at kids to talk more.

You get it by building playgrounds where silence doesn't work.

You don't coach creativity into kids.

You build games where creativity is the only thing that survives.

That's the synthesis. Krashen was right about the foundation—kids need oceans of low-anxiety, meaningful play if you want fluency. You don't build speakers by drilling grammar. You don't build players by drilling technique. Acquisition comes through immersion.

But Swain's immersion kids were a warning label: if the environment never demands precision, the system stalls at "good enough."

The critics were right to complete Krashen. Input alone isn't enough. Output matters. Interaction matters. Noticing matters.

But they were describing what happens in well-designed play—not what happens in coaching.

## The Snow

I was sitting in my office at Joy of the People when the question formed in my head.

The building was empty—early morning, school day, just me and a laptop. I was reading about acquisition versus learning, about the affective filter, about Swain's immersion kids. I was there to dig out a soccer field in the snow.

I walked out of the office. As I threw snow over my shoulder I found myself talking to no one. But getting somewhere. The field and the idea taking shape together.

Acquisition produces fluency. Learning produces accuracy.

Was that it? Was that the split I'd been sensing for years without being able to name it?

The coached kids—the ones from the academies, the ones with private trainers—they were accurate. Their technique was clean. They could pass in rondos. They could scan the field, execute drills. They knew where to stand, when to pass, how to trap.

But the Joy kids—the ones who'd spent all that time in unstructured play—they were something else. They didn't just know the moves. They seemed to speak the game. They improvised. They deceived. They saw things before they happened—and made things happen that shouldn't have been possible.

When you clear snow off a field, each shovel is a little heavier than the one before. Each idea a difficult step. My breath hung in the air.

What if movement is a language? Subject to similar rules of acquisition. Stored in similar unconscious systems. Deployed for the same purpose—to make other people do things.

Krashen's playground—Japanese kids acquiring English through play while the tutored girl struggled with drills—could that be my gym? Were my kids acquiring the grammar of deception, the syntax of timing, the vocabulary of space? No one was teaching them. The game was teaching them. The play was the input.

And Dare—my daughter, the one who barely touched the ball—had she been in the silent period all along? Receiving input. Watching, listening, absorbing. Her brain installing the grammar while she played Legos and faked injuries and wandered off to the playground.

When she finally spoke, the sophistication was already there.

It was a beautiful hypothesis. But I'd been wrong before.

I needed a test.

## The Crossover

First, it should line up. If acquisition was real—if play was the engine of fluency the way immersion is the engine of language—then the proof should be hiding in the developmental histories. Not in theory. In data.

I pulled up the Soberlak and Côté study from 2003—one of the few that tracked play hours and deliberate practice hours across the developmental arc of elite athletes. Everyone who cited that research described a gradual crossover: play declining slowly while practice rose to meet it. The 90/10 rule at eight. The 80/20 rule at ten. A gentle, linear slide from one to the other, like a dimmer switch.

That's not what I saw.

When I looked at the curves closely, the transition wasn't gradual at all. Play didn't taper. It fell off a cliff. And at the same moment—almost the same year—deliberate practice didn't creep up. It spiked. The crossover wasn't a dimmer switch. It was a light switch. On one side: play. On the other: work. And the switch flipped fast.

What was happening at that age?

I took a standard pediatric growth chart—the kind every doctor's office has on the wall—and laid it over the Soberlak data. Peak Height Velocity. The peak of the growth spurt. The moment a child's body begins its transformation into an adult body.

The crossover mapped onto puberty.

Kids weren't gradually shifting from play to practice. Their bodies were shifting from child to young adult, and everything else seemed to follow. The games that had consumed them—the hours of Goalie Wars, the endless dribbling, the mixed-age chaos—suddenly felt childish. The deliberate practice that had bored them at ten suddenly felt serious, purposeful, adult. They didn't choose to stop playing. They grew out of it—literally.

This changed everything. It meant acquisition wasn't half the equation, running parallel to learning the whole way. Acquisition was the first phase—total, immersive, all-consuming—and then it ended. Not gradually. Biologically. The window closed when the body changed.

I saw it with Nick.

Nick was an early starter who seemed to never want to leave the security of the youngest group. He had been here ten years yet spent most of his time playing down, often against five- and six-year-olds.

He would ask, I would tell him to be a good leader. When I poked my head into the gym, Nick would endlessly dribble back and forth against a hopeful five-year-old.

By seventeen he was the most elegant player in the state—ramrod straight, a poised bullfighter, freezing defenders with a shoulder nudge. All of it built in the gym, not challenging the very best, but choosing to play down.

I asked him once to join his age group for a tournament. He was now playing mostly with the oldest group—Z and Marco and the rest.

"Why would I do that?"

"Don't you remember? When you were younger, all you did was play with the little kids."

"No, I didn't."

He wasn't being difficult. He honestly couldn't remember. The laboratory where his fluency was built—those hours toying with five-year-olds, side to side, going nowhere and everywhere—had become invisible to him.

Krashen couldn't have said it better. Acquired knowledge is unconscious. You don't know what you absorbed. You can't access it deliberately. You just have it—the way a native speaker has grammar without being able to recite the rules.

Nick had crossed over. He was in the learning phase now—conscious, deliberate, purposeful. And from that side of the line, the acquisition phase didn't just feel distant. It felt like it never happened.

That's the cruel trick of the crossover: the phase that matters most is the phase you can't remember. And once you leave it, you can't go back.

## The Lens

Forty years after I had sat in his classroom and didn't realize what he was teaching me, Stephen Krashen had handed me a lens.

He didn't know he was explaining soccer. He thought he was talking about Spanish and English and Japanese. But if his theory was bigger than language—if it was about how humans acquire any complex system, how we move from conscious effort to unconscious ease—then everything I thought I knew about player development was upside down.

You don't learn the language and then play the game. You play the game, and the language emerges.

I had the framework. Acquisition before learning. Unconscious before conscious. The arrow reversed.

But theory is cheap. I needed to see it—whether the distinction would show up on an actual field, with actual players, under actual pressure.

I didn't have to wait long.

The test walked into my life when three players ended up on the same varsity team: a captain who had done everything the system prescribed, and two Joy kids who had done almost nothing it recommended.

Same field. Same opponents. Same stakes.

The difference was impossible to miss.

As for Dare—she was still in her silent period, still watching more than playing, still building Lego towers in the lounge. I had no idea how far her acquisition would eventually take her.

# Interlude:

# Dare

"Daaaaarrre!" Z would yell from the open window of the suburban. It was time to go to Joy. Dare was always the last one, running to the truck with dolls, or Lego towers, and a way of seeing the field nobody else did. When she first showed up to play, she wanted to throw the ball in, but a six-year old teammate was not where she wanted them. She put down the ball, picked the teammate up, moved her into position, then threw the ball. A referee shrugged and said, "That is a very different way of playing." So were the hanging dolls. At nine I took some kids to an overnight camp. I had breakfast with Dare each morning. Looking at the all the summer campers she said "Dad, there are a lot of other camps here too, right?" "Yes, that's right." "Well there's soccer camp, we know about that, there's swimming camp, and volleyball camp and band camp." "Yes" "And all the band campers are nerds." I laughed, and then she said, "So, Dad, the question is…where's your band camp T-shirt?"

She spent the week in the nurse's tent drinking Gatorade and winking at me when I checked in. Easy marks At regionals she faced a crowded goal: keeper up, two defenders behind her, no obvious angle. Instead of the usual moves, she stepped on the ball, hopped backward, lured the keeper forward, then lofted the ball over the stumbling keeper and defenders into the net. I've watched soccer for thirty years. I can count on one hand the number of times a player genuinely surprised me. This was one, but I shouldn't have been. The dolls, the Lego towers, the offbeat experiments: all of it fed a richer imagination on the field. Later, when defenses packed the box and dared us to break them down, Dare became the decoder. From midfield she'd launch thirty-yard "passes" that weren't aimed at a winger so much as at a defender's head. The ball invited the defender: "You can win this." They bit. They committed. Momentum and body position betrayed them. The ball was so perfect the defender could not resist, passed over their head and on the winger's foot and the attack was on. It wasn't power. It was persuasion. She didn't drill those passes in some mechanical practice. She built them by watching, by playing odd games, by absorbing the grammar of the sport in strange places. For Dare, a pass was a story you told to everyone on the field—one that made opponents speak her language without knowing it. Her creativity didn't arrive whole; it accumulated, day by day, experiment by experiment, until she could reliably make defenders do what she needed. Dare taught me that creativity compounds: small, odd habits and wide observation create tactics that surprise and succeed.

# Chapter 10:

# The Confession

## The Best Nine-Year-Old

He was the best nine-year-old I had ever seen.

Out of a job, I was working a side gig with Coerver Coaching, a popular program focused on ball control and individual skills through mostly repetitive drills. This kid knew all the named moves and seemed to use them at the right time. He could shoot hard and quickly with both feet. His dad was a smart local coach. This kid was a can't-miss.

Once Joy of the People started up I encouraged his dad to bring him. They came for a while, but eventually the time constraints of his club got in the way. He came less and less, then not at all.

But I kept watch.

His developmental trajectory was textbook—exactly what the system prescribes. Early technical training. Shooting, dribbling, passing, receiving, tactical possession rondos. On the team side, a slow ramp-up of competitive play, eventually joining an elite travel team at the highest level possible.

I saw nothing wrong with this. To me, this was the correct path.

By ninth grade, he made varsity at the local high school. While his size was a concern as a freshman, his ability to control the ball and outmaneuver defenders was evident. The next year he was among the most impactful sophomores in Minnesota. By junior year, he was captain. With years of elite experience, he was poised to become a Mr. Soccer candidate.

Then something strange happened.

## The Joy Kids

That same year, two Joy of the People kids made varsity. One was my son Z, a ninth grader. The other was Nick, an eighth grader.

Both had grown up completely differently than the captain.

The JOTP kids played—most often without direction, certainly without anyone telling them to stop dribbling, or pass the ball, or where and when, much less how. They had spent years in whatever pickup game was happening that day.

Z was the kid every coach pitied. At eight, while other kids swarmed the ball, he drifted as far from the action as possible. Parents gave me sympathetic pats on the back—the director's kid will never be a player. What they didn't see: Z had already figured out how to win. Big Otto was the best player on the field. Z's job, as he saw it, was to stay out of Otto's way and let Otto score. Why chase the ball when someone else would do the work for you? He'd be busy pulling up grass, hear the cheers, turn around, and celebrate. He was eight years old and already underloading.

Then came Joy. Without drills or directives, Z's instinct found a laboratory. He camped near the goal, hunting rebounds like a hawk. Critics hit back. Once a club kid told him to look up the word "pass" in a dictionary. I found him silently crying on the bleachers. But I saw what others didn't—him calculating angles, sitting in spaces. The ball kept finding him.

Nick was seven when he discovered Joy. He treated the gym as his own laboratory. During mixed-age games, he'd toy with five-year-olds—endless dribbling, side to side, going nowhere and everywhere. Some observers called it showboating. I saw pedagogy. His endless dribbles taught him how to manipulate defenders. By high school just a little shoulder nudge or eye wink and the defender would freeze, and Nick went right past.

## The Eye Test

At the very first varsity game, St. Louis Park played Armstrong.

Now I could see all three together. The captain with years of elite training. The two Joy kids with years of play. Same field. Same opponents. Same stakes.

I was as surprised as anyone.

The two Joy kids—one a freshman, one an eighth grader—didn't struggle to pass, to dribble when required, to read the game. Despite having almost no eleven-on-eleven experience, they looked like they belonged. They seemed excited about the higher competition. They made mistakes but moved on.

But the captain?

It looked like he was surprised that someone else might be there. His moves worked on the first defender but looked rushed or disjointed in the chaos of shifting, unpredictable space. He would perform a perfect stepover and then run straight into another defender. He would battle for the ball, or throw a wild pass forward, or shoot from crazy distances.

Z and Nick got trapped too. Everyone does. But when they got trapped, you could see what they were trying to say. The move didn't come off, but the intention was legible—a sentence that came out wrong, not an absence of language. They had something to say and someone to say it to.

When the captain got trapped, there was no sentence. Just a body in traffic. Then the arms went up—that frustrated, palms-to-the-sky gesture.

My brother, who saw the same things I did, put it simply: "He's running out of ideas."

Was he? Or was it something else?

## Z Speaks

In his very first varsity game as a ninth grader, the score still scoreless against a good team, my son came in as a sub. I sat down with Coach Dan. You remember him: he coached that very first futsal team, those crazy ball thieves six years before.

"How long before Z scores?" he said. I smiled, took it as a playful joke.

A few minutes later Nick gathered the ball and played in Z fifteen yards ahead. Z went at a crowded back line of defenders. He jostled a little to move the defenders where he wanted them. He split the defense, moving between two defenders who seemed to let him enter the top of the box.

I have seen Z do this before. Never the most athletic, he would drag a bigger, faster defender toward a second defender. One versus two? When was adding a defender considered a good idea? When they start talking to each other: "You got him." "No, you got him."

Z glided right past with neither taking a stab.

The sweeper attacked the ball quickly. Z pulled it away, spinning with a Maradona turn that would make Zidane proud. Then he calmly passed the ball past the keeper into the net.

Three defenders were around him. Why didn't they attack? They were bigger and faster. It would have been easy.

And the sweeper? Why did he go so hard for the ball, allowing Z to spin around him?

I heard the opposing coach shout something very interesting:

"Too easy!"

Perhaps their coach was right. But why?

## Gween Ideas

Because Z didn't beat those defenders. He moved them. He authored their movement the way Panenka authored Maier's dive. His body told a story, and the defenders obeyed it—stepping toward each other when he wanted space, lunging when he wanted them off balance, hesitating when he needed a beat. They cooperated with their own defeat because they were fluent enough to read the story he was telling—and fluent readers can be fooled by a fluent liar.

Z's movement enlisted the muscles of three defenders and a goalkeeper. They did the work. He walked the ball into the net.

I could see the two younger players trying things. And when a move didn't come off, I could see what they were trying to do. They were attempting to say something—to their teammates, to the opponents, even to the fans.

If deliberate practice were the whole story, the captain should have been the best player on the field. No, it had to be something else. Something the Joy kids had that he didn't.

The captain looked like he wanted to say something too. But he had no way to communicate it. Even when things worked—say, he dribbled past a defender and shot—he was making it up on the fly, throwing out random words, hoping someone would understand.

And there it was. The field shoveled. The question answered.

The difference wasn't speed. It wasn't quickness. It wasn't agility. It wasn't even "soccer IQ"—that vague term coaches reach for when they don't quite have language for what they're seeing.

The difference was fluency.

The Joy kids had acquired the language—unconsciously, through play. The captain had learned techniques—consciously, through drills. His stepover was textbook. The defender didn't move. He had surface structure without deep structure. He could execute moves but couldn't tell stories.

The Joy kids spoke the game. The captain was still translating.

Movement wasn't just like a language. It operated by the same rules, built through the same process, serving the same purpose.

And I was watching the proof.

## The Super Skillers

I was at a convention where a group of soccer freestyle performers spent the week doing everything impossible with a ball. Juggling upside down—keeping it up while standing on their heads, stalling it on their foreheads while performing somersaults. Nutmegging conference goers. Absolutely remarkable. They were there as part of a promotional showcase for a personal skills program with the slogan: "The ball is your best friend."

The convention closed with a fun four-on-four tournament. The Super Skillers signed up a team.

I could not wait to watch. I imagined mesmerizing, crowd-pleasing sequences and defenders standing around wondering what had just happened. After all, the ball was their friend. More than their friend—their dance partner.

It was terrible.

They were fast, fit, technically extraordinary. But when they played against defenders, they seemed to have no idea where or when. Their actions did not fit the environment. They looked like the fancy sword swinger in that *Indiana Jones* scene—all elaborate technique and flourish—while the overweight post-college beer drinkers on the other team just took out their guns and shot them.

The Super Skillers lost four to nothing.

The Skillers and the captain were excellent at playing with the ball. Neither was good at playing with others. The captain had drilled against compliant partners. The Skillers had drilled against no one. Both had developed a private language—technically perfect, socially empty.

If soccer were skills, the Super Skillers would have won one hundred to zero.

But soccer is a language. And a language you practice alone isn't a language. It has no receiver. No response. No one to give your words meaning. Wittgenstein argued exactly this—there is no private language. The four-to-nothing scoreline agreed.

Remember Chomsky's colorless green ideas—grammatically perfect, semantically dead. That was the captain and the Super Skillers.

Now recall Victor's Iowa trip. Z and Nick were speaking gween twee—technically imperfect, but alive with meaning. Especially if you want someone to look at a tree.

## Overloaded and Underloaded

At any given moment, every player on the field is either overloaded or underloaded.

Overloaded means you're doing all the work yourself. You're fighting physics, fighting pressure, fighting the chaos. Your body is tense. Your options are narrowing. You're spending energy faster than you're creating advantage.

Underloaded means others are doing the work for you. The defenders are moving where you want them. The space is opening. The goalkeeper is committing too early. You're creating advantage faster than you're spending energy.

The captain was always overloaded. He only understood what he could do. Even when he beat the first defender, he was immediately fighting the next problem alone. Every step was effortful. Every decision was forced. His movement didn't move anyone. It was a monologue—an impressive one, technically—but nobody was listening.

Z and Nick were underloaded. They had learned—through play—how to get others to cooperate. How to make teammates and defenders move with often conflicting intentions. How to create space by convincing opponents to be somewhere else. Their movement was a conversation. It required listeners, and it recruited them.

They weren't working harder. They were working less. Because others were doing the work for them.

"Too easy!" the opposing coach shouted. He was frustrated. But he was also accurate.

It was easy. Z had made it easy. Through language—through the acquired grammar of movement that let him write a story the defenders couldn't help but follow. After all, what do we say when someone tells us a good story?

That story really moved me.

## Actions Speak Louder Than Words

Richard Dawkins, writing about the evolution of communication, cut through the romanticism: signals don't evolve to convey truth. They evolve because they change the behavior of receivers in ways that benefit the sender. Put brutally: the purpose of language is to enlist the muscles of others on your behalf.

A vervet monkey's alarm call doesn't describe an eagle. It makes other monkeys duck. A baby's cry doesn't explain hunger. It makes a parent feed.

Z's jostling didn't describe his plan to the defenders. It made them step apart. His feint didn't explain the Maradona turn. It made the sweeper lunge. Language is humanity's original underload technology. And movement—five hundred million years older than speech—was the original language.

## The Window

It wasn't the captain's fault.

He had done everything right—everything the system told him to do. But he'd put the hours in the wrong column, during the wrong window. Remember the three charts—the crossing point around fourteen? The captain had spent his critical period learning. Z and Nick had spent theirs acquiring.

And they'd acquired it the only way language can be acquired: as a spandrel of fun. Nobody taught Z to drag a defender into a second defender. Nobody drilled Nick on the eye wink that freezes a man. They discovered these things because the game rewarded them—because easier solutions meant more play, and more play meant more discovery, and more discovery meant deeper fluency. The game was the teacher. Joy was the classroom. Fun was the arch, and fluency was the spandrel that appeared in the space beneath it.

The captain's coaches had tried to build the spandrel directly—drilling the elegant moves without first building the arch of play. The result was a performer who knew the lines but had never lived the story.

Two kids who couldn't stop talking. And one who had run out of words.

## La Jolla

I could see the difference. I still couldn't explain why.

The last place I expected to find the answer was at a coaching conference in San Diego.

The course was called "*La Liga* Methodology," hosted by US Club Soccer. They had flown in three coaches from the Spanish Federation to present on the practice methods and strategies endorsed by the biggest clubs in Spain. *La Liga* had become the global gold standard—FC Barcelona, Real Madrid, their legendary academies *La Masia* and *La Fábrica* producing the finest players in the world. If anyone understood what talent was and how to grow it, it was these people.

One hundred American coaches, including me, gathered at the Marriott in the picturesque, palm tree-lined city of La Jolla, ready for the Iberian secret sauce.

The Spanish coach educators were brilliant, dynamic, engaging, and deeply knowledgeable. Until, during one of the classroom sessions, one of the Spanish presenters let something slip.

"American players," he said, "are … well, not smart."

There was an audible stir. Some low laughter. Zips of air sucked in through pursed lips. Shuffling of chairs.

Then a brave coach raised his hand.

"What is not smart?"

"Not performing the right solution," said the Spanish coach.

"What is the right solution?"

"The correct action at the right moment."

"What is the right moment?"

"Action produced at the right time and space."

"What's the right time and space?"

"That depends on the situation …" There was an uncomfortable pause. "But it doesn't matter. I know it when I see it."

Big laughter.

He won most of the crowd over.

But the sharp laughter contained a double edge. There was disappointment that the Spanish coaches couldn't give us an answer. But there was also relief—we were all in the same boat. The Spanish coaches were just like us.

No one knew what talent was.

## The Martian's Answer

But our Martian from Belgrade would have had no trouble.

It had seen this before, on many planets. Creatures who could author movement in others. Creatures who couldn't. The difference was never speed or strength or technical precision. It was always fluency.

The Martian would have watched Z split those three defenders and known instantly: This one speaks the language.

It would have watched the captain crash into his second defender and known: This one is still translating.

Like Salieri hearing Mozart, the Spanish coaches could recognize brilliance but couldn't write down the sheet music. They could hear the song. They couldn't explain the grammar.

## The Bicycle

Why is talent so tricky to define?

Because it's encased in play—and play is excellent at hiding. Working deep undercover.

We all carry knowledge we can't quite say out loud. Think about riding a bike. You're two hundred meters from winning the Tour de France. "Last bend, gentle left," your director says—and the radio dies. Which way do you turn the bars?

If you say left, you're over the cliff.

The correct move is a tiny right input that leans the bike into a seamless left arc. It's called counter steering. You'd make the turn on instinct—but if you try to think it through in the moment, almost everyone picks wrong.

That's what play does: it builds operational fluency that lives below conscious analysis. We can spot it. We struggle to describe it. And systems that demand explanations miss it entirely.

## Easy Is Hard

To find the pattern, I needed to return to Leslie Orgel—the biochemist from the Salk Institute.

Remember his rule from the fitness landscapes chapter: improvement happens along two axes—faster or easier. It is easy to see faster. It is hard to see easier.

Play is the selection engine. In unscripted games, kids run thousands of micro-experiments. The solutions that feel better, cost less, and hold up under pressure get reused. Over time, they become the player's default.

Watch a striker in the box. The academy kid has been drilled: "Attack the ball! Be aggressive! First to the ball wins!" So he sprints toward every cross, every through ball, every loose ball. He works incredibly hard. He gets there first sometimes. He also runs into defenders, mistimes his jumps, and exhausts himself by the seventieth minute.

The pickup kid does something different. He drifts. He watches the defenders' eyes. He takes a step away from the ball, and the defender follows him—opening up space. Then he checks back into that space at the last moment. The ball arrives. He doesn't have to beat anyone. He just has to be there.

Same ball. Same box. One kid did ten times the work for half the result. Remember Orgel: Evolution is cleverer than you are.

## Messi Walks

Messi walks more than any elite player in the world. During some matches, he spends nearly eighty percent of the time walking or standing still. The hot-take artists call it laziness. The data scientists call it efficiency.

He's not conserving energy because he's tired. He's conserving energy because walking is enough. His positioning, his reading of the game, his ability to be in the right place at the right moment—all of it means he doesn't need to sprint. The game comes to him.

But Messi isn't guessing. He's interacting—authoring and reading the game's information in real time, faster than conscious thought. This is Kinetic Linguistics. Like your native language, Messi picked it up young—during the critical period, the window when fluency installs itself without effort. Miss that window, and you're translating forever.

That's not a coaching decision. That's evolution. That's many years of play on the pitches of Rosario, discovering that the elegant path beats the exhausting path.

Evolution doesn't care about your coaching philosophy. It selects for what works at the lowest cost.

And what works at the lowest cost looks easy.

That's why easy is the signature of mastery: it's what survives the most trials. Effort is beside the point.

## Why Talent Is Invisible

Now we can finally answer the question from La Jolla.

What were the Spanish coaches seeing when they said American players weren't smart?

They were seeing language. Or rather, the absence of it.

Talent isn't a physical attribute. It's not speed, strength, or technical precision. Those are vocabulary words. Talent is fluency—the ability to compose those words into sentences that move other bodies. And fluency is invisible to anyone measuring the wrong things.

Watch the captain. His vocabulary was extensive. His grammar was correct. A scout with a stopwatch would have loved him: fast, technical, well-coached. But his movement didn't move anyone. He had words without sentences. Syntax without semantics.

Now watch Z and Nick. Less polished vocabulary. Rougher grammar. A scout with a stopwatch might have passed them over. But their movement talked. It moved defenders out of position. It recruited opponents into cooperation. It made the hard look easy.

The scouts had built elaborate systems to measure the wrong dimension. They were like literary critics who could only count syllables—missing the meaning that made some poems immortal and others forgettable.

The thing that matters is this: does the player's movement make for easier solutions?

That's why talent feels like "I know it when I see it." Our nervous system can hear the song. Our spreadsheets can't.

## The Thesis

Here, finally, is what I believe this book is really about: Talent is the ability to underload.

Not speed. Not strength. Not technical precision. Those are tools. Talent is the ability to get others to do the work for you—teammates and opponents alike. It requires both. You need someone to speak to and someone to deceive. You need cooperation to compete.

It's fluency in the language of movement—a language that does what all languages do: communicate, convey meaning, follow grammar, and generate new statements never heard before. A language acquired through immersion, through play. Not as the purpose of the game but as its spandrel—the beautiful, unintended byproduct of the arch of fun.

And it exists for the oldest reason language has ever existed: to make things easier. To enlist the muscles of others on your behalf. To get the world to do your work.

The coaches who drill technique are teaching grammar rules to students who will struggle with fluency.

The coaches who protect play are immersing children in a living language.

One produces students who know about soccer.

The other produces players who speak it.

## The Advantage

Underloading has three decisive advantages over every other framework currently in use.

First, it tells you exactly what to value: skill is any action that produces the same or better result with less time and less energy.

Second, it tells you precisely how it works: the fluent player authors a story with the body that the opponent's own reflexes are forced to complete—Panenka making Maier dive, Ricardinho freezing the defender. That fluency doesn't stay individual. It branches into pairs, then triangles, then the full ensemble. The wall pass. The eighteen-pass sequence. Skill is meant to be shared, like a language.

Third, it tells you exactly how to grow it: play down, play mixed ages, keep the stakes low, and let kids discover easier solutions the same way they discover their first language—through joy, not drills.

Everything else in talent development either ignores these truths or actively works against them.

## The Music

The Spanish coaches could recognize brilliance. They just couldn't write down the sheet music.

And until we learn to see what they're seeing—until we stop measuring effort and start recognizing ease—we'll keep missing the truth that was right in front of us all along.

Talent doesn't grind. Talent sings. And the game always knows the difference.

# Chapter 11:

# The Discovery

## The Full Arc

It is rare that a coach can view the whole experiment from beginning to end. Usually you get fragments. One season. One age group. A few years before the kids move on to high school, to college, to life. You see snapshots, never the full arc.

Fifteen years. The same kids. From "he'll never be a player" to varsity goals. From the gym floor to the college roster.

I watched who the system crowned and who it overlooked. I saw Z let Big Otto do the work at age eight, then become something no one predicted. I saw the captain, the one the system loved, hit a ceiling no one could explain.

The experts were building academies. I was watching kids. For fifteen years. And somewhere in year five or six, I started to see something I couldn't name.

## The Pattern

It started as a feeling more than an observation.

The more the kids wanted to play—the more they wanted to avoid getting tired, not lose anybody, keep the game going—the less they seemed to work.

That sounds backward. Everything I'd been taught said that improvement came from more: more effort, more intensity, more volume. The industry had built an entire philosophy around it. Overload. Progressive resistance. No pain, no gain.

But watching the Joy kids, I kept seeing the opposite.

The kids who lasted longest in the gym weren't the ones who sprinted hardest. They were the ones who figured out how to get the same result with less effort. They anticipated instead of chased. They read the game instead of reacting to it. They moved others instead of moving themselves.

And the strange thing was: they kept getting better.

Not despite doing less.

Because of it.

## Two Paths

Remember Nick? Early on he wouldn't play up. He would only play down. In doing so he was facilitating his own long-term development in ways I didn't understand.

The tried-and-true method in American youth soccer was simple: if a player excelled, you "challenged" them by moving them up. Playing up an age group—sometimes two—was the unquestioned marker of special talent. It was overload philosophy in roster form.

But when I reviewed the histories of those kids, I couldn't see the benefit. Over fifteen years, I'd watched thousands of boys and girls play up one or two years. Coaches would point them out like trophies: "See that one? Playing up two years." What they really meant was, "Wait until you see them with their own age group."

More often than not, it was a disappointment later.

Nick was different. I kept catching him in games with the younger kids. Not coaching them. Playing with them.

At first I thought he was just being nice. Or maybe lazy.

But then I noticed: after those sessions with the little ones, Nick would come back to the older games and play better. Sharper. More creative. More confident.

When you play against weaker opponents, you can rely on physical dominance—but that gets boring. If you keep smashing, someone quits. The game ends.

So if you want the game to last, you have to start doing something else. You experiment. You disguise. You find other ways to win—creativity, timing, deception.

And in doing so, you discover solutions you'd never find against peers who are pushing you to your physical limit.

This was underloading. Now I understood the mechanism.

## Best in the World

Nick's path reminded me of something I'd wondered about for years. If the secret weapon is overloading—always playing up, always seeking stronger opponents—how do the best players in the world stay the best? Messi, Ronaldo, Federer, Nadal, and Djokovic dominated their sports for two decades. They're already at the top. There is no "up" for them.

This is such a mental blockade for so many who have believed in overload development that I often give them a simple thought experiment:

"What do the best players in the world, in any sport, do every single day? It's something you could do, but probably don't."

They play down.

Every day. Against opponents who can't beat them. And they get better anyway.

If the theory of overload were true, they'd be constantly leapfrogged by hungrier players using a superior methodology. But they weren't. Instead, being at the top opened a new and better method. Federer talked endlessly about "easy power." Djokovic built his game on elasticity, timing, and angle. Messi's most famous goals look like a man jogging through a crowded park while everyone else sprints and slides.

They weren't doing more. They were doing less. And winning more because of it.

Think of Garrincha at the schoolyard, taking on every kid on the field by himself. One versus twenty, one versus a hundred—the number didn't matter. Nobody thought the ratio was unfair to Garrincha.

If that isn't underloading, nothing is.

## The Slowest Goal

One day, we put a speedometer in the gym to measure shot speed.

At first, it was exactly what you'd expect. The kids competed to hit the ball harder. Forty miles per hour. Forty-five. Fifty. Emmanuel and Joey, the lefties with their Goalie Wars-trained swings, were blasting shots that would have impressed high schoolers.

The speedometer became the new status symbol. The harder you hit it, the cooler you were.

Then Lioul scored a goal at five miles per hour.

The whole gym stopped. Then erupted in laughter.

Lioul was grinning. He'd chipped the keeper—read the goalie's weight shift, waited for him to commit, then softly rolled the ball into the corner. The speedometer barely registered it.

And something shifted.

Suddenly the competition wasn't about the fastest goal. It was about the slowest. Kids started trying to beat Lioul's record. Four miles per hour. Three. The softest possible finish that still went in.

To score slow, you couldn't just blast it. You had to move the goalkeeper first. You had to fake, to wait, to read. You had to make the keeper do the work—commit to a dive, shift their weight, open up space—and then gently place the ball where they couldn't recover.

The kids had way more fun scoring slow than blasting it as hard as they could.

And without knowing it, they were teaching themselves the highest art in soccer: finishing. The thing coaches say it "can't be taught." The thing that separates good players from great ones.

If you apply Orgel's First Rule to finishing, it predicts exactly this: when a five miles per hour chip scores as often as a fifty five miles per hour blast, the five miles per hour goal is better. Same reward, less cost.

Evolution doesn't care how heroic the action looks. It cares about what works at the lowest cost.

The kids had redefined the status game. From "Who hits it hardest?"—visible overload, high cost—to "Who can score the slowest?"—visible underload, low cost, high cunning.

They were learning to make it easy.

## The Payoff

Years later, in the National Futsal League, we hosted a team from Detroit. Their goalkeeper had just returned from the Futsal World Cup in Lithuania, where he'd been the U.S. keeper. On paper, he was as good as it gets.

And then the Joy street kids went to work on him.

One after another, Mika, Bennett, and Dimitri rolled him. They sat him down, rolled the ball across their bodies with almost casual, deadly fluidity, and passed it into the net at walking pace—at a speed Lioul would have been proud of.

Lioul was there that night, sitting on our bench as an assistant coach, watching the slowest-goal game he'd invented as a ten-year-old now being used to dismantle a national team keeper.

We won eight to zero.

The status game hadn't changed. The kids were still choosing ease over power.

Only now they were doing it against professionals.

## Survival of the Friendliest

There's a reason pickup games self-regulate and academies don't.

The political scientist Robert Axelrod ran a famous experiment in game theory. The winning strategy was the simplest: start friendly, mirror what your partner does, and forgive quickly. But it only won when the game repeated. In a one-shot game, betrayal pays. In a repeated game, cooperation wins—because you need the other person to show up tomorrow.

Street soccer is a repeated game. You play with the same kids every day. If you dominate, they leave. If they leave, there's no game. So the game itself selects for inclusion, for calibration, for keeping the weaker kid in so the stronger kid has someone to play with. Nick wasn't playing down out of charity. He was playing down because his nervous system understood what Axelrod's computers proved: the game lasts longer when you cooperate.

Academy soccer is a one-shot game. Tryouts. Cuts. Rankings. Every session is an audition. Cooperation has no future payoff. So kids hoard the ball, play safe, and grind. The environment selects for selfishness—not because the kids are selfish, but because the structure makes selfishness rational.

## Sally

Sally came to us at eleven. Tall, fast, powerful. She had burned through the local club system—too good, too early.

"Our old club wouldn't let her play with the boys," her mom told me. "We want her pushed."

For three years, Sally thrived at Joy. But the logic around her never changed: more. Higher level. Harder games. Next test. At fourteen, they left for "better opportunities."

Sally performed. She was her high school all-time leading scorer. East Metro Girls Player of the Year. The overload theology was paying off. On paper.

Then I saw her play Division I. She came on with fifteen minutes left. The first time she got the ball, she pulled off a couple of classic JOTP moves, gliding past defenders. Then she slipped a pass to the outside.

It was intercepted. Their outside back exploded up field.

Sally took off after her. You could feel the crowd lean forward: can she catch her?

You could feel Sally lean forward too. This was the story she'd been told her whole life: work harder. Want it more. Turn it up.

She did.

And then something very strange happened.

She didn't get tripped. She didn't misstep. It was more like watching a system shut down in slow motion. Her stride began to shorten. Her upper body locked. You could see her trying to push harder—turn the dial from ten to eleven—and her body simply refused the command.

Then, in full view of a silent stadium, with no one around her, Sally's effort just … stopped. She pitched forward and fell flat on her belly.

No contact. No collision. Just a kid chasing as hard as she'd ever chased, and a neuromuscular system that couldn't keep up with the demand being placed on it.

What I saw, watching from the stands, was the overload finally overloading.

## The Revelation

Raymond Verheijen, who has advised Barcelona, Chelsea, and many World Cup sides, once said something that stopped me cold: "Power is overcompensation for lack of ability."

The more you sprint, fight, and grind—the more you overload—the less you're using the more efficient path. The elegant solution. The move that makes others do the work for you.

Power isn't strength. Power is a confession: I don't know a better way.

Play invented underloading.

Not coaches. Not sports scientists. Not training programs. Play.

Play selects for solutions that cost less—ones that preserve energy, keep the game going, let everyone stay in.

Over time, those solutions accumulate. They become style. They become what we call talent.

The kids who overloaded—who sprinted at every ball, who muscled through every challenge—they got tired. They got hurt. They quit.

Johan Cruyff echoed this: "If you see a player sprinting, it means he started too late." Sprinting isn't a sign of speed or effort. It's a confession of poor positioning. And the opposite must be true: the player who always seems lucky—who the ball just finds, who arrives without appearing to rush—isn't lucky. He was there before the question was asked. That's underloading. The work happened in the reading, not the running.

The kids who underloaded kept playing.

And playing.

And playing.

And somewhere in all that playing, they became the best players I've ever seen.

## The Search

Standing in that gym, watching Lioul celebrate his five-mile-per-hour goal, watching Nick come back sharper from playing with eight-year-olds, I finally had the full picture.

Talent isn't built through overload. It's discovered through underload.

The signature of mastery isn't effort. It's ease.

But was I simply seeing what I wanted to see? Was this just one gym in St. Paul, one strange experiment that wouldn't replicate anywhere else?

I needed to find out if anyone else had seen what I was seeing.

So in late 2012, Victor and I traveled to SoccerEx in Rio de Janeiro—a global soccer business conference that brings together the world's leaders in the sport.

We had access to legends: Carlos Alberto Torres, Zagallo, Zico, Bebeto, Jay-Jay Okocha, Ruud Gullit, and others. World Cup winners. Hall of Famers.

We had come looking for clues.

## The Gold Standard

The conference was held on a giant rock at the edge of a peninsula between Copacabana and Ipanema, offering otherworldly views of the beach and

Sugarloaf Mountain. They built a street court on the sand with music and a DJ. You could walk back and forth and hang with Ruud Gullit or join Roy Hodgson on his morning beach walk—he couldn't get enough of the foot-volley games, transfixed by the Brazilian ease with the ball.

At the Brazil CBF booth, they had a loop of film showing all the goals from their five World Cup championships. Between 1958 and 1970, Brazil was untouchable. Light years ahead of the world.

What was their secret?

A moment from their 1958 World Cup final gives us a hint.

The ball is rolling toward the corner of the box. Two massively athletic Swedish defenders are charging toward it—bodies low, knees driving. A terrible beauty of human movement.

From outside the picture glides a slim figure, moving carefully as if on an icy walk, but surprisingly quickly. The three of them will arrive at the ball at the same time.

It's not a fair fight.

The little man is Mário Zagallo, who will become the beating heart of Brazilian soccer—part of all five World Cup wins as player, head coach, and assistant.

Zagallo is gliding, controlled, smooth. Then he does something strange. He turns himself sideways, like a fencer giving away little to contact.

The big Swede gets to the ball full-on with force. But Zagallo lightly swings his right foot—surely too lightly?

He contacts the ball at just the correct time. He catches the defender using too much force, trying too hard.

The big defender struggles for a split second, but momentum carries him forward. Zagallo pauses to let gravity do its thing. The defender stumbles by, face-planting in the turf.

Zagallo glides in alone and slots it under the keeper.

Effort, strength, endeavor—meet your master: skill.

That little sideways turn, that soft contact that let the defender do the work for him—that was pure underloading. He wasn't winning the collision. He was refusing to be in a collision in the first place.

The skill Zagallo used is only born of the street. There is no drilling this. No coach would think of it, and if they did they would have no idea how to teach it.

In 1958, 1962, and 1970, Brazil simply out streeted the world.

Victor and I took a picture with Zagallo at the conference. I asked Victor to tell him I liked his tackle on the third goal. He smiled and nodded.

## The Blind Spot

That evening, we were talking with Roberto Ayala at the Copacabana Palace Hotel. The balcony overlooked the beach—crashing waves, bossa nova, beach soccer goalposts white against the black ocean.

Ayala was a dominant yet elegant center back who had captained Argentina more times than Maradona.

"What was the most important time in your youth development?" Victor asked.

"When I was nineteen and I joined River Plate."

This was what we'd been hearing all week. We would ask about the most important part of their development. It was always the same: When I made the first team. Getting to Feyenoord. Signing with Botafogo.

Always something formal. Always between fourteen and twenty-one.

Then we would ask what they were doing as kids.

And everything changed.

They would lean forward. Their eyes would light up. They spoke faster, looking directly at us as if to say: Listen to me. This is important.

"Play. All day. Every day. In the street, at the park. On cobblestones. Barefoot."

Every single one. Caju, Alex, Denílson, van Hooijdonk, Winter, Carlos Alberto, Mendieta, Gullit, de Boer, Okocha, Zagallo—play every day.

But this didn't add up. If it was the play that developed them, why weren't they giving it credit?

"Victor, ask him if he thinks that had anything to do with his development."

There was a long pause.

"I never thought of it that way," Ayala said. "That free play I was doing when I was eight, nine, ten, eleven was important to my development … I thought I was just better than everyone else."

There it was. The blind spot.

When you ask experts how they got good, you're not getting a documentary. You're getting a story their brain has stitched together after the fact. Experts attribute their success to formal training while minimizing early playful engagement.

The play had been so natural, so deeply integrated into their childhood that they didn't even recognize it as development. The skills they acquired were so deeply embedded that they became second nature—like learning a first language.

You don't remember learning to talk. You don't credit the hours of babbling that built your fluency. You just … talk.

## This Message Will Self-Destruct

True skill has a self-destruct mechanism.

Learned as a spandrel—a byproduct, not a target—you never give it credit. To do so would expose your skills to your own conscious knowledge. And if you know what you're going to do, so does your opponent.

The evolutionary biologist Robert Trivers proposed a disturbing idea: natural selection favors self-deception. If you don't know you're lying, you're a more convincing liar. Your body doesn't leak the truth. Your face doesn't betray the bluff. The best deceivers are the ones who've deceived themselves first.

The underloader acquires the skill unconsciously—through play, below the radar. They don't know what they know. So there's nothing to give away.

## Why It Hides

Andre Agassi couldn't beat Boris Becker, who had burst onto the scene with an almost unreturnable serve. After losing his first three matches, Agassi spent hours studying video and discovered a subtle tell that gave away one of the greatest serves in tennis history.

Just before Becker tossed the ball, he had a peculiar habit with his tongue: if it stayed in the middle of his lips, he was serving center or at the body. If he slid it to the left corner of his mouth, he was going wide.

The hardest part for Agassi wasn't returning the serve—it was hiding the fact that he knew. He intentionally underloaded his advantage. He ignored the tell for most of the match, allowing Becker to hit aces and winners so Becker wouldn't realize his code had been cracked. Agassi only used the information on break points—high-stakes moments when breaking serve actually mattered.

He won ten of their next eleven matches.

Boris Becker learned his serve consciously. Somewhere in that learning, his tongue became linked to his toss—a tell he never knew was visible. Agassi read it for years.

That's the risk of conscious learning: it leaves traces. Traces become tells.

But there's a second layer.

Maier dove the wrong way. But he didn't feel tricked. He felt like he chose wrong. His read, his reflexes, his decision. The underloaded person believes they were in charge.

If Maier had felt manipulated, he'd have been angry. He'd refuse to play next time. But he didn't feel manipulated. He felt like he lost.

Losing is acceptable. Being deceived is not.

So both parties walk away whole. The underloader doesn't know what they did. The underloaded believes they acted freely. No one feels wronged.

No trace. It works next time.

Years after they both retired, the two were sharing a beer at

Oktoberfest. Agassi finally confessed: "Did you know you used to give away your serves with your tongue?"

Becker almost fell off his chair. He told Agassi he used to go home and say to his wife, "It's like he reads my mind."

He was. Agassi was reading the language of movement that Becker didn't even know he was speaking.

If we learn things consciously, we cheat ourselves. We lose the ability to self-deceive—to tell a story that's one hundred percent believable, both to the teller and the receiver.

Becker's tongue was a spandrel for Agassi. He didn't know it existed. That's what made it work.

The moment he knew, it would stop working.

## The Warning

In Rio, one voice pushed back.

At one presentation, Zico—one of the greatest Brazilian players of all time—issued a warning.

"We have always had a formidable free play culture, but that is going away," he said. "The lack of space, the safety issues are keeping kids from interacting. And clubs are robbing the most vibrant free play environments too early—from the age of eight, they are signing street kids into academies."

If Brazil's vaunted pickup games disappear, Zico warned, so will that special play at the World Cup level.

We left Rio with a pattern we couldn't ignore.

Every great we talked to had a version of the same story: endless childhood play, followed by formal training, followed by success they attributed to the formal training.

They couldn't see what had built them.

But we could.

Now I needed to find out if the science agreed.

# Interlude:

# Khalid

As Director of Coaching for a big club, I once sent a very talented U13 player to participate in a U16 practice.

Khalid had been raised in a refugee camp in Kenya. He'd built a foundation of play on dirt pitches with nothing but a ball and other kids. His ball skills were world class. He went on to join the U.S. Men's National Team at the U15 level.

I was hoping this skillful player and the team would bond.

The practice began with small-sided games in very tight space. Khalid scored seven goals in thirty minutes. Some were quite spectacular. He was thirteen, playing against sixteen-year-olds, making them look like they were standing still.

At the end of practice, the coach asked the players to run eight two-hundred-yard repeats.

Khalid made it through one.

The other players had no trouble giving effort to the sprints. They finished all eight, breathing hard, hands on their knees, proud of their work.

The coach called me that night.

"He won't make my team," he said. "He didn't complete his sprints. Bad attitude. Low capacity for work."

Because he could not make himself run those sprints, he would not be on the team.

I asked the coach a question. "What if you took one of your regular players—one of the kids who finished all eight sprints—and put three defenders on his back. Passed him the ball in tight space. Told him: 'If you don't score here, you're off the team.' Would you demand that player finish those chances? Would you cut him if he couldn't?"

Silence.

That player has no more capacity to complete the task in front of goal than Khalid has to complete the two-hundred-meter runs.

But we only see one kind of inability.

The U16 players understood work. They'd been brought up under strict supervision and organization. They knew how to suffer through sprints because coaches had demanded it since they were eight.

Khalid understood play. He'd been brought up with no rules, no objectives, no adults timing his runs. He knew how to beat three defenders because that's what ten thousand hours of joyful chaos had taught him.

One capacity is visible. Measurable. Controllable.

The other is invisible. Unquantifiable. Built only through fun.

We put too much emphasis on work because we can control work. We can design it, schedule it, measure it, and post the results on a whiteboard. We can point to it and say: "See how hard we push them."

We can't control play. In fact, if we try to control it, it stops working. It's built up over time with only joy as the objective. These hours of mindless fun are an invisible learning tool used by every great player who ever inspired us.

The coach saw a kid who quit after one sprint.

He didn't see the open play in that refugee camp. He didn't see the language Khalid's body had acquired. He didn't see the seven goals.

He saw the thing he could measure. He missed the thing that mattered.

***

Khalid later came back to help coach. The kids loved him. He would often dribble end to end—some of the most amazing dribbling skills—moves, flicks, combinations that made teammates, fans and even opponents, smile.

At twenty-five, he was teaching what no sprint repeat could ever build.

# Chapter 12:

# The Science

## The Secret Underground Lab

By 2015, Joy of the People was starting to show results. Our oldest kids were making high school teams and playing well.

It reminded me of what I heard in Rio. "Nothing for the first five years," said Ginés Meléndez, head of the Spanish youth development system. "At five years we started to see progress, not much before that," said Houllier.

Development, these leaders were telling us, was a very long-term process.

We had a building. We had kids. We had stories. We had enough small miracles on video to fill a Nike commercial. Parents swore their kids were different now—more creative, more confident, more in love with the game.

From the outside, it looked like the theory was working.

From the inside, I had a problem. I didn't really know why.

I had six years of watching kids in free play. I had patterns. I had names for what I thought I was seeing. But I didn't have proof. I didn't have mechanism. "Play works" is a nice slogan; it is not an explanation.

So when I got invited to the first-ever Scientific Conference on Motor Skill Acquisition, it felt like being summoned to the secret underground lab. This, I thought, is where the people with the brain scanners and grant money tell me if I'm crazy.

I went to Finland to learn.

What I found was more unsettling than confirmation. By the end of the week, I had reached a conclusion the science seemed to share but couldn't quite say: play works, and we still can't fully explain why.

## The Fab Four

Late fall, 2015. Kisakallio Sports Institute, about sixty kilometers outside Helsinki.

Imagine a 1950s Indiana high school gym smuggled into a Finnish fairy tale. Dark wood floors. Arched ceiling. A giant window from floor to apex that, in Finland in November, lets in exactly zero usable light. The gym sits on a small campus carved out of birch and aspen woods. Walking between buildings feels like stepping into a live-action Hansel and Gretel.

A quiet older professor took the stage.

"Welcome to the First Scientific Conference on Motor Skill Acquisition," he said. Then he smiled. "We have the original Beatles—the who's who of skill acquisition—here, playing live."

He wasn't wrong. The program read like the bibliography I'd been struggling through for years: Al Smith, Richard Shuttleworth, Wolfgang Schöllhorn, Jean Côté, Jia Yi Chow, Duarte Araújo, and the man who just welcomed us, Keith Davids.

There was a charge in the room, the feeling of a field finally giving itself a name. Like early powered flight—Wright brothers era—only with more graphs and fewer crashes.

These were the people who'd spent entire careers asking the same question that kept me up at night: How does skill actually develop? They had data. They had theory. They had the rigor I lacked.

I had kids in a gym in St. Paul.

## Bernstein and Gibson

Davids opened by walking us through the intellectual foundations of this new thing called Ecological Dynamics.

First up: Nikolai Bernstein, a Russian neurophysiologist from the early twentieth century who worked on motor control. Bernstein's big idea was the degrees of freedom problem.

Your body has a ridiculous number of joints, each moving in multiple directions. Any "simple" movement—like kicking a soccer ball—requires coordinating dozens of muscles in space and time.

For that one kick, there are thousands of possible combinations of hip angle, knee bend, ankle position, timing, and force that could get the ball where you want it.

The traditional coaching answer was always: repetition. Drill the correct movement until it becomes automatic. Groove the pattern.

But Bernstein noticed something odd: expert performers never actually repeat the same movement exactly. And yet the result is consistent.

That suggested expertise isn't about memorizing one perfect movement pattern. It's about building the ability to assemble a good enough solution on the fly, every time, from a huge range of options. A flexible family of movements tuned to the moment.

Second pillar: James Gibson, the American psychologist who created ecological psychology. Gibson's heresy was simple: perception and action are not two separate stages.

We don't first "see" the world as neutral objects and then decide what to do. We perceive the world directly in terms of what we can do with it. A chair isn't just wood and fabric. It's "something to sit on." A ball isn't a sphere. It's "something to kick, catch, head, trap."

Gibson called these possibilities affordances.

For motor skill learning, that means: learning doesn't just happen "in the head." It happens in the relationship between person and environment. Change the environment, and you change what actions are visible, attractive, and possible.

These ideas had been lying around for decades. Ecological Dynamics was about applying them directly to sport.

## The Car Ride

I'd ridden to Kisakallio with Jia Yi Chow and his teenage daughter, who were heading north for a ski trip afterward. Chow is one of the pioneers of Nonlinear Pedagogy—a coaching framework that treats learning not as "drill the correct technique," but as "set up the right problems and let players discover their own solutions."

In his work, you don't tell a player exactly how to swing or kick. You mess with constraints—space, time, rules, equipment—so new solutions become necessary and obvious.

In the car, he asked what I did.

"I run a free play space for kids in Minnesota," I said. "We just let kids play."

He was quiet for a moment. Then he said, "I can't wait to hear what you've found. Practitioners are regularly ahead of the research."

His words landed like quiet confirmation. For six years I had watched the same kids move through that exact environment—no drills, no curriculum, just play. What I was seeing on the ground every day looked a lot like what Nonlinear Pedagogy described in theory. One of its leading voices had just suggested that sometimes the people inside the long experiment see things the models haven't measured yet.

## Puckelball

Midway through the conference, Davids gave a talk about "environments of the future." Up on the screen popped … our park.

Or at least, the strangest part of it: Puckelball.

Puckelball was a wild, roly-poly soccer pitch designed by Swedish artist Johan Ström. Imagine a field with rolling humps, odd angles, a hoop, goals without nets—more Dr. Seuss than FIFA.

Johan had come to St. Paul to design something for Joy—an artist with movie star looks, a musician, even a world-class fencer. He spent a week with us—talking with Victor, Glenn, Raffi, walking the neighborhood, watching kids play.

We held a meet and greet so the community could grill this Scandinavian mad scientist.

"Why is the field all lumpy?"

"Is this a competitive game?"

"Why no nets on the goals?"

Johan's answers were always delightfully unhelpful: "It can be whatever the kids decide." "It's worth exactly what you agree to." On the "no nets" question, he paused. Before he could answer, a voice from the back—Raffi, leaning against the wall—called out: "Actually, most goals around the world have no nets."

Johan's real objective was absurdly simple: create a fair playing field by building an unfair one. Warp the space so kids couldn't rely on standard solutions. Force creativity by design. Let the environment do the teaching.

So when Puckelball's lumpy cartoon field appeared on Davids' conference PowerPoint—held up as an example of future-thinking skill environments—I couldn't help smiling. Practice had snuck onto the slide deck before the science caught up.

## We Didn't Wait

But here's what mattered most: we hadn't waited. We didn't wait for a control group study. We didn't wait for peer review. We understood that if we followed the cleverness of play, it would lead us safely to the answer.

Find the play and you find the answer.

Kids don't wait for the research either. They just play. They've been running the experiment for thousands of years.

Later, I told Johan his crazy field was starring in an elite science conference, that practice is often ahead of the science.

"Yes," he said. "But art is ahead of both."

Touché, Johan.

## Differential Learning

All week, the Beatles of skill acquisition took the stage. Wolfgang Schöllhorn, a kinesiologist from Mainz University, presented his work on Differential Learning.

He was the most fun of the bunch—weaving stories at breakfast, telling everyone who would listen how he offered every grad student an "A" if they could beat him in a forty-yard dash. ("No A's yet," he said, smiling.)

Traditional coaching: pick the right technique, repeat it until it's automatic, correct errors.

Schöllhorn: do the opposite. Introduce variability on purpose. Have players do things differently every time. No repetition. No "This is wrong, fix your elbow." The errors are the process.

"The idea is that there is no repetition of drills, no correction, and players are encouraged not to think about what has gone wrong if they have made a mistake," he said. "Players have to take responsibility. They have to be creative and find the optimal solution."

To any traditional coach, this sounds like malpractice. If you're not correcting mistakes, what is a coach for?

To Schöllhorn, the answer was obvious: the coach designs the buffet of variability and then gets out of the way. Learning emerges from the player's nervous system sorting through the mess.

## Sport Sampling

Of all the researchers whose work shaped Joy of the People, Jean Côté hit closest to home.

Early on I leaned heavily on Côté's work. He seemed to be fighting off the specialization wave by himself. His continuum from Free Play to Deliberate Practice helped me visualize where the casual games of the sítio fit alongside the intense sessions that deliberate practice prescribed.

Most counterintuitive was this idea of multi-sport sampling—Côté's data said that early specialization, locking into a single sport year-round from age six, is usually a bad idea. Kids who "sample" multiple sports tend to do better long term.

David Epstein picked up on this in his book *Range*, using the example of Roger Federer, who would skateboard, play soccer and basically do anything but tennis. Federer has said publicly that kids should play many sports for fun and delay specializing until their mid-teens.

On a walk with Colleen I told her about this.

"But it's more than that," she said. "The missing piece here is 'for fun.' You played five sports in high school. If you did that today you'd go from structured soccer to structured baseball to structured hockey. It wouldn't be sampling. It would be specializing five times."

## Sampling Within Sport

Côté's theory had one problem: Brazil.

Brazilian soccer players don't "sample" other sports. They just play soccer. A lot of soccer. Yet they're among the best in the world. How do you explain that?

In his keynote, Côté presented his elegant solution: Brazilians do sample—they just do it inside soccer. Futsal. Street soccer. Beach soccer. Different ball sizes. Different surfaces. Different formats. The variety doesn't come from switching sports; it comes from constantly switching constraints within the same sport.

"Within-sport sampling," he called it.

From the outside, that looks like "just soccer." From the inside, it's an all-you-can-eat buffet of affordances.

Côté wasn't inventing a methodology. He was giving a name to something that already existed. The games on the beach, in the favela, on the street—those weren't designed by sports scientists to optimize "within-sport sampling." They were just fun. Engaging. Inviting.

Kids played them because kids play. The favela didn't need the label. It just needed a ball and some friends. For fun.

## The Pattern

As I watched talk after talk, a pattern snapped into focus.

Nonlinear Pedagogy, Differential Learning, Constraints-Led Approach, Ecological Dynamics—every one of these methods was circling the same insight: the best learning environments share qualities that already exist naturally in play.

Variability? No two pickup games are the same. No two possessions are the same. The ball never bounces exactly the same way twice.

Constraints? Play is nothing but constraints—space, time, score, number of kids, age gaps, skill gaps, weather, shoes or no shoes, all constantly shifting. You don't need a lab; you need a cracked parking lot and a flat ball.

Self-organization? Nobody tells you where to stand. You figure it out or you lose the ball.

Affordances? Every second of a pickup game is packed with I could do this or that—and the kid's nervous system is surfing that wave all day.

My Brazilian mentor's words echoed: "Change the ball. Change the surface."

At Joy, that's what we'd been doing—volleyballs, futsal balls, tennis balls, dodgeballs on gym wood, turf, grass, dirt, wet asphalt. We thought we were screwing around. Schöllhorn would have called it Differential Learning. Côté would have called it sampling within sport. Davids would have called it manipulating constraints.

The scientists were archaeologists as much as inventors—brushing the dust off an ancient learning machine kids had been operating for as long as humans have had games.

## A Cleaner Test

A couple of years after Finland, at another motor learning conference, I heard a talk by Rob Gray, a baseball researcher and skill acquisition coach. Gray wanted to see what actually improves batting performance. Specifically: launch angle.

He tested three approaches.

An internal focus group got body-focused instructions: "Keep your hands loose on the bat." "Shift your weight like this."

An external focus group got environment-focused cues: "Watch the spin on the ball." "Drive it to the back net."

A constraint group got no cues at all. Instead, a barrier was placed in front of them, and the only instruction was: "Hit the ball over that." No lectures about elbows or hips. No talk of swing path. Just a simple, concrete problem space.

The constraint group improved the most.

The closer the setup got to real play—a clear goal, a problem to solve right now—the better the learning.

Remember the soft volleyball from Chapter 5? That was Gray's constraint group in real time. No cues, just a different ball, and the six-year-old became a finisher.

## Play Did It First

The scientists weren't wrong. Their methods worked. Their research was careful. Their insights were gold for any coach willing to listen.

But they weren't discovering a new learning technology. They were finally finding evidence for the oldest one.

This doesn't diminish the science. It reframes its job. The big discovery isn't "We've invented a clever new method." It's "We finally have language and data to respect what play has been doing all along."

## The Open Question

But there was still a question I couldn't shake.

I spent the whole week in Finland listening, asking questions, silently comparing their slides to what I was seeing every day in St. Paul. The science confirmed that play works. Every study, every method, every theoretical framework pointed in the same direction: the best learning happens when you stop prescribing exact solutions and start designing environments where many solutions can emerge.

And yet for all the talk of variability, constraints, and affordances, the scientists rarely said the word itself. Play. The silence was deafening.

The science could only describe how play behaved. Self-organization. Affordances. Degrees of freedom being harnessed. It could not quite tell me what was actually being built underneath.

Bernstein had named the problem: too many degrees of freedom. But what is the thing that orders them?

Gibson had shown that perception and action are coupled. But how does that coupling form and refine itself over time?

The scientists had mapped the terrain. They had named the patterns. But the engine underneath—the thing that orders all those degrees of freedom, that makes a six-year-old stand tall against a cannon shot, that lets a lefty learn to chip without a single word of instruction—was still hidden.

# Interlude:

# Edison

I got the Minneapolis Edison boys varsity job three days before the start of the 2022 season. Edison—celebrating its hundredth year—is a beautiful river-sandstone building that looks like it has been holding its breath for most of them. The state titles in the gym read 1923, 1932, 1944. Nothing recent.

One of the last grass fields in the metro, the stadium sits elbow to elbow with the working-class neighborhood. The North Star rail line cuts through, bowing to no one—sit in the top bleacher and the aluminum rumbles in deference to the powerful steel wheels just overhead.

The year before, Edison boys soccer was ranked 187 of 201 Minnesota teams. I expected learned helplessness.

I found the almost inexhaustible power of hope.

Most of the kids had never played club. Preseason was three days at a local park with no nets and grass seven inches high. Thirty players. No equipment. I let them play. Coach Daniel kept the program alive on two phones, Spanish, English and all languages in between, zero budget, indefatigable energy—turning soccer into the most popular sport at school. Soon we had seventy boys and one secret weapon: lunchtime soccer. Every day thirty kids skipped lunch and played for an hour straight. No coach. No structure. Just a ball and whatever teams they invented.

## Magic

Comebacks became our signature. Down six to zero in the playoffs, Anwar scored with one second left and grinned on the bench: "Last goal wins." The next year brought last-second winners and the night the boys scored three goals in three minutes to beat perennial power Southwest for the first time in school history. Sam from basketball sent it down the line to Oli from volleyball. Oli stumbled just before the cross—the whole stadium leaned forward—then somehow got the ball off anyway. Theo rose and headed it in at the buzzer. Polyathletes speaking a language none of them had ever drilled. One morning an administrator stopped me in the hallway.

"We got calls about the noise from the stadium last night."

My stomach dropped.

"Not what you think," she said. "They called to say it was good to hear cheering again."

## Collective Fluency Is Cinema

Individual skill is vocabulary—Panenka's chip, Z's Maradona. But vocabulary alone is a monologue. Collective fluency is cinema. When kids acquire the same grammar through shared, unstructured play, twenty-two bodies start telling a story no coach could write. The wall pass becomes a plot twist. The run that drags three defenders is a sacrifice. The goal after eighteen passes is a climax the whole stadium feels in its chest. That's what Guardiola meant: "We move the ball to move the opposition." A fluent team doesn't issue commands—it writes a story so compelling the opposition can't stop turning the page. The kids wanted the comebacks. They played loose early because the story was better that way. The deficit, the final minute, the harvest moon—these weren't threats. They were the third act. Comebacks were stories. They wanted stories they could tell at lunchtime–except that they couldn't because they were playing.

## What Play Wants

Play isn't searching for fitness or titles. It's searching for connection—the moment separate voices become one story. That story feeds the game, and the game feeds the story. The oldest teaches the youngest. The game makes a new game. Not because of curriculum, but because the story wants to be told again. The language of movement reaches past the field—into the stands, the neighborhood windows, the young kids watching from the barrier. It turns strangers into witnesses and opponents into fans who stay and cheer. I don't have a study for this. My evidence is the phone calls. My evidence is Anwar's grin. My evidence is three goals in three minutes, Leo under the harvest moon, and a neighborhood remembering what joy sounds like. The language of movement is older than any academy. All it asks is that we let it play. Then sit back and enjoy the show.

# Chapter 13:

# The Proof

## The Roster

I was at USA Cup. We put our oldest team—Marco, Z, Eman, Danielson and company—into the tournament. A coach approached me.

"You must be playing these kids up," he said. "They are really small."

Coach speak for: good for you, you really believe in these kids, you are pushing them by playing up an age group or two.

"Actually they are the same age as yours. Just younger."

He was confused.

"Let's compare rosters."

He had fifteen of his eighteen born in the first half of the year. Joy had four.

"Your team is older. It's called the Relative Age Effect."

I am not Sherlock Holmes. It was an easy guess. His team was the top team in the state for that age group—which meant years of tryouts and selection, which meant years of selecting bigger and faster, which often means slightly older. Something called the Relative Age Effect.

That coach may still be staring at that roster.

## When Birthdays Beat Talent

If you line up a random group of kids, birthdays scatter across the calendar. About twenty-five percent in each quarter. That is what random looks like.

Line up elite U13 players from almost any traditional soccer country, and the calendar looks rigged. Q1 (Jan–Mar): forty percent. Q4 (Oct–Dec): ten percent. Same birth year. Same sport. Completely different odds of being labeled talented—all because one kid happened to be born in January instead of October.

A 2020 study of FC Barcelona's male football academy—one of the most celebrated youth programs in the world—documented a stark Relative Age Effect across age groups. Of the players in their academy, fifty three percent were born in the first quarter of the year. Just six percent were born in the last quarter.

*La Masia*. The crown jewel of youth development. The numbers don't describe talent. They describe a calendar.

That's RAE. The Relative Age Effect. It is not a talent filter. It is a selection bias.

The system pulls off a magician's trick. Start with a small biological advantage—a few months older means stronger, faster, more coordinated at eight through twelve. Rebrand that advantage as talent, drive, coachability. Pour disproportionate opportunity into it. Watch the performance gap grow. Call the gap proof.

We mistake a head start for destiny.

## Why Coaches Choose Overload

They choose it because it works. At twelve.

The early-born kid is bigger and faster. He can outrun opponents, outmuscle them, outjump them. Overload—more effort, more force, more intensity—produces visible results. The coach sees a dominant player. The scout sees a prospect. The system selects him, promotes him, celebrates him.

Nobody is wrong at this stage. Overload works beautifully when your body is your advantage.

Each coach is aware of RAE. They just think they are the exception to the rule. RAE is everyone else's problem. Not mine. Our January birthday kids have talent.

The problem is what happens next.

## The Reversal

At the very top, the pattern reverses. The players who dominate professional sport are disproportionately late birthdays—the kids the system tried hardest to keep out.

A study of Canadian NHL players found this exactly. Only seventeen percent of All-Stars were first-quarter births. Canada's 2010 gold-medal team? Just thirteen percent.

The 2026 Olympic final between the US and Canada featured fully NHL rosters on both sides—by general agreement, the highest level of international hockey ever assembled. The 2026 US roster answers the question the whole system is afraid to ask: forty-three percent of the team was born in the last quarter of the year. Twelve percent in the first. The USA won the gold medal with a team of predominantly late birthdays.

At the youth level, Q4 births make up just ten percent of elite rosters. At the highest level of hockey ever played, they made up forty-three percent of the US team. The system discards them at thirteen. The gold medal belongs to them at twenty-five. The pipeline is pointing in the opposite direction of the destination.

## Why the Pipeline Reverses

The late-born kid at eight is smaller and weaker. He can't overload—can't outrun, outmuscle, or outjump the January kids. So his nervous system does what Orgel's First Rule predicts: it finds the easier path. He learns to read. To anticipate. To make the defender move first. He discovers underloading—not as a philosophy but as a survival strategy. He learns to make his movement do more work so his body can do less.

Meanwhile the early-born kid never needs to. Size works. Speed works. Power works. The system rewards him for it—select team, premier league, academy invitation. He climbs the nearest peak. By twelve he's on top. By sixteen the peak is a local maximum and he can't get off it. His body solved every problem with force, so his nervous system never built the vocabulary of deception, timing, and ease.

But here's the part the selection story misses. Most late-born kids don't rise through the system. They rise outside it. Cut at ten, passed over at twelve, never invited at all—they go back to the park. Back to the driveway. Back to pick-up. While the selected kids accumulate coached hours, the rejected kids accumulate play hours. Their play hours climb precisely because the system didn't want them. Every year outside the academy is a year of acquisition the academy can't replicate.

The late-born kid's disadvantage was his development. His weakness was his teacher. The system that excluded him gave him the one thing academies can't provide: years of play with no physical advantage to fall back on.

The implication is uncomfortable but the data is clear: once early selection enters a sport, being chosen may be the worst thing that can happen to a young player's long-term development.

## Why Underloaders Win at the Top

At the adult level, bodies even out. Everyone is big. Everyone is fast. Everyone is strong. The physical advantages that separated kids at twelve disappear.

What doesn't disappear is language.

The Q4 kid who spent years reading, timing, and deceiving—because he had no other option—arrives at the professional level with a vocabulary the Q1 kid never needed and therefore never acquired. The overloader runs out of advantages. The underloader is just getting started.

Q1 kids are overloaders who got selected for overloading. Q4 kids are underloaders who got ignored into fluency.

It's the Reverse Relative Age Effect—the rise of the underdog.

I call it the Rise of the Underloaders.

The coaches think he's lazy. The scouts think he's small. The system thinks he's behind.

He's not behind. He's been acquiring a language they don't have a metric for. And by the time they notice, he's on the national team.

## Recent Phenomenon

But here is the part that should keep you up at night.

The 1962 World Cup rosters show no relative age effect. Birthdays spread evenly across the calendar. Quarter by quarter, almost perfectly random. The best players in the world, drawn from every continent, and no birthday bias at all.

That means RAE is not a law of nature. It is not an inevitable consequence of child development. Kids born in October were not at a disadvantage in 1962. They are at a disadvantage now.

Something happened between then and now. What happened was us. Tryouts happened. Academies happened. Age-group cutoffs paired with early selection happened. We built systems that mistake maturity for ability, and those systems began filtering children before the game had a chance to sort them on its own.

The Rise of the Underloaders is a beautiful story—the late-born kid who survives the bias and outperforms everyone at the top. But it shouldn't need to be a survival story. In 1962 it wasn't. The underloaders didn't have to rise because no one had pushed them down yet.

## The Editor, Not the Author

In summer 2014 we hosted coaches from GNK Dinamo Zagreb—one of Europe's top academies. By day they ran formal, precise sessions. Individual to small group progression, technical ladders, pattern play.

Their mantra was relentless: we will do everything with two feet. Half the kids cried by the end of the first morning.

In the afternoons we inflated futsal courts and let the kids loose. The hard-bitten coaches lightened up. They sat on the sidelines, joined teams, tried to hold a court. “These are great,” one said. “We need some of these.”

In the evenings they put their transfer fees on the whiteboard. One name stood out: Mateo Kovačić.

That night I found a two-minute Kovačić highlight video. At about twenty-four seconds: ducking into traffic, then zipping out—an explosive outside-of-the-foot turn at full speed. This was not a bilateral academy drill. I could see the coach now: Hey Kovačić, turn with your left foot. No. This was a street move. So I went back and counted: right foot used roughly 123 times, left about nine. There is no way he grew up under this system. A kid who had taught himself to skate with a ball.

The next day I asked.

“When did he come to you?”

“Fourteen. Street soccer, small club, playing every day.”

To bring him in, Dinamo released a kid who had been there since age six. But this was not uncommon. According to the coaches, only one of Dinamo’s top ten transfers joined before age fourteen.

Think about the kid they released. Fourteen years old. In the academy since six. Nine years. Every drill, every two-footed exercise, every tactical session. His parents drove him three times a week for almost a decade. Bought the gear. Skipped the vacations.

Then one day the director calls him in and thanks him for his service.

Nine years of compliance traded for nine years of play—the very thing that would have given him a real chance. He was never being developed. He was holding a place. Propping up the team while the eventual stars slipped the line—street kids who had spent their childhoods playing, not training.

That is not just a bad prediction. That is a theft.

Top academies provide structure, polish, and the platform for big transfers. But the raw grammar of the game for their best players comes from messy, unstructured play. The academy is world-class at what it does. It just isn't the origin of the player's deepest gifts. More often, it is the editor of a story that was first authored in parks, courts, and driveways.

## The Relative Play Effect

We have a name for the birthday bias: the Relative Age Effect.

We need a name for what we just saw.

I call it the Relative Play Effect—RPE. It's simple: the ratio of play hours to coached hours in a player's development history.

When Kovačić arrived at Dinamo at fourteen, his RPE was extremely high. Street soccer every day. No drills. Just play. The kid Dinamo cut to make room for him? Low RPE. In the system since age six. Eight years of being coached while Kovačić was living in the language.

High RPE beat low RPE. The native speaker replaced the tourist.

The pattern repeats everywhere. Zidane grew up in La Castellane—concrete pitch, mixed ages, no coaches, joined a formal club at fourteen. Maradona learned barefoot on the potreros. Pelé played with a sock stuffed with rags.

Play early. Learn late. That is high RPE in four words.

Ford and colleagues tracked elite youth soccer players in England—same system, same coaching, same talent label. The only factor that differentiated professionals from washouts: hours of unstructured play between ages six and twelve. Not practice hours. Play hours.

RAE tells us we are selecting the wrong birthdays. RPE tells us we are selecting the wrong histories.

## The Eiffel Tower

Imagine you're standing under the Eiffel Tower. Your job is to find the kids who speak the most fluent French. But you don't speak a word of French yourself.

What would you do?

You'd probably pick the loudest kids. The most confident ones. The ones who look like they're communicating well. You'd have no idea if they were actually fluent or just faking it with memorized phrases and aggressive hand gestures.

That's RAE. That's the entire youth sports selection system, trying to identify fluency by watching from the outside.

But there's another way.

What if, instead of trying to evaluate fluency directly, you asked a different question?

Which kids grew up here?

Which kids have been immersed in the language since birth—playing in the streets, absorbing the grammar, speaking it every day with native speakers of all ages? And which kids just got dropped off for a weekend immersion program?

You don't need to speak French to answer that question. You only need to ask: how did you grow up?

That's RPE.

## The Same System, Opposite Results

The US Women's National Team has won four World Cups. The US Men's National Team has won zero. Same country. Same federation. Same massive youth-sports infrastructure built on Title IX and decades of investment. Opposite results.

The conventional explanation is Title IX. True, but not the whole story. The whole story is RPE.

Boys around the world play. Street corners, dirt pitches, concrete courts, parks at dusk. They accumulate play fluency before anyone decides to develop them. Their RPE is high before a coach ever sees them.

Girls, historically, have not had the same access. Marta played in the streets. Megan Rapinoe played with boys. But the broad cultural permission for girls to play freely, unsupervised, mixed ages, for no reason except the game—that has been slower to arrive.

When the Women's World Cup launched in 1991, the US women were not competing against play cultures. They were competing against other overloaded systems. When everyone's RPE is low—when every team is built on coaching, structure, and intensity—the best overloaders win. The US had the best overloading infrastructure in the world. Overload beat overload.

That's not a compliment. It's a description of a landscape with no higher peaks.

The men's game is different. Other factors matter—academy overcoaching, cultural preference for other sports, limitations in the MLS pathway—but when the US faces Brazil or Argentina, they face players whose movement was acquired in the streets before anyone coached them. Fluency beats overload. It has always beaten overload. The US men keep climbing the overload hill, and the play cultures keep winning from the valley next door.

The world is already changing. Girls are playing more. The real tipping point for women's soccer isn't better coaching—it's the arrival of underloading. The moment a country builds a genuine play culture for girls, the moment they start accumulating the same unstructured repetitions and RPE that street boys have always had, then that country's female fluency will finally emerge. At that point, the old overload advantage disappears

The 2023 Women's World Cup offered the first glimpse. Spain won, the US went home early. Spain has been deliberately building a culture where girls play, not just train, for a decade. They didn't out-coach the US. They out-played them. The underloaders arrived.

That is not a crisis. That is the game catching up to what it was always supposed to be.

## The Arbitrage

Play is more valuable for girls than for boys. Minute for minute. Not because girls need it more developmentally—the acquisition process is identical. But because the competitive landscape is different.

Invest in play for a boy and you are competing against Brazil's street soccer culture, Argentina's potreros, a hundred years of pickup tradition. The underload cultures already exist. A hard gap to close.

Invest in play for a girl and you are competing against overload everywhere. The global infrastructure of play-based development that produced Pelé and Maradona and Messi simply does not exist for women. Every national team in women's soccer is still climbing the overload hill. The valley is empty.

The country—or the club, or the program—that builds a play culture for girls first will dominate women's soccer for a generation. Not by overloading better. By underloading first.

If you want to produce the next Marta, give girls what the favela gave Marta: a ball, friends, no schedule, and years of play before anyone decides to develop them. You are not competing against street cultures. You are competing against programs that forgot to let girls play.

The gap is yours for the taking.

## The Proof From the Body

Here is the number that stopped me cold.

American girls playing year-round soccer have greater than a one-in-six chance of tearing their ACL before finishing high school. More than fifty-seven percent of those tears are non-contact. No collision. No opponent. The body simply failed to protect itself during a normal athletic movement.

The injury prevention industry has responded with prehab protocols, activation programs, and structured warm-ups—real science, real commitment from researchers and coaches who care deeply about this problem.

The ACL epidemic continues. Rates are rising, not falling.

The problem may not be the programs. It may be a mismatch between the solution and the system it is trying to reach.

I watched it happen in real time. A fifteen-year-old at a showcase tournament—fast, well-coached, her team up by two. She received a pass at the top of the box, planted her right foot to cut left, and her knee simply buckled. No one touched her. She crumpled to the turf holding her knee, and the stands went silent. Her coach later told me she had done every ACL prevention protocol her club prescribed. Twice a week, all season. Band walks, single-leg squats, Nordic hamstrings. She could describe the exercises in detail. Her knee couldn't execute the protection in real time.

Motor learning researchers call it the Constrained Action Hypothesis—one of the most replicated findings in sports science over twenty years. When you direct an athlete's attention to their own body during movement—keep your knee aligned, watch your landing—you activate conscious control of the motor system. Conscious control is too slow for sport. A reactive athletic movement happens in fifty to one hundred milliseconds. Conscious processing takes three hundred to five hundred. The conscious mind doesn't just fail to help. It interferes.

The system that protects the knee is automatic. It fires in milliseconds, below awareness. It may not be fully reachable through verbal instruction, however well-designed.

Where does the protective reflex come from? The same place the movement vocabulary comes from. Thousands of hours of unstructured play movement during a critical developmental window, where the child's attention is directed entirely outward—toward the game, the ball—and never inward toward the joint.

The child chasing and being chased is not learning to stabilize her knee. She is solving spatial problems at full speed. And as a byproduct, her neuromuscular system is quietly building the unconscious movement architecture that will protect her for the rest of her athletic life.

A meta-analysis in the *American Journal of Sports Medicine* found neuromuscular training before age fourteen reduced ACL injury risk by seventy-two percent. After age eighteen: essentially no benefit. The window opens and closes.

## Fifteen Years in One Building

I want to be careful here. I am not a researcher. What I am about to share is observational. The numbers are small. I offer it as a directional finding that the theory predicts.

In fifteen years of running Joy of the People, boys and girls who trained exclusively within our play-based model have not torn an ACL.

Three girls who trained with us and also trained with high-level club programs did tear their ACLs—all three outside of JOTP, all three in environments defined by structured, coached training.

Small sample. Observational. No controls. I know this.

But the pattern is exactly what the theory predicts. High RPE correlates with no ACL tears. Lower RPE correlates with injury.

Low play leads to coaching filling the gap leads to overload leads to ACL. And then the sports medicine community arrives to treat the injury at the end of the chain while the chain keeps running.

Play is safe. It is a safer warm-up, it is a safer everything. It is nature's masterpiece. Remember, play is cleverer than you are.

## What the Villain Built

There is a system that looked at all of this and went the other direction.

Not out of malice. The people who built these systems believed they were solving a real problem. England's academies wanted more homegrown players. MLS NEXT wanted to give American kids a professional pathway. ECNL wanted a national platform for elite girls. Every one of these programs was built by people who loved the game.

What they built instead was a system that consumed the very resource it was trying to develop.

Elinor Ostrom won the Nobel Prize in Economics for a deceptively simple observation: communities self-govern shared resources better than top-down management systems. When a fishing village manages its own waters, the fishermen have a stake in the long-term health of the commons. When a government agency takes over—however well-intentioned—the local knowledge disappears, the incentives shift, and the commons collapses.

Play was the *commons*.

The park, the pond, the street corner, the swamp—self-governing systems. The oldest kid ran the game. The rules emerged from the players. Access was free. Rob passed it to Debbie and me. We passed it to whoever showed up. The game made new games.

Then the top-down systems arrived.

England's EPPP delivers up to ten thousand contact hours across a player's academy career. Güllich et al. found that self-directed play in childhood was the strongest single predictor of adult elite performance. Not coached hours. Play. The EPPP looked at this literature and built the opposite.

In the United States, the Development Academy required year-round commitment that eliminated high school soccer for many players. Elite programs like ECNL and MLS NEXT demand regional and national travel that prices families out. ECNL funnels girls into expensive travel structures at ages when they should be accumulating free play hours.

## Local Commons

When we first started JOTP, our goal was to be a free play center for all kids. And at first that is exactly what happened. Kids came from all over and played and played, had fun, told their friends, and played even more.

Then tryout season came and all those kids got promoted. They had improved so much they made some of the most elite teams in the metro. Kids were happy. Parents were happy.

Then they stopped coming.

I asked a twelve-year-old named Johnson why he hadn't been around. "My coach said I'm a good player now. I need to stop goofing around at JOTP." He was scheduled five days a week—dome training and technical sessions.

We were putting ourselves out of a job. Those kids who stopped returning left with their rainbows, their Maradonas, their Goalie Wars shots, their smiles, their gentleman's sweeps, their friendships, their language. And the system that took them had no idea what it was receiving.

We went along at first, believing this is how it works. We waved kids goodbye. Z, Marco, Nick, Lioul, and others stayed.

When the club kids came back, we couldn't wait to see the results. But like the high school captain, the kids had spent the winter in deeply overloaded environments and had somehow fallen behind.

I could see it. And so could the kids. How was Nick able to dribble like that? Why can't I ever get past Z? Why is Marco always smiling? They don't even play on a serious team.

Ostrom would have recognized it immediately.

The commons does not fail because the fishermen are lazy. It fails when those managing it stop having a stake in its long-term health and start optimizing for short-term yield. Those clubs that took our kids were trying to help their teams. They were good people making rational decisions. But every kid they pulled out of the gym lowered the RPE of a child who needed to keep playing.

What Ostrom also found: the commons can be restored by returning governance to the people closest to the resource.

So Nick, Z, and Emmanuel stayed and played. To avoid the exodus at tryout season, we started offering ways for kids to play together on teams—not because we wanted to create teams, but because it kept those smiles together. No tryouts. No cuts. No selection. No required travel. Just a gym, a ball, and the oldest kid running the game. The resource sustains itself because everyone who uses it has a stake in keeping it alive.

It has been running for fifteen years. The resource is not gone. It just needs room to run.

# Interlude:

# Mika

There's an iron law of coaching: if a coach has a kid, that kid will be either the best or the worst, never in the middle. And the second law: that kid never comes out of the game. Mika got caught in both. He arrived with his mom and a chip on his shoulder—cut from a top club, hungry to start over. Quiet and determined, he immediately played differently. He walked the ball. Never sprinted. Never seemed in a hurry. Defenders reacted like some invisible field repelled them: Mika was unthreatening until suddenly he wasn't. Most kids announce themselves—"Look at me! Hero entrance!" Mika did the opposite. He played like a shrug: "Oh, never mind me. I'm no threat. Take it if you want." Then, casually, the ball was in the net. Nicknames followed: the Soft Bullet. He had no Plan B; he invented a Plan A that felt like doing nothing and worked like everything. He weaponized ease. He told defenders, by body and tempo, not to commit. He moved so unhurried they didn't feel pressure—so they relaxed—and in that relaxation he found openings. The trick wasn't stealth; it was timing and persuasion.

The moment that made this undeniable came in high school. All year Mika rode the bench behind the coach's kid—classic iron-law injustice. Central made the state semis and trailed with fifteen minutes left. Mika came on and produced perhaps the best fifteen minutes of soccer I've ever seen. At US Bank Stadium he moved like a slow-motion burglar: defenders admired his calm, then watched in disbelief as he threaded impossible runs, slid balls forward, created chance after chance. Ten minutes left, a cross, and Mika arriving exactly where he always arrived. He finished. Redemption looked like a quiet man in a noisy stadium. In college he kept exploring easy—languid runs that left defenders stumbling, pristine assists to Phil, and a reputation: "He doesn't run. He floats." The coach's kid still got minutes. Mika got the game. Easy can look like nothing. Then, in a moment, it looks like everything.

# Chapter 14:

# The Underload Index

## The Metric

In the 2022 World Cup in Qatar, the United States covered more total distance per match than any other team in the tournament. Canada ranked near the top in both total distance and high-intensity running. Coaches, analysts, and commentators loved it. "Unbelievable engine." "Relentless work rate." "This is what American and Canadian soccer should look like—fit, athletic, never stop running."

They thought they were seeing greatness. They were watching the opposite.

The teams that went the farthest—Argentina, France, Croatia, and Morocco—were not the ones who ran the most. They made their opponents do the running. While the USA and Canada chased, pressed, and covered ground, the best teams underloaded: using positioning, deception, and timing to force the other side to do the heavy lifting.

We have spent decades celebrating the wrong metric.

RAE tells us we're selecting the wrong birthdays. RPE tells us we're selecting the wrong histories. But neither metric captures the thing itself—the actual skill that separates players who make it from players who don't. We know who tends to develop it. We haven't measured it directly.

I call it the Underload Index.

## The Logic

Underloading means making others do the work. The fluent player doesn't beat you with effort—he beats you by convincing your body to move the wrong way. His movement speaks; your movement answers incorrectly.

If that's real—if underloading is measurable and not just metaphor—it should show up in the data.

Here's where to look: penalty kicks.

A penalty is the purest test of kinetic conversation in soccer. One shooter. One keeper. Twelve yards. No chaos. Just two people and a question: Can the shooter get the ball into the net?

## xGOT and Its Limits

Analytics departments use xGOT—Expected Goals on Target—to measure how hard a shot is to save based on placement. Corner shot? High xGOT. Central shot? Low xGOT.

But central is only "easy to save" if the keeper stays home. Research shows keepers dive left or right ninety-four percent of the time. They commit early—the ball travels too fast to wait.

The question xGOT doesn't ask: Why did the keeper dive the wrong way?

Maybe he guessed wrong. Or maybe—and this is the underloading hypothesis—the shooter's body told him to dive. The hips said left. The eyes said corner. The run-up said power. And the keeper believed every word.

Then the ball went down the middle.

I know what you're thinking: how can you know Maier wasn't just guessing? It doesn't matter which explanation is true. The meaning of the shooter's run-up isn't in his intentions. It's in the keeper's dive. If the keeper moved wrong, the language worked.

Wittgenstein's principle applies here—meaning is use, not intention.

## The Formula

UI = Goals - xGOT

For penalties, this isolates everything except placement. Score from a low-xGOT location—a spot the keeper should have saved—and it means the keeper wasn't there. The keeper was moved.

The real fingerprint of kinetic fluency is overperformance on easier shots: central, body-height, moderate xGOT. When a player scores consistently from shots the keeper should save, it means the keeper wasn't there to save them. That's more than luck.

Watch Messi's slowest penalty kick goals. The ball barely crosses the line—rolling, almost apologetic. The keeper is nowhere. He's been moved so completely that Messi doesn't need pace, doesn't need placement, doesn't need power. He just needs the keeper to not be there.

The speed of the ball crossing the line is almost a proxy for underloading. Fast finish into the corner? Precision beat the keeper. Slow roll into an empty net? Language beat him.

Orgel's Rule for finishing: the slower the ball crosses the line, the more work the shooter made someone else do.

## The Data We Already Have

Israeli researchers studied 286 penalty kicks: twenty-nine percent went down the middle, but keepers stayed central only 6.3 percent of the time. That twenty-three-point gap is what underloading theory predicts.

Central shots convert at eighty-seven percent—higher than corners at eighty-three percent. Because the keeper is almost never there.

The data confirms the gap. But what happens if you follow the logic all the way down?

## The Hierarchy

Watching a game one day, Colleen walked past the TV just as the team I was cheering for gave up an own goal.

"So unlucky," I said.

She kept walking. "Actually, an own goal is the highest level of skill. You got the other team to do the work."

If you follow underloading theory to its logical conclusion, a hierarchy emerges:

**The Overload Goal.** You beat the keeper with power and placement. You did all the work—generating force, executing technique, putting the ball exactly where it needed to go. The muscles were yours. The effort was yours. The glory is yours.

**The Author Goal.** You moved the keeper yourself. Zidane against Casillas, World Cup 2006. Your body wrote the sentence that made his body respond. The hips said left. The eyes said corner. The keeper did almost all the work—he beat himself. You just wrote the story that made him do it.

**The Collective Goal.** Your team moved the keeper. A run dragged him left. A pass shifted his weight. The collective language of your teammates pulled him out of position before you ever touched the ball. The underloading was collective. Your skill was team literacy: seeing the space your team's movement had written into existence, and finishing what others had already started.

**The Own Goal.** You've gotten the other team to score for you. A defender trying to clear. A keeper palming it into his own net. You created the conditions—the cross, the pressure, the chaos—and they did the rest. The effort was entirely theirs. The muscles were entirely theirs. And in the locker room afterward? The blame is entirely theirs too.

This is underloading perfected.

The ultimate underload move turns the shooter into a smooth-talking grifter and the keeper into the classic mark. A slick run-up, a hip fake, a knowing glance—the shooter sells a beautiful lie so convincingly that the keeper dives like he just made the smartest read of his life. The ball rolls gently down the middle into an empty net. It's exactly like my brother Glenn proudly buying those worthless speakers out the back of a van, declaring "I'm the last guy who gets conned."

The overload goal makes highlight reels. The underload goal wins quietly. The own goal is the logical extreme—proof that the best outcome requires the least effort from you and transfers everything, including the psychological cost of failure, to the opponent.

## The Testable Prediction

The Kinetic Linguistics framework predicts:

Players with high RPE will have higher Underload Index scores.

The kid who grew up playing—thousands of hours reading bodies, learning to manipulate movement—should be better at making keepers move than the kid who spent those hours in drills.

The street player's body learned to speak. The academy player's body learned to execute. Speaking moves people. Execution requires precision.

The penalty data exists. The test is waiting. Connect Underload Index to developmental history and I believe you will find that the kids with high RPE don't just have better "feel" or "vision"—they have higher UI. They move keepers. They move defenders. They make others do the work.

The youth-sports industry has had decades and still hasn't asked.

The Underload Index is a starting point, not a finished instrument. It works cleanest on penalties because the variables are isolated—one shooter, one keeper, one moment. Extending it to open play means accounting for teammates, opponents, game state, and a thousand other factors the penalties strip away. That work hasn't been done yet. But the logic holds: if underloading is real, overperformance on savable shots should correlate with developmental history. The first test is simple—connect penalty UI to play hours before age twelve. Someone needs to run it.

RAE. RPE. UI.

Three numbers that tell us everything the highlight reels can't.

## The Opportunity

Youth sports in America is a forty-billion-dollar industry.

Travel teams. Club fees. Private coaching. Speed training. Camps. Showcases. Tournaments. Facilities. Equipment.

A family in Minnesota pays four thousand two hundred dollars a year for their nine-year-old's travel soccer team. That money buys three practices a week, weekend tournaments, matching warm-ups, and a coach who runs passing patterns and three-layer possession drills. It does not buy a single hour of unstructured play. The kid's schedule is so full of organized soccer that he comes home and plays video games—not because he doesn't love the sport, but because every available hour with a ball has already been claimed by an adult with a clipboard.

His parents think they're investing in development. They're investing in the opposite. Almost every dollar is lowering his RPE.

That family is not unusual. They are the market.

Every dollar of that forty billion is spent on the same thing: more training, more intensity, more reps, more games, more coaching, less play.

The industry has Phase Two—refinement—covered: coaching, clubs, travel, facilities, leagues, equipment, and more.

But Phase One—acquisition, the play years where fluency is built through immersion and joy—is completely unaddressed.

If acquisition is half of development, and the evidence suggests it's at least that, then the market has built an expensive machine to address half the problem.

Which means the other half is wide open.

Play—real acquisition, the kind that builds fluency—is worth at least as much as the training industry built on top of it. Probably more. And unlike travel fees and GPS vests and private coaching sessions, it costs almost nothing to provide. A ball. A space. Some friends. The oldest kid running the game.

That's not a forty-billion-dollar mistake. That's a forty-billion-dollar opportunity.

## The Mispricing

The clubs charging premium fees for eight-year-olds? They're selling Phase Two to kids who haven't finished Phase One. They're lowering RPE when they should be raising it.

The academies selecting at ten? They're interrupting acquisition to start refinement too early.

The parents spending thousands on travel teams? They're buying low RPE when their kids need high RPE.

Meanwhile, the late bloomers—the silent-period kids, the ones acquiring fluency in parks and driveways—are being discarded. Priced at zero. Told they don't have what it takes.

But they're the ones who keep showing up in World Cup squads. They're the ones Dinamo Zagreb sells for millions. They're the ones with high RPE.

The market is mispriced. Massively.

## Reaping Without Sowing

There is an Airbnb that we rent in Kansas City. It is normally eight hundred dollars per week. During the weeks when Kansas City is hosting the World Cup the price is fifty-six thousand dollars a week.

We should be careful of underestimating the value of play.

One hundred and fifty years ago, children in England kicked a ball around on a field. Nobody designed it. Somebody watched. Somebody said: I could charge money for this. An industry was born.

You cannot monetize the harvest while destroying the seeds. Outdoor pond hockey in Minnesota is dying. The warming houses are gone. The rinks are empty. The game that produced Herb Brooks and the Miracle on Ice is quietly disappearing. When the last player who grew up on outdoor ice retires, the game will be a little less surprising. A little less capable of producing the moment everyone paid to watch—when a player does something nobody taught them, something that could only have come from thousands of hours of invented solutions in conditions no coach designed.

Lioul's chip, Bennett's roll, Z's rainbow. The academy produces technically correct players. The swamp produces Messi. The market knows the difference even when the industry does not. Kill the play environments and you don't kill the game immediately. You kill it in twenty years, when the Airbnbs quietly drop back to eight hundred dollars a week. Because nobody wants to watch technically correct. They want a story.

The industry did not create fluency. It inherited it. And it is spending the inheritance without knowing what it is.

The solution is not a better warm-up. It is not more mentors at the exit door of the academy. It is not a softer version of the same model. It is designing environments that build the architecture. Measure the right thing at the right age. Stop selecting at age six for performance under instruction. Start asking how many hours of unstructured play a child has accumulated before anyone decided to develop them.

Give the girls the swamp. Because it will make them unstoppable. Give everyone the swamp. The late-born kid who learns to underload because he has no choice. The street kid who arrives at fifteen and outplays the nine-year academic. The girl building her neuromuscular architecture through hours of chasing and being chased, attention entirely outward, nobody watching.

The published evidence is not ambiguous. The system has a belief problem, not a data problem. High RPE beats low RPE. In the data. Across genders. Across sports. The solution isn't more coaching. It's more play.

I believed this. Living through it was different.

## The Driveway

Somewhere right now, a kid is playing in a driveway. No coach. No uniform. No pathway. Just a ball and a sibling and hours of joyful conversation in a language no adult is monitoring.

That kid's RPE is through the roof.

And in ten years, some academy is going to pay millions to "discover" what was there all along.

# Interlude:

# The Gift Of Play

My dad was a tile setter—and also a good sport.

He'd pack up after a job, the back seat of that month's rusty station wagon stacked with mastic, Portland mix, and silica sand, pants and knees grout-splattered. Instead of heading straight home he'd take the scenic route—every tennis court in the neighborhood, one by one—until he found someone hitting serves alone. Then he'd pull over, grab his racquet, introduce himself, and play. Almost forgetting I was still in the car. It was never about me. He couldn't have made me a better tennis fan.

My mom had seven kids and was always outside. Maybe because there was no air-conditioning in the three-bedroom house. Maybe because she grew up on a farm with ten brothers and sisters (my dad came from nine), and for both of them the neighborhood was the world. She knew every kid on the block better than their own parents did.

This particular evening was the race of the century. Record heat, but the sun was setting and cool air had finally arrived. Troubles—our dog, and really the neighborhood's dog too—was back. My mom had given him the name, which told you everything about her sense of humor and something about the dog. The previous Friday a tornado had ripped through Golden Valley—the real kind, the kind that tears streets apart. In the scramble to get to the basement, Glenn lost track of him. Troubles had been out back fetching fly balls, which was his idea of a full life. For three days we searched and cleared debris while little Amy told anyone who would listen that the tornado had taken Troubles to heaven. On the third day he came trotting down Independence Avenue carrying a branch so wide it nearly spanned the asphalt—late to the cleanup, but doing his part. So when Troubles took his place at the starting line that evening, he had recently returned from the dead. He looked like he knew it. Peggy stood at the start, Paul at the finish, Glenn holding baby Gabe. Neighbors drifted off porches and out from under trees. I sat next to Debbie on the hill. Bill leaned over and whispered that men's sprint records ran about twenty percent faster than women's—so Dad would probably win. A reasonable prior. My dad in work clothes splattered with mastic. My mom in three-quarter pants, tank top, and bare feet. They were off. Dad had built another bathroom that day. Mom had the light feet of a girl who grew up chasing siblings across open fields, and she ran like that now—easy, certain, like the outcome was never in question. Dad crossed the finish line smiling, the best loser on the block.

The neighbors laughed. Amy chased Troubles down the hill.

Dad with his racquet and his detours. Mom with her bare feet, her seven kids, and every neighbor's name. Debbie on the hill. The swamp gang. The Friday Tornado. Troubles, risen.

We were hard to beat.

# Chapter 15:

# The Monarch Rules

## Butterflies in the Cage

The city is upgrading all the parks, including ours. For our park—with its futsal courts and cages and kids—they proposed a theme: Butterfly and Caterpillar.

It sounded cute. Then August came.

Every August, maybe because we're close to the Mississippi flyway, monarch butterflies flood our park. Kids are playing cage ball underneath while hundreds of orange wings drift overhead. They gather on the milkweed, their own bleacher, watching kids at play. On the ground: eleven-year-olds trying to find themselves in tight spaces. All around them insects that weigh less than a paperclip commuting three thousand miles to Mexico.

Same park. Two journeys.

The monarch's life cycle looks like this:

- Egg (on a safe milkweed leaf)
- Caterpillar
- Chrysalis
- Butterfly—then the long migration

It's beautiful biology. It's also a brutal development manual.

You can't skip stages. You can't reverse them. You can't "speed them up" with motivational speeches.

And every stage has its own kind of joy.

The monarchs don't chase where the warmth was. They follow where it's going—but only because they honored every stage that came before. The egg didn't try to migrate. The caterpillar didn't try to fly. Each stage did its own work, and the result was a creature capable of crossing a continent.

Human development is messier than insect development. Kids stall, loop back, surge ahead. But the order of operations still matters.

That's what this chapter is about: the stages of development and the sequence of joys that actually work.

I call them the Monarch Rules.

And I know they work because I watched a kid named Phil live every single stage.

## Stage 1: Egg—Home Before World

Monarchs don't start in the sky. They start glued to a leaf.

The egg stage is tiny, protected, hyper-local. Everything that matters is within a few centimeters. The job description is simple: exist, be safe, wait.

For kids, that's the living room, the backyard, the schoolyard. Parents and siblings, not scouts and standings.

The first games are on the couch, in the hallway, against the garage door. The first opponent is a brother, a sister, a parent. The first crowd is whoever looks up from the kitchen.

Phil's first crowd was his dad, Amilcar.

Amilcar was a Brazilian who loved soccer so much he'd been kicked out of every adult league in town. Too passionate. Too competitive. Too Brazilian. He had nowhere to put all that joy—until he had a son.

By eight, Phil was ready to quit. The local clubs had done what local clubs do: turned play into work, turned joy into obligation. The spark was almost out.

Then Amilcar brought Phil to a futsal tournament at Joy. Afterward, he found me.

"I want to thank you for letting the kids play," he said. "Phil showed that Brazilian joy again."

That was the egg finding its leaf.

No one looks at a monarch egg and says, "You can't even fly yet? Hustle. Wings up."

But we do something very close to that with six-year-olds.

## Stage 2: Caterpillar—Acquisition Before Learning

Then the egg hatches.

The caterpillar does one thing, obsessively, for weeks: it eats.

Crawl, eat, molt. Repeat. The entire job description is acquisition.

The caterpillar is not "training for migration." It has no concept of Mexico. It's taking in fuel and raw material. It's building the body that will later be torn apart and rebuilt into wings.

After that tournament, Phil started showing up at Joy. Every day. Always alone at first—he would arrive somehow, leave somehow—but never alone once he got there. He was either watching or playing with others. Always.

Here's what I never saw Phil do: practice by himself.

No ball against a wall. No solo drills in the backyard. No grinding alone to "get better."

Phil was driven by something simple: I love soccer. I don't want to practice on my own. I need a game. For that I need a ball, a space, but most importantly—friends.

He wasn't the outgoing, charismatic type. He just slid into the group like a stray runt puppy, hoping no one noticed. Quiet. Present. Small for his age. Always attacking.

He may have played more hours than any kid who ever came through Joy. But he never "practiced" in the traditional sense. He just played.

The philosopher Ludwig Wittgenstein argued that there is no private language. Language requires community. A word only you understand isn't a word—it's noise.

If movement is language, then movement cannot be acquired alone. You need someone to talk to. You need the conversation.

Phil ate with friends.

No one stops the caterpillar to explain lift and drag. No one diagrams optimal wing beats on a whiteboard.

We do that to kids all the time: tactical lectures for eight-year-olds, "shape" diagrams for kids who still trip over the ball, "principles of play" before they've even fallen in love with finishing.

We are explaining flight to caterpillars.

The monarch manual is clearer: Let them eat. Let them acquire. That's their entire job right now.

## Stage 3: Chrysalis—Protect the Rebuild

Then comes the weird part. The caterpillar hangs upside down, sheds its skin, and turns into a chrysalis. Inside, the body literally dissolves. It becomes a kind of genetic soup, then reorganizes into something new.

That's adolescence. Peak height velocity. Feet suddenly too big for the body. Limbs growing faster than the brain can track. Kids who once moved like water now look like they're wearing someone else's legs.

Inside, everything is under construction: bone growth plates, neural wiring, strength and coordination patterns.

This is not the moment to pile on extra tournaments, double training load, or turn every practice into a test.

Every youth coach has seen the human chrysalis: the twelve-year-old who used to glide now stumbles through basic moves, the thirteen-year-old who was fearless now looks hesitant and self-conscious. Parents panic; coaches "raise standards." We are stress-testing chrysalises.

The chrysalis period was brutal on Phil.

He was so small. Other kids hit their growth spurts and started flying—physically bigger, faster, suddenly dominant. Phil stayed earthbound. The gap that hadn't mattered at ten became a canyon at fourteen.

Amilcar saw his son struggling. He did what loving parents do: he tried to help. He sent Phil to a traditional club, thinking structured training might give him an edge.

It got worse.

The club saw a small, quiet kid and treated him like a project to fix. They didn't see the endless camp days of acquisition underneath. They saw size and speed deficits. They saw a kid who didn't fit the template.

Phil still showed up at Joy. But he didn't break down the door anymore. The spark was dimming again.

This is the cruelest phase. The caterpillar has dissolved. The butterfly hasn't emerged. You're genetic soup hanging in a shell, and everyone around you is demanding you fly.

Linguists talk about critical windows—periods when the brain is uniquely primed to acquire language. Miss that window and you can still learn words and rules, but native, accent-free grammar gets harder and harder. Children up to age six acquire language effortlessly. From six to puberty, acquisition becomes steadily harder. After puberty, native fluency is rare.

A similar window appears to exist for movement. Roughly ages five to twelve seem to be the critical period for physical fluency.

The chrysalis—adolescence—is when everything reorganizes. The window is closing. The brain is consolidating what it acquired, not eagerly opening new grammatical categories.

This is why overloading the chrysalis is so destructive. You're not just making kids tired. You're corrupting the installation process.

Remember Sally? Her body shut down mid-sprint at the Division 1 level. That's what happens when you crack open the chrysalis to check progress. You don't get a butterfly. You get a mess.

Phil almost became a mess. We almost lost him.

But we didn't crack open his shell. We let him keep playing while his body reorganized. We protected the chrysalis.

Biology's rule is brutal: Mess with the chrysalis, kill the butterfly.

Phil made it through high school. Some progress, but not much. He didn't grow until after his senior year. Most programs would have written him off years earlier. We let him keep hanging in the chrysalis.

## Stage 4: Butterfly—Learning and Migration

Then the shell goes clear, splits, and the butterfly emerges.

At first, it doesn't fly. It hangs there, pumping fluid into its wings, letting them dry. It tests short hops. It gets a feel for this completely new body.

That's learning in our terms: you already play fluently, now you start to care about why certain decisions work. You rewind your own game in your head. You refine on purpose.

This is where film study tastes good. Where pattern names finally mean something. Where tactical diagrams attach to thousands of hours of felt experience.

You have wings now. Instruction hooks.

Phil took a gap year just as the pandemic hit. Everything shut down—except Joy. During that strange, difficult time, the kids played every night. It was the only thing that felt normal.

Z called me one evening. "Phil's back," he said. "And he's doing amazing."

The chrysalis had finally cracked open on its own schedule. Phil had grown. But more than that, all those years of acquisition—all that eating, all that quiet relentless play—had reorganized into something new.

He wasn't just bigger. He was fluent.

He saw passes earlier. He manipulated defenders with little hesitations he didn't know he had. Whole games started bending around his choices.

But the adult monarch's job is bigger than flying around the park.

It has to migrate.

Three thousand miles. Over highways, cities, cornfields, storms. Some cross the Gulf of Mexico on paper-thin wings.

Phil's migration began with Joy AC's first season. He was a huge part of our run to the second national title. Then he went to St. Cloud State University with Z, Noah, Emmanuel, and Mika—a flock of Joy kids migrating together.

By his senior year, Phil led Division II in scoring. Conference MVP. National Player of the Year finalist.

The small, quiet kid who showed up alone every day. The one who almost quit at eight. The one we almost lost in the chrysalis.

He made it to Mexico.

Migration is overload with a purpose. It's not "try harder in drills." It's travel, pressure, fatigue, playing for something beyond you.

And it only works because the sequence was honored:

- Egg: Amilcar's joy, the tournament that rekindled the spark
- Caterpillar: years of pure acquisition at Joy, always with others
- Chrysalis: protected through the brutal waiting
- Butterfly: learning and, finally, migration

You don't strap weights to the caterpillar to "build grit." You don't crack open the chrysalis to "check progress." You don't demand a Gulf crossing from a butterfly whose wings are still wet.

We do all three to kids—and then wonder why they hate flying.

## Sequence, Not Ratio

The Monarch Rules are not about ratios. Not "ninety percent individual, ten percent collective." Not "mostly fun, with a little bit of grind."

They are about sequence. Acquisition then learning.

You can't have a conversation before you have vocabulary. You can't compose stories before you've acquired grammar.

The favela kid, the street-hockey kid, the backyard kid—they experience each stage's satisfaction naturally. No one needs to script it. The modern industry skips straight to the butterfly's rewards—competition, rankings, results—for kids who are still eating. And then we act surprised when nothing feels good.

## The Empty Kid vs. the Fluent Kid

You've seen him.

He's in the right line in the 4-3-3. He knows the pressing trigger. He's memorized the build-out pattern from the goalkeeper. The coach is happy with his "shape."

The ball rolls past him and he doesn't move.

Not because he's lazy. Because he's empty.

He's standing in the right position with nothing to say. He knows the system. He doesn't feel the game. He has no language.

He never acquired the grammar of movement—the kinetic language that lets you tell stories with your body. He can follow instructions. He can't author action.

The fluent player doesn't just occupy space. They compel. Their feint pulls the defender. Their run creates the passing lane. Their stillness freezes the backline.

The empty kid has positions. The fluent kid has sentences.

Phil had sentences. Thousands of them, built over years of quiet, relentless play with others. When he finally emerged from the chrysalis, he wasn't just physically ready. He was fluent—and that fluency stayed, even as his body kept changing.

## The Underloading Thread

There's one more pattern hiding underneath the four stages.

Every first involves underloading. The caterpillar eats before it flies. The chrysalis reorganizes before it migrates. The sequence is the underload—each stage doing less than the next one demands, building exactly what the next stage requires.

The monarch doesn't flap frantically all the way to Mexico. It rides thermals.

That's what the Monarch Rules are designed to build.

## Where Everest Will Be

The landscape will keep changing. The game will keep evolving. What counts as mastery will keep shifting.

But this part doesn't change: sequence still matters more than ratio. Underloading is still where fluency gets built. Joy still changes as you develop—and flow is still the compass.

The Monarch Rules don't tell you what Everest looks like. They tell you how the path has to unfold if you want people to actually enjoy the climb.

Honor the sequence, and every new level of challenge feels strangely good, even when it's hard. Each stage is satisfying because the previous stage prepared you for it.

Skip it, and nothing feels right, because the order is wrong. You're asking a child to enjoy adult problems with a child's toolkit.

Phil followed every rule because he played at Joy, and Joy was designed to let the rules unfold naturally. Egg to caterpillar to chrysalis to butterfly. Ten years. One kid. The whole journey.

Our job is not to outsmart that compass. It's to stop fighting it.

Every August, the monarchs still flood our park. The kids still play cage ball underneath. And every once in a while, one of them looks up and watches a butterfly drift toward Mexico on paper-thin wings.

They don't know it yet, but they're on the same journey.

Follow the butterflies.

# Interlude:

# Sean

Running programs for my old club, I thought we would run out of space in our little gym.

We had one kid at our first program.

His name was Sean.

***

His grandfather brought him. His name was David, and he was a well-known unbeliever.

A professor of anthropology, David was skeptical about everything. Possession-based soccer? Guided discovery? Play-first methodology? He'd heard it all before and demanded proof.

At my old club, he'd volunteered coaching the younger age groups and butted heads with the Directors of Coaching who wanted nothing to do with him. He asked too many questions. He didn't accept "because that's how it's done" as an answer.

I walked him around Orchard Park one afternoon. He watched the kids playing, shook his head. "You think you can solve everything with play?"

I enjoyed his skepticism and saw it as a challenge. We would sit for long periods talking about development—what we could actually know, what was opinion dressed up as expertise.

His own son, Max, had grown up with me at Monroe Skills. I believe that earned some capital with David. He understood I had been around. Did the work. Max became a great player, then built a successful business in personal training, then took over the head coaching position at the fabled soccer school SPA, where he won two state titles.

So for David to bring his grandson to Joy, I felt half proud that he trusted me and half embarrassed that I could not round up more kids.

Victor and Glenn walked into the gym that first night and sat down. Later Victor told me, "Well, this will never work."

***

Sean kept coming.

A very quiet kid, he found his voice playing with others. Which is not always the case.

The club kids who came in for summer camp free play were louder, more boisterous, less empathetic. Their currency was who's good and who's bad. They needed to communicate those rankings constantly. They looked to adults to confirm their assessments.

"I'm the best player here, right?"

One kid said to me, "Why are you cheering? Every time my team plays your team, we beat you."

"Really?" I said. "Joy is undefeated."

He didn't know what to do with that.

***

The club kids were strong players—stronger than the best of ours at the time. They made sure to let you know, and then backed it up. They did not care how they won. Get the lead. If you have a lead, get in goal and stop the other team. Keep the weaker kid on the bench, or if he's in the game, certainly don't pass to him.

Win the game.

The youth sports system doesn't have much space for the quiet kids.

Z. Phil. Mika. Sean.

The system wants loud. It wants "show your stuff." It wants winners.

Everyone is welcome at Joy.

That means more October-December birthdates. Faster kids, slower kids. Taller kids, shorter kids. Louder kids, quieter kids.

But then also: kids used to those differences. Used to getting along in diversity. Forming something welcoming.

The quiet kids find space to become themselves.

***

Sean stayed quiet. Kept coming. For a junior high project, he produced a science poster board on the physics of a Volley-lite versus a soccer ball in Goalie Wars. I still have that poster.

Sean played varsity soccer starting in ninth grade. He eventually went to Yale.

***

The first outside kid who chose Joy. Quiet. Calm. With an anthropologist grandfather who demanded proof, who was tired of all the subjective coaching opinions, who had fought with every director of coaching he'd ever met.

David wanted evidence. He got it.

When David's son Max won state at SPA, he sent me proud texts.

When Sean tears it up on futsal teams at Yale, David sends me a photo.

Three generations. One skeptic who finally believed.

And it started with one kid in an empty gym.

***

"You think you can solve everything with play?"

I've thought about David's question for years.

The answer is no. Play isn't a solution to a problem.

Play sees problems as play.

Sean didn't need to be fixed. He needed space to play.

He found it.

# Chapter 16:

# The Environment

## Two Sidelines

Walking my dogs through the park one evening, I passed a youth soccer game. Coed groups of jerseyed-up kids running off for water bottles. The sidelines were lined with lawn chairs—moms, dads, grandparents holding their kid's water bottle in one hand and coffee in the other. Referee. Inflated ball. Thick long grass. Perfectly marked lines. Starting on time.

A soccer machine.

One problem: we are modeling the wrong behavior.

The kids look to the sideline and see parents sitting, drinking Diet Dr. Pepper. They say to themselves, "That's what I want to do when I grow up."

In St. Paul, at the Hispanic league, it's different.

All day Sunday. Adults of all ages—with boys, and sometimes girls, as young as sixteen—play hotly contested games. Their uniforms are whatever shorts they can find and a knockoff jersey. It is usually Barcelona versus Real Madrid. *El Clásico* redux.

Young kids are not allowed in the competition. That is the work of the adults.

Instead, kids by the dozens play in kid-structured games on the sidelines while dad, or uncle, or big brother plays in the important game. They stop to watch. They see the skill, the intensity, the joy.

They look and say, "That's the game I want to play in. That's what I want to do when I grow up."

The food. The music. The camaraderie. The community ties it all together from morning to night.

The kids on the sidelines of the Hispanic league acquire movement, soccer skills, social and cultural skills—even how to lose is picked up as a byproduct of the fun of play, food, family, friends.

To the structured kids, fun looks like a comfortable lawn chair and a nice cold Diet Dr. Pepper. Two sidelines. Two futures.

## Building the Container

No one ever sat the favela kid down and explained the progression: "First you will experience intimate, low-stakes inner-circle play. Then you will naturally move into more challenging and socially complex environments…"

They just opened the door.

The alley was there. The other kids were there. The ball was, more or less, round.

The environment did the work.

You understand the theory now: acquisition before learning, play before practice, author before editor. You cannot force acquisition. You cannot mandate play. You cannot instruct someone into fluency.

So what can you actually do?

You can design the container—and then learn to move with it as the landscape shifts.

## Why Principles, Not Rules

Charles Goodhart was a British economist who noticed something that should have been obvious: the moment you turn a measure into a target, it stops being a good measure.

A basketball coach wants better shooters. She tracks shooting percentage. The kids figure out what gets measured and start taking only easy shots. Shooting percentage goes up. Actual shooting—the courage to pull up from twenty-three feet with a hand in your face—goes down. The metric climbed. The player got worse.

Goodhart's Law is the story of modern player development. Passing completion? Kids play safe. Sprint speed? They run straight. Goals per game? They stop trying the move that might not come off. Every metric becomes a hill the system climbs, and every hill turns out to be a local optimum—a peak that feels like progress while the real mountain sits in the next valley.

You cannot coach the landscape with a clipboard. The landscape shifts under your feet with every touch, every new player who walks in, every change in mood or weather or energy. A rule that works on Tuesday is wrong by Thursday.

So we need principles—not instructions, but a compass for reading the shifting terrain in real time.

## The Five Principles

### 1. The landscape is shared

This comes first because it changes everything that follows. You are an independent agent moving through the landscape, making your own decisions. But as Wittgenstein showed us, there is no such thing as a private language. Language—Kinetic Language included—exists only between people. The other player is not an obstacle or a feature of the terrain. The other player is the only part of the environment that is also navigating. When two people play, the landscape changes shape because both are moving through it and responding to each other's movement. Think of Eman playing against the six-year-old. Each adapted, each changed the landscape, creating a new and different problem to solve. The best environments feel like a family cookout—conversation, play, laughter, and the kind of learning that no one notices is happening.

### 2. Beware of local optima

What feels like progress can be a false peak. More reps, more structure, faster visible improvement—you climb higher on the hill you are on while the real mountain sits in the next valley. In the landscape, up means anxiety—more challenge, more pressure, the territory flow theory tells you to seek. Down means what looks like boredom—less challenge, more slack, the territory every coach is trained to avoid. The whole system corrects upward because anxiety looks like effort and effort looks like development. Nobody corrects downward because boredom looks like waste. Keep asking: are we still building language, or just climbing because climbing feels like progress?

### 3. Play down when given a choice

This is the heretical one. Every other system says climb. The landscape says the opposite: when offered an easier, lower-stakes path, take it. The elite travel team or playing rec with your friends. The mixed-age game, the extra round of Goalie Wars. Nick playing with the five-year-olds—these are not steps backward. They are descents into the valley where acquisition lives. Ideas are born in boredom. The kid with surplus attention is the kid who tries the thing nobody taught her. Anxiety compresses. Boredom expands. The *trivela* did not get invented under pressure. It got invented when a kid had enough slack to think—what if I hit it with the outside of my foot?

### 4. Follow your interest

Javi playing hide and seek, Duncan playing keeper—interest is the only reliable signal that you are moving toward real acquisition and not following someone else's route up someone else's hill.

The moment curiosity fades, the landscape has changed. Adjust immediately. A kid who is interested is acquiring. A kid who is trying to win is performing. You can see the difference from across the room.

### 5. Climb when it's fun

This is not anti-effort. This is anti-obligation. What is fun for kids—tag, hide and seek—may not look like fun to adults. Fun for adults is different. It is doing what you are interested in. Gardening. Fixing a classic car. A painter working on a canvas. Montessori said play is the work of the child. At Joy of the People we say work is the play of the adult. When persistence is joyful—when the kid tries the move again and again not because someone told her to but because she has to know if she can do it—keep climbing. The moment climbing becomes a grind, you have left acquisition territory. Stop climbing that hill. Look for the next one.

These five are not a checklist. They are a compass for reading the landscape in real time.

## The Physical Container

Raffi was one of our founding coaches at Joy. Brilliant coach, world-class talker. Could fill a gym with words and still have some left over for the parking lot.

One day, watching kids trickle into the gym—some sprinting in, some drifting in shoes half-tied, some hanging back—Raffi said something I have never forgotten: "The environment should call the kids to play."

Not drag them. Not require them. Not bribe them. Call them. The room itself should feel like an invitation before any coach says a word. Attraction, not compulsion. If you have to constantly push kids to play, the container is wrong.

You don't need much. A ball. A space. A way to say: "This is in, that's out." Maybe small goals. Maybe pennies. Maybe some music. The quicker you can go from "we're here" to "we're playing," the better. Every extra minute of setup is a minute stolen from the real teacher: the game.

## Change the Ball, Change the Surface

My Brazilian mentor said it first. Wolfgang Schöllhorn's Differential Learning is the science behind it. Every variable you change—space, surface, ball, boundaries, time, goal size—creates a new problem that demands a new solution. The physical container is not a fixed stage. It is a set of dials you turn.

### Space

Big fields reward big solutions: run faster, kick harder, cover more ground. Speed and power are overload strategies. They don't build fluency as well as small spaces. Shrink the space and the language elevates. In a small space there's nowhere to outrun anyone. You have to solve problems with communication and deception, not horsepower. Futsal courts. Street cages. The gym at Joy with seven small courts jammed into a space built for three. Ricardinho grew up in school gyms in Gondomar. The tight spaces weren't a limitation; they were a teacher.

### Boundaries

Kids are like puppies—they like to be penned in. A fenced-in futsal court will be more popular than an open field one. The boundary says: this is where the game lives. Like life itself boundaries can be clear or delightfully flexible. The weekly Jundiai Saturday *campinho* was bordered by a wall on one side and street curb on the other, but street play was also allowed, as long as you didn't get run over. Walls add variation—the ball comes back at angles, ricochets, surprises. Play with lines and you will soon witness tightrope walkers—a street soccer signature—the dangerous dance partnership wily veterans have with the line—using every inch of the space to make the game easier.

This maps beautifully to life. Good boundaries—rules, values, deadlines, social norms—aren't oppression. They're the silent teacher that says *master this domain first.* Once you internalize the lines, you can play with them: bend them creatively, expand them thoughtfully, or occasionally vault over them when the moment demands.

## Surface

The kids at academies train on perfect grass. The kids in the favelas train on concrete, dirt, broken pavement, sand. Who gets better touch? Every surface is a different teacher. Sand slows the game and builds balance. Gym floors speed it up. Asphalt punishes falling, so trickery and patience emerge. The imperfect pitch trains you for the real world. The perfect pitch trains you for a museum. At JOTP we went all in. We even had a giant inflatable bounce field made. Kids bounce, flip, and sometimes play soccer. If we didn't take it down, they would never get off.

## Ball

Legend has it that the original futsal was created by Portuguese longshoremen in Brazil. The ball kept bouncing into the water. One of the workers stuffed a ball with rope to slow it down, and futsal was born. What the longshoremen understood: a ball with less bounce is a decision-making device. With less time to corral it, the next action is imminent. Players can tell stories instead of gambling. Different balls bring out different games. Dodge balls are keeper-safe and fun to shoot. Volley-lites are perfect for young keepers learning to save without fear. Vinyl play balls fly with opposite spin, rewarding strikers who can bend it. What I like most is that kids see a giant vinyl ball and smile. They let go of overload and relax.

## Time

Some games never end. The pickup hockey game on Lake of the Isles in Minneapolis starts around nine in the morning and never really ends—it only slows to retrieve a puck. To join, you get in line on the boards. Players move in and out as they tire. It's a good place to acquire skill, to practice your Canadian—"He skates like a Ranger, eh"—and just enjoy the languid game. Pond hockey scoring—play to a hundred, sub in and out live—creates an underloaded rhythm. Other games are all urgency. Make it, take it with three teams can tip into overload fast. Time is invisible architecture. Change it and the whole game feels different.

## Goals with keepers

When I first saw Brazilian futsal courts, my first thought was: why is the goal so big? But when I joined the game, that's where they placed me. The new guy plays goalie. The striker/keeper problem is the first sentence of kinetic language: how do I get the ball past this person who is trying to stop me? Kids like problems. You couldn't just blast it. You needed to fool them, chip them, send it to the far post. Want better finishers? Train everyone to play keeper.

## Bleachers

Every great play space I have visited had places to sit close to the action. In Jundiai cement steps. In Asuncion a giant fallen Guapo'y tree. In Santos a cut-out hillside. This perplexed me. Were these just conveniences? Nice to haves? Or something more?

But once you look at this through the Krashen lens, the bleachers become essential acquisition machines. Our inflatables are great examples. Kids sit inches from play. They absorb the grammar of movement without anyone explaining it. They see how fluent speakers solve problems. They feel the rhythm of the game before they enter it.

Bleachers are not for parents. They are for the next wave of players. An academy coach that read this manuscript noted that he witnessed this. The Minnesota United academy kids sat as close and as silent as they could as they watched Colombian legend, James Rodriquez practice free kicks—it was pure acquisition.

## The Social Container

The first landscape a kid navigates is the family. A parent kicking a ball in the backyard, an older sibling who lets the little one play but does not let them win every time—these are the first co-authors of kinetic language.

Friends come next. Lower anxiety, higher risk-taking, more laughter. You will try something ridiculous in front of your friends that you would never risk in front of a talent ID scout.

The modern system skips family and friends entirely. It puts strangers in matching jerseys and calls them a team. At Joy, kids bring friends. Friends become the team. The team is real because the relationships were real first.

## The Expanding Conversation

Often we see two strong players wanting to play together. The assumption is they just want to win. But watch what they actually do.

They try wall passes. One-touches. Give-and-go's that require both players to read the same moment at the same time. They are not trying to dominate—they are trying to expand the reach of their language.

The wall pass is the first sentence of group underloading. Underloading scales. One-on-one first. Then pairs. Then triangles. Then the full ensemble, where five players write a sentence together and make eleven opponents do the work.

But it always starts with two people who want to see what they can say together.

## Mixed Ages

The system slices kids into birth-year cohorts and never lets them mix. Mixed ages do three irreplaceable things. Older kids demonstrate without demonstrating. The big kid naturally dials down against the little kid—underloading—while the little kid stretches up. And the oldest kids lead because they want the game to keep going.

There's an iron law of play: the oldest and best lead. Not out of charity. Out of self-interest. They need bodies to play. If they bully everyone away, they're stuck alone with a ball and a wall. So they accommodate, include, and instruct—gently, selfishly, beautifully.

And here's where the underloading magic happens. The older kid has to dial back against the younger one—the game would die otherwise. That self-imposed constraint is where the highest skills get built. When you can't rely on being faster or stronger, you have to make your movement do more work so your body can do less.

The older kid playing down isn't wasting time. They're practicing the most advanced skill there is.

## Adults at the Edges

Every adult in the room changes the room.

Kids behave differently when adults watch. They perform. They seek approval. They hide certain behaviors and exaggerate others. Even a silent adult is constantly instructing: a raised eyebrow here, a sigh there, a "nice job!" that tells kids which actions win praise.

The best acquisition environments are adult-light. Not zero adults—safety matters. But fewer, farther away, and quieter than feels comfortable.

The less I did, the more they learned.

## The Cultural Container

Culture is not a poster on the wall. It is what happens between people.

At Joy, we celebrated the move that made everyone gasp—even if it failed. That single shift produced more experimentation, more creativity, more underloading. When achievement is what gets noticed, kids chase achievement. And because the safest path to reliable results runs through less risk, kids stop trying weird things. They lock into early solutions—simple sentences, repeated forever. When joy is what gets noticed, kids chase joy.

But culture is not only what the group celebrates. It is what your face does when you think no one is watching. Kids read your eyes instantly. If your eyes light up for goals and wins, they will chase goals and wins. If your eyes light up for the beautiful attempt, the impossible pass—they will chase that instead.

When a player makes a move that surprises you, do not just see the move—see what it reveals. That is their voice emerging. The pigeon-toed *trivela*. The hesitation that freezes defenders. These are not mistakes to correct. They are the player showing you who they are. If you accept what emerges—if you don't immediately edit it into something "proper"—they'll feel that trust. And they'll repay it by going further.

What you notice becomes what they practice.

## Winning

And in the end—yes—it is about winning.

But play kids win differently. They have already won and lost ten thousand times before the scoreboard arrived. A pickup game is a referendum every five minutes: whose team wins, who picks next, who gets the ball back. By the time the lights come on and a referee blows a whistle, the play kid has been here before. The score is just a louder version of a conversation they already speak.

They learn to win in style. They learn to win in community. They learn to lose without losing themselves. And in time—because style, community, and a clear head are exactly what pressure rewards—they learn to win on the scoreboard.

Leo under the harvest moon. Zinedine's last-second volley. Those moments were not surprises. They were the predictable arrival of kids who had spent years winning quietly, in small ways, until the big moment looked familiar.

The play kid knows how to face down pressure and find the joy.

## Safety to Fail

Early on in my time working with kids, there was a grade school habit of making fun when someone mis-hit a shot.

"Fail!" they would shout.

"That word is never spoken here."

That was fifteen years ago and I have not heard it since.

Experimentation requires failure. Failure requires safety. High standards and high safety can coexist: "We go hard here. We try ridiculous things here. And nobody gets punished for blowing it."

## The Oldest Kid at the Park (OKP)

This is the most important idea in the book for anyone who works with kids.

The culture creates the expectation. The environment provides the stage. But someone has to start the game.

That someone is the Oldest Kid at the Park. OKP.

The day my friend's dad drove up and took my friends to Golden Valley hockey tryouts, I was left with four eight-year-olds looking up at me, tilting back their helmets. What was I going to do? I set up a game and played. I had fun. Twisting, teasing, dangling, putting the puck through their floppy ankles. I scored goals.

But not every goal. Not every time.

An OKP is just the game's way of making a new game.

The oldest kid does not run drills. They play. They model. They start games. They pick teams. They settle disputes with the only currency that matters: if you do not figure this out, we do not play.

I did it selfishly. I needed the game to happen. You score on the eight-year-olds because you want to. You help them score because you need them to come back tomorrow. You accommodate, you include, you calibrate—not because someone taught you character, but because the game demands it. Coaches talk endlessly about character as if it can be lectured into kids. Like the Spanish coaches, they can feel that it matters. But they can't explain where it comes from. It comes from here. The oldest kid at the park learns generosity the only way it can be learned—by needing other people. Kids see this and say, "That's what I want to do when I grow up."

A few years later those kids were the best skaters at the park.

## The Gentleman's Sweep

Here's what the oldest kid learns, eventually: you don't win every time.

Researchers studying play in rats found something interesting. When experienced rats wrestle with less experienced rats, they let the younger ones win about one in three to four times. A gentleman's sweep.

If the older mouse wins every single time, the younger mouse stops playing. The game dies.

The best competitors don't have killer instincts. They have play instincts.

Back at the rink with those four eight-year-olds, I let them get a few. I set them up. I celebrated their scores louder than my own. Not out of charity. Out of self-interest.

I wanted the game to keep going. For that, I needed them to come back tomorrow.

## The Trap

The moment you start thinking about what is good for the kids, you stop being the oldest kid at the park. You become a coach. And coaches cannot help but teach.

The coach thinks: these kids need to work on their weak foot. The oldest kid thinks: I want to play.

The coach thinks: this game would be better with a constraint that forces switching. The oldest kid thinks: I want to play.

Every time you modify the game to make it "better for development," you step out of the oldest kid role and into the coach role. And the kids feel it. They know the game isn't real.

## Do Nots

Do not play to small goals without keepers—you remove the first conversation. Do not add touch restrictions—you create a false environment where the fast play that works does not transfer. Do not set up rondos—no oldest kid ever said, "Let's stand in a circle and keep the ball away from Tommy." Do not add scoring rules—now the game is about your constraints, not about the defender.

Every modification sends the same message: the real game is not enough. You need my improvement plan. The game becomes medicine. And nobody takes medicine for fun.

## What to Do

Set up a real game. Two goals, keepers, a ball, teams. Play on one of the teams. Try to win. Self-constrain to keep the game going—the gentleman's sweep. You're constraining yourself, not the game. The game stays real. You adjust your effort to keep it alive.

## No Correction

Vanuatu is the most language-dense nation on Earth—roughly one hundred and thirty indigenous languages for three hundred thousand people. They have a cultural practice called *Kastom* that governs interaction across language groups. They discourage open correction. When someone is learning your language, you do not fix their mistakes.

This keeps language in acquisition. It keeps anxiety low. And it lets the learner build their own feedback system. The game tells them what worked. Not you.

## Model Joy

This is the most important one.

If you're having fun, they're learning that this is fun. If you're grinding through it like a job, they're learning that too.

The Hispanic league kids don't just see skill on the main field. They see adults who desperately want to be out there. They see joy.

That's what you're modeling. Not technique. Joy.

## Play Your Music

Not kids' music. Not what you think they'll like. Your music.

The oldest kid at the park doesn't curate an experience for children. They do what they love, and kids want to be like them.

At Joy, I can't play anymore, so I Hula-Hoop on the sidelines. I play the music I like. Colleen does the playlists. The kids don't get a vote—and they don't want one. They want to know what the oldest kid listens to.

How can kids take themselves too seriously when their coach is Hula-Hooping?

## What to Look For

You want kids playing in underload—curious, relaxed, experimenting—not overload: stressed, pushing, performing. Fluency and transferable skill grow in underload. Overload produces polished but brittle behavior.

The high-level rule: every player, every session, is either underloaded or overloaded. Underload equals acquisition. Overload equals performance. Your job is to nudge the session toward underload.

Signs of overload: furrowed brow, clenched jaw, anxious expression. Eyes darting, shifty, locked on scoreboard or parent. Arms rigid, clenched fists, flailing. Movement all gas, sprinting blindly, everything at full power. Behavior: contesting every call, refusing to pass, not including weaker kids.

Signs of underload: calm face, relaxed, often smiling. Eyes scanning, soft focus, reading teammates. Arms quiet, relaxed, in service of movement. Movement flowing with the game, timing over force, playful risks. Behavior: inviting others in, laughing at mistakes, experimenting with new moves.

Two quick diagnostics. The Smile Test: are you having fun? If the adults are enjoying themselves, you're probably underloading. The Duct Tape Test: could you run this session with tape over your mouth? If not, you're coaching, not playing.

What looks wrong but isn't: the kid standing on the outside watching is acquiring. The kid making lots of mistakes and not seeming to care is acquiring—and calibrating their own feedback. The kid who barely touches the ball is acquiring. These kids do not need correction. They need time.

If kids are overloaded, do not lecture. Change the game. Different ball—softer, bouncier, bigger. Play in socks. Two balls at once. Smaller space. Different teams. Monitor the fun. Stay in OKP mindset: what keeps the kids playing?

## The Thread

Culture → Environment → Individual. Remove any one and the chain breaks.

Culture without environment is nostalgia. Environment without individual is empty ice. An individual without culture is lonely obsession.

Your gym on Tuesday is all three. You carry the culture. You provide the environment. You are the individual—the oldest kid at the park, the one who wants it most.

## The Quiet Revolution

The simple mistake is to look at this and pretend it's easy. It isn't.

In 2018 Life Time Fitness converted the old Vikings Winter Park into a 150,000 square-foot free-play facility dedicated to unstructured pickup soccer. When they launched Life Time Sport that fall, I couldn't help but smile. They were attempting the same philosophy we had been quietly testing with the JOTP kids for years. They spared nothing: twelve concierges with iPads, a full play lounge, perfect indoor turf courts, referees, and official balls. It lasted about a year and never gained momentum.

I offered to help, but they saw no need. Play was easy—why would they need me? With numbers dwindling they turned it into isolated individual skills training and then eventually closed.

Providing real play is thankless work. Skills arrive as unconscious operational fluency, so the kids never realize they are learning. They never say thank you. That silence is the confirmation you are doing it right.

At JOTP everything took time and mistakes. Sergei's son Andrei was essential as Joy's GM, shaping the environment so we wouldn't suffer the same fate as the bigger, better-funded experiment. Later he moved to Omaha, started Joy Omaha, and in 2024 became the oldest kid at the park there—a true co-author of the JOTP environment.

Over time the kids started showing up early and staying late. They organized their own games, developed weird, idiosyncratic styles no coach would ever teach, and learned the language of movement: the glance that says I'm going, the body shape that says play it here, the pause that says I'm about to do something ridiculous. One day the eight-year-olds who once stared up at you become the oldest kids at the park. They start the games. They pick the teams. They do the gentleman's sweep. The game makes a new game.

# Interlude:

# Ace

The tryout was over.

Sixty of the best U15 players in the state had just spent two hours proving themselves inside the St. Paul auditorium while Charlie Ball and I took notes and made the quiet calculations tryouts require. Now the gym was emptying, parents collecting sons, and Charlie and I were packing up, stepping out into a November night that human beings had no business inhabiting.

Negative six degrees.

We pushed through the door and there he was: tall, quiet, standing at the bus stop with his bag.

Just standing there the way someone stands when standing there is the plan.

"You just tried out, right?"

"Yes," he said.

"Do you need a ride?"

"No. I'm good."

Charlie and I kept walking. Got maybe twenty feet.

"How about that," Charlie said. "Taking a bus to a tryout in below-zero weather."

I stopped.

“You’re going to take him on the team, aren’t you.”

“Yes.”

His name was Arinze. We called him Ace.

He was athletic, tall, powerful, and very raw. What he had instead of polish was something harder to name and impossible to manufacture—the devotion of someone who understood, at fifteen, that he had been given a chance. When he played you found yourself hoping you had ever wanted something that much. Hoping you still did.

I have never regretted that choice.

Ace took the chance and kept growing. Division I. The Internationals. He kept playing long after Sergei and Victor and I had faded into the background like good soldiers do. He is still playing, carrying on the tradition.

When we started Joy of the People he was always there. Keeper of the Internationals. The leader of the Goats—the Joy men’s team. He has a young son now picking dandelions. He’s right where he should be.

# Chapter 17:

# The Game

## Viva La Vida

Before the Minnesota State Hockey Tournament, they show a video. Two kids stand in falling snow.

A girl in a Warroad jersey. A boy in a Johnson jersey. The ancient powers—the Rangers from the frozen lakes up north, the Grand Army of Phalen Creek. They're dressed to play, sticks in hand, breath visible in the cold.

And then the music starts. Coldplay's "Viva La Vida." The montage rolls...A range kid weaving through defenders. The Phalen Creek kids on outdoor ice. Zagallo gliding sideways, refusing the collision.

The message is clear—play used to rule the world.

Play had its day.

Johnson doesn't have a hockey team anymore. The outdoor rinks sit empty. The warming houses are gone. But every year, Minnesota gathers to watch this video and remember what play looked like when it ruled the world.

Why?

Why does a state that dismantled its play environments still romanticize them? Why do the same parents who drive their kids to year-round travel tryouts get misty-eyed watching footage of pond hockey? Why does the machine that killed play keep showing videos that mourn it?

Because somewhere, in the gut of every Minnesotan who grew up on outdoor ice or park soccer or pickup basketball, there's a memory. A feeling. The way the game used to feel before someone turned it into work.

Minnesota loves play. Exposed to the real thing, it would choose play. It just forgot that play was still possible.

## The Talent Thief

River City Football Club wasn't the villain. They were the giant. The windmill that, when you got close enough, turned out to be real.

Every city has one. The club with the best facilities, the biggest social media presence, the slickest branding. River City FC was just the local version of what's happening everywhere. They weren't the disease. They were the symptom.

The best with the best with the best coaching. Push every day. Optimal training environment. Climb, overload, compete. Ambition, wanting more, dog eat dog. Vanquish your opponents, then make fun of their fans going out the door.

You've felt it in every chapter—the thing that empties parks, replaces friends with tryouts, mistakes winning for learning. Now it has a name. This is the Talent Thief.

A hunger. The inability to play because you're hooked on the drug of killer instinct. The bully at the park who dribbles the eight-year-olds and then flexes.

The Talent Thief is ambition untethered from joy. And it's everywhere. In facilities, in overcoaching, in the culture of overload. It knows where to get its future talent—find where the kids play. It comes for the oldest kids at the park first—then empties rinks, courts and gyms. It replaces neighborhood play with an hour's drive to train. It steals the opportunity for kids to interact and build a language. It does not look back, and it does not want you to.

We build playgrounds of climbing structures, balance beams, monkey bars, rope bridges—because we understand, without being told, that five-year-olds learn through unstructured exploration.

Nobody puts a five-year-old in a periodized monkey bars training program. The jungle gym is our last act of biological honesty.

And then they turn seven, and we put them on a team.

Not because the science changed. Because our anxiety did. Because waiting feels like losing. Because the kid down the street is already in an academy. Because we love them, and love makes us want to protect them from the valley—from the wandering, the losing, the looking lost. We want to point them at a peak and watch them climb.

So we skip the language. We pull them off the jungle gym and hand them a training schedule.

The Talent Thief doesn't steal talent with malice. It steals it with the best intentions in the world.

That's what makes it a perfect crime.

## The Origin

River City FC started in the lower divisions. Two guys from Ohio, professional marketing backgrounds, who'd come to Minnesota and fallen in love with the game. They were good at telling a story. They built a team, worked the lower rungs of the pyramid, and looked up at the NPSL—the highest level of amateur competition in the country—and decided that's where they needed to be.

The Internationals had ruled the top division for thirty years. Fifteen championships, nine state cups. Franklin had built something nobody had ever done before in this state. Ignoring warnings. Twenty nationalities. The best players in Minnesota, assembled not by salary or contract but by love of the game. The MSA board—the old guard, the ethnic clubs who'd run Minnesota soccer for decades—said it wouldn't work. Germans with Germans. Serbs with Serbs. Brits with Brits.

That was how it was done.

Franklin proved them wrong fifteen times.

He created a powerful pull to play. Youseff drove across the city with his whole family just to make training. Nate lived next door. Andy and Jose would show up just on time and never warm up. Some of those practices at Richfield High School were at a skill and tempo that are legend to this day. Franklin ran it with Patton-like devotion—fierce, loyal, impossible to replace.

Then his health faltered. Victor told me he was worried—all the work required to keep the Internationals together was killing Franklin. The club fell behind on league fees—just over three thousand dollars, after three decades of dominance. The River City group—a club no one had heard of in 2014—went to the league directly, paid off the debt, and took the spot.

Victor asked to just keep the name.

They got to work. They created the story: River City FC. The Ravens, long history, success over time, local roots, cutting-edge jerseys and a store to sell them. Packed stadiums and an influencer-style social media following known for its get-in-line devotion to the Raven badge.

They wanted in.

Everybody wants in. That's how you know it's real.

And then they put this on their website: "Fifteen league championships and nine state cups."

Those titles belonged to Franklin. To Victor. To me. To Youseff and Ahmed and Pedro and Andrei and Sasha and Jose and Sly and Ace and the foul-mouthed Scottish keeper.

I told Colleen, "It's like the United States taking over Brazil and then claiming five World Cups."

Five years later they were undefeated. Ranked number one in the country.

Parents wanted their kids there. Everyone wanted to play for them.

Everyone except a handful of skinny gym rats from a weird free-play program in St. Paul who didn't know what they were supposed to be afraid of.

## Real Rivals

The Internationals had a formidable rival. The Cougars. A South St. Paul team, full of college kids, and they could play. Their sweeper Keith Peterson and their keeper John Swallen were longtime teammates of ours on the Minnesota Select team and the Thunder. Every game was life or death, decided by a goal, fought to the whistle. Real rivalry. Real stakes.

One year at Thunder Bay we didn't make the final. The Cougars did. We were sitting in the hotel lamenting it when somebody had an idea. We dressed Victor in a homemade cougar costume—ears and whiskers, giant claws, mock-up cougar jersey, the works—and sent him out to entertain the Canadian crowd at halftime. Victor wowed the packed stadium with the Russian dance in full costume. Then he stood in goal and let a line of Canadian kids take penalty shots at him, stopping just enough to make it interesting and letting just enough through to make it joy.

That was the Internationals' rivalry with the Cougars. Fierce on the field. Family off it. The kids in that crowd absorbed something nobody could have taught them with words.

River City bought a history, not to erase one but to prove one. *Look at us. We have the trophies. We do what it takes. We don't mess around with play.*

Victor in a cougar suit, doing the Russian dance for Canadian kids who would remember it forever.

River City claiming Franklin's trophies on a website. Same sport. Same trophies.

Different game entirely.

That night, on their field, we were about to see which one was real.

## 1969

This battle is older than any of us.

Let's revisit that important 1969 Minnesota High School hockey final: Warroad versus Edina. Kids who grew up on outdoor rinks versus kids drilled on indoor ice. The old versus the new. Play versus program.

Warroad had Henry Boucha—a tall, powerfully built Ojibwe forward who rarely came off the ice. He learned to play hockey on frozen ponds and rivers, often using a taped-up tobacco tin as a puck and rolled-up magazines for shin guards. He was the top-ranked hockey prospect in the country.

Herb Brooks was asked, "What can Boucha do with the puck?"

"He can make it talk."

I watched on black-and-white TV, my face inches from the screen. My dad was shaking his head, almost to himself, "Look at him go."

For two periods Boucha was unstoppable. Then Edina knocked him out of the game—ruptured eardrum, fractured cheekbone. Even without him, Warroad scored twice late to force overtime.

In overtime, Edina finally wore them down. They won five to four.

The template was set: indoor, organized, coached-up teams as the model to copy. Edina has won fourteen state titles.

But look closer. Warroad—population fifteen hundred—has produced seven Olympians, including Boucha who won silver in 1972. Edina has produced zero male Olympians.

That's what it looks like when you solve the problem "How do you beat play?"

Fifty-two years later. Different field. Same question. The soul of the sport was on the line again. The kids didn't know it. But if they did they would have said, "This will be easy."

## Friends vs. Giants

In a gym in St. Paul, the game survived.

Kids playing Goalie Wars, chasing slowest goals, learning the gentleman's sweep. For years they played—not because someone told them to, but because they wanted to. And somewhere along the way, those kids became good.

Not drilled-good. Good the way Boucha was good. Easy good. Speaking a language the machine had forgotten existed.

Z, Emmanuel, Marco, Noah, Jorge—they'd grown up together in that gym. No tryouts. No cuts. No selection. Just play. For ten years. Together.

River City FC was the opposite. Selected. Sorted. The biggest and fastest culled from a thousand tryouts, assembled into a roster, drilled into shape. They had trained for exactly this moment. They were daunting, confident, ready. By every measure available to them, the system had worked.

They weren't wrong to believe that. That's what made them dangerous.

Friends versus giants.

## What Z Carried

When Z was fifteen, we drove to Fargo to see one of the best knee doctors we could find.

Part of his cartilage had lost blood supply and was deteriorating rapidly—a large section was dying.

They tried a screw system in surgery, but it didn't hold. We chased every option: experimental injections, stem cells, everything. The doctor spoke right to Z.

"You will never be able to continue playing," the doctor said. "Maybe a year, but it will give out."

We drove home in near silence.

Unable to walk and out of ideas, a friend recommended Mayo. The surgeon said he couldn't restore the cartilage, but he'd do what he could. He removed seventeen pieces of damaged cartilage, including one from the back of Z's knee.

His knee responded. Every day of play after that felt like a prize—a bonus.

Later that year, Z called to tell me he'd made varsity. I was at McMurray Field marshaling a group of U10s. I stepped away from the game I was coaching and cried.

High school turned him into a leader. By his senior year he'd helped carry a top-ranked team. Nick was there, of course, as well as other Joy kids who'd learned the same dialect; they were formidable.

Z was first team all-state and a Mr. Soccer finalist, an electrifying player. The local papers did features; the *Tribune* ran an interview about his season and an upcoming trial in Germany. "My dad was never disappointed in me," he told them. "People said, 'Sorry about your son. He's never going to be that good.' But my dad had his own thought process."

Z always came through.

We had tried for futsal nationals five years running and kept losing to the same KC Legends team. But when it counted most, he was the best player and leading scorer as Joy won the 2019 Futsal Nationals. As a junior he scored an impossible volley to knock out top-ranked Washburn. As a senior he scored a generational goal—with Rudy in the stands cheering, hands over his head. Time and again, when everything looked lost, when scores, doctors, or doubters had written the end, Z made the play.

Fifteen years ago we were driving home from Joy with the usual suspects in the Suburban—Marco, Z, Joey, Lioul, Eman, and Dare stuffed together in the back. The heater was broken, or rather, it worked only if you knew the trick: six-year-old Dare would hop out, swing the passenger door closed with exactly the right force, and the heat would snap on. She did it without being asked, every time.

The kids were holding their Joy of the People jerseys—faded, spray-painted T-shirts made an hour before—like trophies. Tomorrow they would play in their first futsal tournament. From the backseat came a small, triumphant voice: "Dad, you finally came through."

But it was always Z. And he would have to do it again.

## The Build-Up

The week before the River City game, we played in Moorhead.

It was a difficult match—a tie against a team we should have beaten. The kids were flat. The long drive home was quiet.

I watched and questioned everything. Every loss felt like evidence against me. Every kid who left for a "real" program felt like a verdict.

Ace did something interesting that week. Instead of practice, the goats—the college kids—played in the gym with the younger ones, playing Goalie Wars and taking on the twelve-year-olds.

Underloading. Exploring the low-stakes landscape. The older kids not trying harder, getting the young kids to try harder. Garrincha playing against a hundred grade-schoolers.

It was exactly right. The week before the biggest game of their lives, Ace brought them back to where it all started. Back to play.

I should never have doubted. Neither should any of us.

All season, we'd been building toward something. The Joy kids had won games they shouldn't have won. They'd lost games too—we weren't undefeated, weren't claiming to be. But something was different. The way they moved. The way they found each other without looking. The way they made the hard things look easy.

Now they'd face River City FC. Undefeated, ranked first in the country. Their field. Their crowd. Their coronation. For more than ten years I had taken these kids on a journey many felt would end in disaster. The eight-year-olds whose parents trusted me. The twelve-year-olds who chose our gym over the showcase circuit. Their hopes. Their parents' hopes. All of it riding on a theory the establishment insisted was wrong. But this was never about theory. It was about proof. And the proof was about to walk onto River City's field with fourteen players and spray-painted memories.

## July 2021

We showed up with fourteen players. Our U19s were in Kansas City for nationals. We were thin, but it was a tight band of friends: Marco, Z, Eman, Noah, Jorge, and Danielson. From the outside it looked like that very first game in spray-painted shirts made the night before.

The announcer made sure everyone knew.

"Joy Athletic, not really a full team tonight," he said, chuckling.

You could hear the condescension. The Ravens had a packed stadium, a full-production livestream, and raven-call sound effects for every special play. This was a juggernaut facing a short-handed squad from the weird free-play program across the river.

This wasn't supposed to be a game. It was supposed to be a footnote.

## The Mezzanine

I wasn't there. I was in Kansas City with our U19s. We'd just won Futsal Nationals—our second in three years, the validation of everything we'd built, earned by kids who'd grown up in our gym. But while the team celebrated downstairs, I slipped away, found a quiet mezzanine in the convention center, pulled out my laptop, and dialed up the stream.

The score was still zero to zero.

## The Defiance

Early in the second half, Marco clipped a ball to Emmanuel.

Emmanuel—the kid who'd been there since the beginning, ungodly fluid, the one who could sprint up a wall and do a backflip, the kid who'd scored the winner in their first tournament twelve years earlier—took one touch and then just ran.

To see him run those first fifteen yards was to witness a real thing of beauty. He carried that beauty into River City's box. Past one defender. Past another. The River City backline—structure, training, overload—folded. Emmanuel glided through it like it wasn't there.

He finished and turned up field. Not celebration. Defiance. The face of a young man who had won his share of Goalie Wars—who knew how to celebrate, but always with respect. His whole body saying it now: you want to see champions? Striding up the field, hands clenched, chin up, eyes on the crowd.

Joy 1 – City 0. The stadium went quiet. Then nervous.

## The Response

River City equalized. Of course they did. They were undefeated for a reason: talent, organization, depth. They weren't going to fold because of one goal. Joy 1 – City 1.

But we weren't folding either.

## The Brothers

Whitney and his brother Martin had been River City's best players. Their most talented. Their future.

And they'd left.

They'd walked away from the giant and shown up at Joy. They just came. Asked if they could play. Asked if they could help.

Don't ask what that meant. Instead look at what it did.

Whitney just scored. Joy 2 – City 1. But the way he scored—the combination, the ease—that was the answer the giant couldn't give.

Whitney and Martin matched the Joy kids. They spoke it too—you could see them enjoying the language, the stories. And they had some of their own.

## The Rainbow

Then Z did something.

A defender closed on him near midfield. The smart play was to pass—to keep possession, to manage the clock. We were up two to one against the best team in the country. Z held him off, but River City used the second to trap him—three Division I, uber-athletic ball-winners surrounded him.

With nowhere to go, Z pulled off a rainbow.

The ball arced over the defender's head, over his own head, and Z collected it on the other side like he'd done it a thousand times—which he had—in the gym, in pickup, in all those hours of play the critics said would never amount to anything.

River City's crowd erupted. Not in anger. In joy. They couldn't help it. It was that beautiful.

Three defenders stood looking for the ball. One walked like a zombie toward the bench, his mind temporarily fried. Z ran free down the line.

Somewhere, a Martian settled back and smiled. It had seen this before, on many planets. Creatures who could author movement in others. Creatures who couldn't. The difference was always the same.

This one speaks the language.

For Z it wasn't a show; it was a tool. Don't ask what it meant—look at what it did.

The fifteen titles they'd bought for three thousand dollars? Z was taking them back, one rainbow at a time.

## The Sequence

Remember Pep Guardiola: "We don't move the ball to move the ball; we move the ball to move the opposition."

Eighteen passes.

River City tried to break it with a long ball over the top. Noah went up to meet it.

At twelve he'd been tiny; now he was six-foot three—soft-spoken, funny, and as easy on the field as he was quiet off it. His mom had brought him to Monroe at seven and to Joy at nine. She'd been there for every step.

He was up against their center forward from Division I New Hampshire: a big, strong, teeth-grinding effort machine, the kind of player you're supposed to lose that duel to.

Noah didn't out-jump him. He out-timed him. He rose early so when the River City striker exploded off the ground his momentum lifted Noah higher. Noah met the ball comfortably and won the header.

The ball dropped loose in midfield.

Marco, with his mom and dad in the stands, saw the ball falling loose in the midfield. He shaped like he was going to jump for the bouncing ball. The River City midfielder bit—left his feet too early, stretching. Marco stayed on the ground, waited that half-beat, then reached out with his right foot and poked it to Z.

Z's defender closed fast. Z dropped his shoulder, hinting at a sprint, and the defender froze—another rainbow? Z used the sliver of time to drive a ball on a rope to Whitney, who chested it down to his brother Martin.

Martin—a tall, liquid passing machine—rolled a ball so smooth the gods were jealous, right into the path of Danielson.

Danielson killed the ball under his feet. The defender rushed in—

too hard. Danielson waited, then spun a pass into the space behind him—the old broken-wing trick. The ball gripped the turf and fed back to Whitney, then on to Marco and back to Danielson again. The defender was now caught behind the play; the broken wing was fine.

Each player a part of the story.

The eighteenth pass set Martin Brown free. His shot was blocked. The ball rolled toward the right wing.

The camera didn't cover the right wing. Was someone there? It should be Z. I twisted my head as if I could see past the edge of my laptop.

## The Voice

In that moment, a voice came back—the one we'd been listening to for fifteen years: Listen to me. This is important. Everyone is invited. Everyone can do this. Just show up. Play with your friends. Make it fun.

I watched the ball rolling toward the right wing.

Come on, Z.

## The Goal

He slammed it in.

I don't remember if I shouted. I might have.

Somewhere in the stands, Rudy was watching. The Austrian ski coach who'd taught me that all kids do better when they just play. Who'd let me sit beside him for nine years before I ever stood in front of a team. Who'd thrown his hands in the air when Z scored that incredible volley at sections.

Rudy had passed the joy onto me. I had tried to pass it to Z and his friends. Now they were passing it to everyone watching—the twelve-year-olds in the gym, the parents on the sidelines, the young River City fans leaning over the barrier.

That's how it works. That's how it's always worked. The oldest kid at the park teaches the younger ones. The game requires it.

## Would He Speak?

Many years earlier I'd watched an eight-year-old wander behind the goal during a game. That day, watching him blow the seeds into the wind, I asked myself the question that had haunted me ever since: Would he speak?

I should have never worried. Z, like all kids, was born to move, born to play, born to speak. All we have to do is build the environment and show them how much fun it is.

Now Z ran toward the crowd, shirt off, arms out, flapping his wings like a raven—like their raven, their symbol, thrown back in their faces.

He was speaking now. Not in words. In movement. In everything he'd been acquiring since he was five, playing Goalie Wars with kids twice his size. The grammar of deception, timing, and ease—no coach taught it because no coach could.

Early on others had looked at him and seen nothing.

They should have listened.

## The Champs

Then the kids came running up—Dare first, having just finished second with her team, then the others, Bennett, Mika, Henry, Phil, and Lioul still buzzing from their championship. They came to see their friends face down the giant.

We crowded around the laptop. Tinny speakers. Bad lighting. A thousand miles away. River City had answered. Would Joy hold on?

## The Final Minutes

On the screen, River City poured everything at us. The last fifteen minutes were relentless—waves of crosses, set pieces, desperate attacks.

More pressure. The Joy kids—fourteen of them, short bench, already gassed—hung on. Clearances. Blocks. Noah rising again to head one away. Marco throwing his body in front of a shot. Jorge blocking a sure goal at the last second. Danielson, with his light feet, stealing a ball off a foot. Z back defending, removing the ball from their star striker.

Everyone played.

The whistle blew.

Joy 3 – City 2. Final.

The kids around me erupted—national champions themselves, watching their friends, their family, do something impossible.

## What It Proved

I could say the game proved I was right, and they were wrong. But play taught me something quieter: when you summit, you must go down. Tomorrow there's another game, another group of kids, another gym full of possibilities.

That River City FC night was satisfying. So was the U19 national title. But when I think about what Joy actually built, I don't think about the scoreboard.

I think about the gentleman's sweep. The oldest kid leading the game so the youngest kid could stay in it. The way Lioul took care of Emmanuel. Dare slamming the truck door for heat. Bennett's smile. Javi's eyeball. Z and Eman still arguing over Goalie Wars. Duncan pushing his glasses up and making save after save against the kids who wanted him cut.

That's the beauty—the skill, the connection.

Rudy passed it to me. Victor, Zé, and Franklin passed it to me. My duty was to pass it on. Z and his friends were proof it could be passed on.

## The Photo

A photographer caught the moment. Z, shirt off, flexing at the crowd, hugged from behind by a teammate. Six Joy players around him, mid-celebration. River City FC's undefeated season, their coronation, hijacked by some free-play kids.

Look closer.

Five young faces lean over the barrier. Not adults. Kids. Beaming. Two of them in River City jerseys.

River City kids cheering for Z.

The River City supporters should have been furious. But that's not what happened. No adults in the frame. Just kids—from both sides—recognizing something the grownups missed.

The oldest teaching the youngest. The language passing from body to body. The joy that Garrincha carried, that Rudy protected, that Colleen reminded me to look for, that Victor handed me in a parking lot when everything had fallen apart.

That's talent. That's what play builds.

Everyone invited.

Everyone plays.

Everyone goes home happy.

That's Joy.

# Epilogue:

# Playing At Life

*"There is no better way to learn everything for your life than football."*

—Paul Breitner

It was one of those classic fall days in St. Paul—sun washing through clear, cool air, the ground dusted with maple leaves crunching under the feet of a group of hustling ten-year-olds in a hurry to jump up on the three-foot cement wall to pause the game for a water break.

Around the corner on tree-lined Summit Avenue, runners were finishing the Twin Cities Marathon. Encouraging cheers wafted up past the nineteenth-century mansions. F. Scott Fitzgerald once lived here, as did Sinclair Lewis.

The kids fought for positions on the wall, their legs dangling halfway down, rapping their cleats against the cement to create a matching rhythm. The sound brought conspiratorial smiles to their faces. *Look at the noise we can make together!*

I had asked Raffi to coach this group—the best U11 age group we had ever developed. Sitting on the wall, they were almost eye to eye with Raffi as he went down the line with a question.

"What do you want to be when you grow up?"

"Professional soccer player," said the first.

"Pro," said the second.

"Professional soccer player," said the third.

Down the line it was the same, until the tenth and last player.

"*Futbolista*." He didn't speak English.

Raffi and I looked at each other. We knew we had to try something different.

That very night the club let me go.

## What I Was Looking For

I started looking for play as the developmental answer. The secret sauce. The thing that would make better players faster, deeper, with less injury and more joy. And play did not disappoint—though it dragged its feet at first, didn't show up right away, cried in the candy aisle. For years it looked like I was doing something very wrong. But it came through. It came through on a different timeline for each kid. The Joy kids got good. Most got very good. A few got famous.

I like to joke that the second-most-asked question on the planet, after "Why do we exist?" is "How do I get better at soccer?" Now I am confident that fifteen years from now every club and every federation will adopt this model. It is too powerful, too inventive and too efficient. The economic and cultural pressure will win out.

Play is the master waiting for the students to appear.

That part of the story—the development part—is what this book has been about. *Play makes better players.* I believe it. The evidence is in the gym. The proof was on River City's field that night in 2021.

But that wasn't the real find.

## What I Actually Found

The real find was something Colleen saw before I did. Maybe because she was outside the trade. I was on the field, in the language, too inside it to notice it as a language. She was on the sidelines. She watched.

What she saw was that the kids who learned to play together were learning something that had almost nothing to do with soccer. They were learning to read each other. To dial back when the younger kid couldn't keep up. To celebrate the move that failed. To negotiate the rules. To repair the game when it broke. To take turns being the oldest kid at the park. To include the small kid, the slow kid, the new kid, not because anyone told them to—that would have been instruction, and instruction doesn't take—but because the game required it. The kid who couldn't include the others ended up alone with a ball and a wall.

The game was teaching them how to be in a community. The soccer was almost incidental.

Colleen grew up in Edina—yes, that Edina. Her family still tells the story, over and over at barbecues. It was a pickup softball game at Chowen Park. Edina Park and Rec staff told the kids they had to leave the field. The kids refused to budge. They held a sit-down protest. Turns out play is bigger than sport.

I had been calling it Kinetic Linguistics. The ability to enlist the muscles of others through movement. But somewhere along the way I started to see that the "muscles of others" meant something larger than pass receivers and defenders. It meant the way humans get other humans to do things—to cooperate, to follow, to lead, to listen, to forgive, to keep showing up. The kids in the gym weren't just learning to move a soccer ball. They were learning to move each other. *Kids are playing at life.*

That's the deeper lesson. I should have written it on the wall fifteen years ago.

## The Grand Army

Most of the Grand Army of Phalen Creek didn't become professional hockey players. Most of them became St. Paul. Mechanics, plumbers, schoolteachers, firefighters, fathers, and neighbors. They built the city the way kids who grew up playing together build cities—by being able to work with each other without needing to be told how.

One of them was Herb Brooks. He went on to coach the most famous American hockey team that ever played, and what he taught them wasn't a system or a set of drills. He taught them how to be a team—which is exactly the skill the Grand Army had built on Phalen Creek when nobody was watching. The Miracle on Ice was not the product of a great coaching innovation. It was the product of a developmental environment that had quietly produced a coach who knew what a team felt like because he had grown up inside one.

Brooks didn't invent the language. He inherited it. From the older kids on the creek who let him into the game when he was small. From the rinks that stayed open because the community wanted them open. From the version of childhood that no longer exists in most American neighborhoods.

The system that produced Brooks doesn't produce anyone like Brooks anymore. We dismantled it. Not on purpose. Not with malice. We dismantled it because we got anxious, because we wanted to give our kids more, because we believed the system that replaced it would do the job better. It does not.

What we lost when we lost play was not a generation of athletes. It was the cooperative play that builds the kind of person a free society depends on.

## Why This Matters Beyond the Field

George Orwell warned us that "who controls the past controls the future." Elinor Ostrom showed us, in her Nobel-winning work, that the commons—the shared resources humans manage together—can only be governed from the bottom up, by communities that know each other and trust each other and have learned through long practice how to cooperate without being supervised. Top-down management of a commons destroys it. The science is clear.

Play is the developmental commons. It is the place where children learn the bottom-up skills that bottom-up governance requires. Take it away and you do not produce better-managed children. You produce children who have never learned the skills that adult cooperation depends on. They will, in adulthood, look for someone to manage them. They will be drawn to top-down authority because they have no other model. They will not know how to govern themselves because they were never given the developmental space in which self-governance is learned.

That's the civic cost. It is not abstract. It is happening now, around us.

A society that cannot play together cannot govern itself. It will reach for an outside hand to do the work it should be doing for itself. The disappearance of pickup play in American childhood is not unrelated to the political instability of our time, to the loneliness epidemic, to our unhealthy need for confirmation and attention. These are not separate phenomena. They are, in part, what happens when an entire generation of children grows up without the cooperative play that builds the muscle for living together.

I am not saying soccer will fix this.

I am saying that the children in the gym were doing something we have stopped letting most children do, and the consequences of stopping go well beyond athletic outcomes.

## The Way Back

The lost language of play hasn't gone anywhere. It is waiting in every driveway, every park, every gym floor where someone is willing to set up a real game and step back. It is in every card game played for nothing, every made-up rule, every argument about whether the ball was in or out.

We do not have to invent anything. We have to stop interrupting.

> **For parents:** find pickup. Find older kids who want to play with yours. The most valuable thing you can give your child is time without adults telling them what to do.
>
> **For coaches:** set up a real game. Play on one of the teams. Model joy. Step back. The best work you do will often be the work nobody notices.
>
> **For everyone:** notice the kid who is walking instead of running. Notice the kid who is barely touching the ball. Notice the kid who

looks bored. They are not failing to participate. They are doing the work that fluency requires. They are watching, listening, reading, building the language. Leave them alone. The game will reach them.

Twenty years ago, ten kids sat on a wall in Saint Paul and told me their dreams.

*Professional soccer player. Pro. Futbolista.*

They were asking: "How do I get good?" I have spent twenty years answering them. The answer in this book is the answer I would have given them then, at the wall, if I had known how to say it: *Find some friends. Start a game. Play it every day. Make it fun. Trust the game to teach you. The lost language is waiting.*

The deeper answer—the one I have only learned by writing this book—is this: *What you are about to acquire on that field is not a sport. It is a way of being in the world. It is the language of how humans become human together. A professional career is a possible outcome. The way of being is a certain one. Acquire that, and the rest takes care of itself.*

Fitzgerald and Lewis lived just around the corner from that wall. They acquired a language so deeply it made millions of readers do the work—feel what they felt, see what they saw, lean into every sentence. Movement is a language. The language of the game, of play.

Let it do the work, so you don't have to.

## My Hope

My goal has always been simple. Twenty years from now, a dad is driving his kids past Joy of the People. He slows down. He points.

"That's JOTP. That was the best place to grow up."

That's enough. That has always been enough.

# The Tuesday Manual

## Start a Game on Tuesday

If you're holding this book, you are now the Oldest Kid at the Park in your neighborhood—whether you want to be or not.

The game is waiting.

You don't need a curriculum. You don't need a license. You don't need to understand any of the science you just read. You only need to remember the kid you were before someone turned play into work.

Pick a Tuesday. Find a space—a driveway, a parking lot, a gym, a patch of grass. Bring a ball. Bring whoever shows up. Make the youngest kid feel like they belong. Let the oldest kid run the game.

Then ask yourself two questions:

*Are you having fun?*

*Could you run this hour with tape over your mouth?*

If your answer is yes to both, you're doing it. The architecture is building itself underneath the laughter. The kids are acquiring a language they will speak for the rest of their lives. The neighborhood is becoming the kind of place that produces fluent humans.

If the answer is no—change the ball. Change the surface. Change the rules. Change yourself.

Show up Thursday. Do it again.
That's the whole book.
Everyone invited. Everyone plays. Everyone goes home happy.
Now go.

# Acknowledgments

This book began in a gym in St. Paul, but it was built by a community.

Victor believed before anyone else. When he stood up at that parent meeting and said "gween twee," he gave me the words I'd been searching for. He took me to Brazil, where the game showed me what it was supposed to look like. He's been my best friend and co-conspirator for thirty years. Nothing in these pages would exist without him.

Colleen saw what I missed. She noticed the Noisy Arms before I had a name for them. She watched thousands of hours of kids playing and told me what mattered. She's in the dedication because this book is for her—but she belongs here too, because this book is also by her.

To my brother Glenn, who first led me through the landscape. To Raffi, for showing me how. Raymond Verheijen, who set the bar high. Zé—thank you for the show. Franklin, who formed the Internationals and showed me that a good player is a good player, no matter where he's from. Charlie Ball for the greatest mentorship on a lifetime of play.

To Sergei Gotsmanov, who was the best midfield partner a forty-seven-year-old could ask for. His sons Sasha and Andrei became family—Sasha coached with me for six years; Andrei serves as JOTP's GM, built Joy's infrastructure and is now bringing it to Omaha.

And to Coach Dan, who believed in the ball thieves. And Coach Daniel, who built the culture at Edison. And to Ace and the coaches, who played on teams when they could have stood on the sidelines. To

Bill Lydon who encouraged me to lead. To Rudy, for showing me how to pass it on.

Stephen Krashen doesn't know what he started. I took his class at USC in the late 1970s and forgot about it for thirty years. Then one snowy night in 2012, his ideas came back and changed everything. If he ever reads this: thank you.

The researchers in Finland—especially those who shared their work on ecological dynamics, constraints-led learning, and the science of play—gave me the language to explain what I was seeing. Wolfgang Schöllhorn, Keith Davids, Jean Côté, and others: your scholarship made this book possible.

Romeo Jozak and the coaches from Dinamo Zagreb came to Minnesota and taught me humility. They also couldn't beat us at basketball.

To Alex Manning—for your scholarship, for leading the recovery mission after a child was forgotten in Canada, and for the foreword to this book. And Johan Ferner Strom for creating a fair playing field. Thank you, Martí Cañellas Trias, Stuart Armstrong, Jamie Munro, Adam Belz, 3four3, and Ernesto Diaz—for your podcasts and for helping get the word out.

To my mom and dad, for showing me how to play.

To Debbie, who loved sports when girls weren't supposed to.

To Ian Graham Leask and everyone at Calumet Editions, whose direction helped shape this book into what it became.

To the parents who trusted the chaos: you let your kids play when everyone else was drilling. You ignored the whispers. You showed up at the rec center and voted yes. This book is proof you were right.

And thank you to the kids: the Leos and Nicks and Phils, the Noahs and Emmanuels and Liouls, the Marcos and Bennetts and Duncans, and all the others who came through Joy: you were the finches. I just had the notebook. Thank you for letting me watch.

And finally, to my own kids, who showed me everything: Dare, who Hula-Hooped on the sidelines and found her own notes. Who taught me that the silent period isn't empty—it's full. You were acquiring while the world thought you weren't paying attention. You were. And Z, who picked dandelions at eight and made defenders do his work at nineteen. You answered the question I'd been asking your whole life.

Would he speak?

You're speaking now.

# Questions

## Questions for Everyone

### 1. The Martian Test

Think of a moment in sports (or life) when someone's movement "spoke" to you so clearly that you reacted exactly as they wanted—without them saying a word. What did that body language actually say? How does this idea change the way you watch a game now?

### 2. Underloading in Action

Panenka, Ricardinho, and Z all made their opponents *do the work for them*. Describe a time you (or someone you watched) underloaded an opponent instead of trying to overpower them. What felt different about that moment compared to "trying harder"?

### 3. Play vs. Work

The book argues that the most valuable skill-building hours happen when no adult is "teaching." Looking back on your own sports childhood, what percentage of your development came from free play versus organized training? Would you change the balance if you could?

## Questions for Coaches

### 4. The Oldest Kids at the Park

The author realized his real job wasn't coaching—it was being "the oldest kid at the park." How would your next practice or season change if you ran it that way instead of as an instructor? What's one small experiment you could try this week?

### 5. The Duct-Tape Test

"If you can't run your session in silence, you're talking too much." Try it: run one full practice without giving a single verbal instruction. What happened? What surprised you about what the kids already knew?

### 6. Acquisition vs. Learning

The book says most youth programs skip acquisition (through play) and jump straight to deliberate practice. Where does your program sit on that spectrum right now? What would it look like to protect more acquisition time for the kids you coach?

## Questions for Parents

### 7. The Relative Play Effect (RPE)

The book claims high-RPE kids (more play, less training) are the ones who reach the very top. Looking at your child's weekly schedule, what is their current play-to-training ratio? Are you comfortable with it, or does something need to shift?

### 8. The Talent Thief

The Talent Thief is described as "ambition untethered from joy." Have you ever felt it pulling at your own family—maybe through tryouts, showcases, or the fear of falling behind? What would it look like to say "no" to the Thief in one concrete way this season?

### 9. Would He Speak?

Ted watched his eight-year-old son Z pick dandelions and wondered if he would ever "speak" the language of movement. Think of a child you love who seems quiet, late-developing, or overlooked. What would trusting their silent period look like in practice?

## Questions for Players

### 10. Your Own Language

Every fluent player eventually develops a personal dialect (the pigeon-toed *trivela*, the rainbow, the five-mile-per-hour chip). What move or style feels most "you"? Where and when did you first discover it?

### 11. Making Others Do the Work

The Dawkins Test asks: Does your movement make other bodies do things? Pick one skill you're working on right now. How could you practice it so that the defender or goalkeeper ends up doing more of the work than you?

### 12. Everyone Goes Home Happy

The book ends with the idea that real play leaves *everyone*—winners, losers, and spectators—feeling something good. Think of your favorite game or moment in sports. Why did it feel that way? How can you create more of those moments for yourself and the kids coming up behind you?

# Glossary

**Affective Filter**: Stephen Krashen's term for the emotional barrier that blocks language acquisition when a learner feels anxious, judged, or self-conscious. In youth sports, coaching corrections, sideline pressure, and performance anxiety all raise the affective filter and interfere with the unconscious installation of movement fluency.

**Ball Thieves**: A defensive style that emerged organically through free play at Joy of the People. Rather than traditional "first defender" technique—stay low, contain, deny forward progress—ball thieves charge the attacker and tap the ball away from behind. A skill discovered through thousands of hours of unstructured play and never coached.

**Collective Fluency / Cinema**: What happens when multiple fluent speakers play together. Individual fluency is vocabulary—a chip, a rainbow, a feint that moves one defender. Collective fluency is what emerges when those voices combine: drama. The wall pass becomes a plot twist. The overlapping run becomes a sacrifice. The eighteen-pass goal becomes a climax the stadium feels in its chest. It is the invisible matter every coach senses but none can articulate—the thing the Spanish coaches meant when they said, "I know it when I see it." You don't see it. You feel it.

**Competitive Cauldron**: Anson Dorrance's training system at the University of North Carolina. A data-driven, hyper-competitive environment where every action is tracked, ranked, and published. The summit of overload methodology. Twenty-two national championships. Used throughout this book as the counterpoint to play-based development.

**The Crossover**: The developmental moment, mapped onto Peak Height Velocity (puberty), when a child's primary mode shifts from acquisition (unconscious, play-based) to learning (conscious, deliberate). The transition is abrupt—a light switch, not a dimmer switch—and biologically driven. The acquisition window closes when the body changes. The phase that matters most is the phase you can't remember.

**Fitness Landscape**: A visualization from evolutionary biology (Sewall Wright, 1932) describing the terrain of player development. The landscape has many peaks (local maxima) and valleys. Overloading climbs the nearest hill. Underloading explores valleys to find higher peaks.

**Futebol de Salão**: The original Brazilian indoor game, played with a small, low-bounce ball. Precursor to FIFA-standardized Futsal. One origin story credits longshoremen on the docks of Brazil who stuffed a ball with rope when it kept bouncing into the water.

**The Gentleman's Sweep**: A self-handicapping behavior observed in play. In animal research, experienced rats let younger partners win approximately thirty percent of encounters; without this, the younger partner stops playing and the game dies. In human play, the best competitors have play instincts, not killer instincts. They calibrate their effort to keep the game alive.

**Goalie Wars**: A game invented by Joy of the People kids using a lightweight volleyball shot at futsal goals. Players take turns shooting and saving. The light ball allows fearless goalkeeping, creating natural selection pressure on finishing quality. The most popular game in JOTP's fifteen-year history.

**Kinetic Linguistics**: The book's central framework. The theory that movement operates as a language—acquired through immersion and play, stored in unconscious systems, deployed to make other bodies move. Movement is older than speech by hundreds of millions of years and serves the same evolutionary purpose: to enlist the muscles of others on your behalf.

**Local Maximum**: A peak on the fitness landscape that is higher than everything immediately around it but not the highest overall. A player or program trapped on a local maximum cannot improve further without first descending. The Western Roll, the Competitive Cauldron, and the Dan Plan are all examples.

**Monarch Rules**: The book's developmental framework, modeled on the monarch butterfly's life cycle. Four sequential stages: Egg (home, safety, family), Caterpillar (acquisition through play, always with others), Chrysalis (adolescence: protect the rebuild, do not overload), Butterfly (learning, refinement, migration). The key insight is sequence, not ratio: each stage must be honored before the next can succeed.

**Noisy Arms**: A diagnostic marker for overloaded movement. A brief, involuntary flutter or spasm of the arms during ball reception, dribbling, or passing. Observed in players whose movement has been developed through isolated, decontextualized training or under excessive conscious control. Absent in players whose skills were acquired through conversational play. First observed by Colleen Kroeten.

**Oldest Kid at the Park (OKP)**: The person who starts the game, models play, picks teams, and settles disputes—not through authority but through self-interest. The OKP wants the game to happen and will do whatever it takes to keep it going. The most important concept in the book for anyone who works with kids. The OKP role is incompatible with coaching: the moment you start thinking about what is good for the kids rather than wanting to play, you become a coach.

**Overloading**: Doing all the work yourself. More effort, more intensity, more force. The dominant paradigm in youth sports development. The overloaded player fights physics, fights pressure, and spends energy faster than he creates advantage.

**Polyathlete**: A multi-sport athlete. Players whose movement fluency was built across multiple sports rather than through early specialization in one.

**Relative Age Effect (RAE)**: The statistical bias in youth sports selection toward children born earlier in the eligibility year. Q1 births are overrepresented in elite youth programs; Q4 births are underrepresented. The bias reverses at the professional level (Reverse RAE), where late-born players disproportionately reach the highest levels.

**Relative Play Effect (RPE)**: The ratio of unstructured play hours to coached hours in a player's developmental history. High RPE (more play, less coaching before puberty) correlates with higher adult performance. Low RPE (more coaching, less play) correlates with earlier peaks and earlier plateaus. The author's original framework.

**Spandrel**: In architecture, the triangular space between two arches—a structural byproduct, not a designed feature. In evolutionary biology (Gould and Lewontin, 1979), a trait that was not directly selected for but emerged as a byproduct of other structures. In this book: the skills that emerge from play without anyone intending or designing them. The *trivela*, ball thievery, McEnroe's volleys, and Zlatan's tricks are all spandrels—skills built through fun that were later co-opted for competition.

**Underloading**: Making others do the work for you. The fluent player's body tells a story that compels opponents and teammates to move, creating advantage with less effort. Talent is the ability to underload. Skill is any action that produces the same or better result with less time and less energy.

**Underload Index (UI)**: The author's proposed metric for measuring kinetic fluency. Formula: UI = Goals minus xGOT (Expected Goals on Target). A positive UI indicates a player scoring from locations the keeper should have saved—suggesting the keeper was moved by the shooter's body language rather than beaten by shot placement. Currently applicable to penalties; extension to open play requires further development.

**Variation, Replication, and Differential Survival**: The three ingredients of evolution as applied to play. Variation: different attempts and solutions. Replication: successful solutions get repeated. Differential survival: some solutions work better than others and persist. When all three are present, improvement occurs. Fun is the signal that all three are active.

# Notes

These notes are organized by chapter and referenced by key phrase. No superscript numbers appear in the text. Where the author was personally present at an event or conducted firsthand interviews, those sources are noted as such. Where peer-reviewed citations exist, they are given in full. Several frameworks introduced in this book—the Underload Index, the Relative Play Effect, Kinetic Linguistics, the Monarch Rules—are the author's original work and are presented as testable hypotheses rather than established findings.

## Chapter 1: The Perfect Crime

- "The European Championship final has gone to penalties": 1976 UEFA European Championship final, Belgrade, June 20, 1976. Czechoslovakia defeated West Germany five to three on penalties after a two-to-two draw. Antonín Panenka's chip on the decisive fifth kick lead to the technique being named after him.
- "Ricardinho—O Mágico, named Best Player in the World": Ricardinho (Ricardo Filipe da Silva Braga) won the FIFA Futsal Player of the Year (Futsal Planet Awards) six times: in 2010, 2014, 2015, 2016, 2017, and 2018. He grew up in Gondomar, Portugal, playing futsal in school gymnasiums.

- "futsal Euro qualifiers, Portugal versus Serbia": UEFA Futsal European Championship qualifying, Belgrade, 2016. The author was present.
- "the data from Dinamo Zagreb": Based on conversations with GNK Dinamo Zagreb academy coaches during their visit to Joy of the People, summer 2014. According to the coaches, only one of Dinamo's top ten transfer earners had joined the academy before age fourteen.

## Chapter 2: The Swamp

- "Zoilo Versalles": Zoilo Versalles (1939–1995), Cuban-born shortstop, won the American League Most Valuable Player Award with the Minnesota Twins in 1965.
- "The Kicks—Minnesota's brief NASL professional phenomenon": The Minnesota Kicks played in the North American Soccer League from 1976 to 1981, regularly drawing crowds of thirty thousand to forty thousand people to Metropolitan Stadium in Bloomington.
- "In 1990, at Tampa Stadium—the 'Big Sombrero'—the Minnesota Select team won the Donaldson Cup": The James P. McGuire Cup (commonly referred to as the Donaldson Cup in Minnesota) was the top prize in U.S. amateur soccer, contested annually by state select teams. The author was on the team.
- "Sergei Gotsmanov—one of the supersonic Soviets who finished second to Holland in the 1988 Euros": Sergei Gotsmanov played for the Soviet Union national team. The USSR reached the final of the 1988 European Championship in Munich, losing two to zero to the Netherlands.
- "Jundiaí is one of the birthplaces of Futebol de Salão": The origins of Futebol de Salão (later codified as futsal) are disputed. The game is generally attributed to Juan Carlos Ceriani in Montevideo, Uruguay around 1930, though

Brazilian accounts give credit to the game developing in São Paulo gymnasiums and on the docks of Santos. Jundiaí is recognized as one of the early centers of the game in Brazil.

- "Rudy Martignacco at Richfield High School": Rudy Martignacco coached at Richfield High School in Minnesota. The author assisted him for nine years.

## Interlude: What Happened to Play?

- "It was the twenty-fifth anniversary of the Minnesota High School State Hockey Tournament": The Minnesota State High School Hockey Tournament began in 1945. The 1969 tournament marked the twenty-fifth.
- "the new Metropolitan Sports Center": The Metropolitan Sports Center in Bloomington, Minnesota, opened in 1967. Capacity: approximately fifteen thousand for hockey.
- "Since 1945 the state tournament had been dominated by environments": State tournament champions from 1945 through 1968 were predominantly from northern Minnesota towns and St. Paul. See Minnesota State High School League historical records.
- "St. Paul Johnson… the 'Grand Army of Phalen Creek'": St. Paul Johnson High School's hockey dynasty is documented in Minnesota hockey histories. The "Grand Army of Phalen Creek" nickname refers to players who grew up on Phalen Creek and nearby outdoor ice. Johnson won four state titles and posted twelve top-four finishes.
- "A number of the Grand Army played in the 1960 Olympic gold-medal team": The 1960 U.S. Olympic hockey team won gold at Squaw Valley. Several St. Paul-area players were on the roster, including Paul Johnson (West St. Paul) and Jack McCartan (St. Paul).
- "Another Grand Army kid, cut from that roster, was Herb Brooks": Herb Brooks (1937–2003) attended Johnson

High School and won the 1955 state championship there. He was the last player cut from the 1960 U.S. Olympic team. He later coached the 1980 "Miracle on Ice" team to Olympic gold. See Coffey, Wayne. *The Boys of Winter: The Untold Story of a Coach, a Dream, and the 1980 U.S. Olympic Hockey Team*. Crown, 2005.

- "In 1960 Minnesota had four indoor sheets. By 1970 it had twenty-five": The growth of indoor ice facilities in Minnesota is documented in state hockey histories. These figures are drawn from Minnesota Hockey and Minnesota Amateur Hockey Association records.

## Chapter 3: The War

- "Cruyff, Michels, and Neeskens lost the 1974 final": The Netherlands lost the 1974 World Cup final to West Germany two to one in Munich. Johan Cruyff, Rinus Michels (head coach), and Johan Neeskens were central figures on the Dutch "Total Football" team.
- "Garrincha": Manoel Francisco dos Santos (1933–1983), known as Garrincha ("little bird"), won the 1958 and 1962 World Cups with Brazil. His nickname *Alegria do Povo* (Joy of the People) reflected his status as a beloved folk hero. See Castro, Ruy. *Garrincha: The Triumph and Tragedy of Brazil's Forgotten Footballing Hero.* Yellow Jersey Press, 2004.
- "Before the critical group-stage match in Gothenburg, 1958": Brazil vs. USSR, June 15, 1958, Nya Ullevi, Gothenburg, Sweden. Group-stage match. Brazil won two-to-zero.
- "The Swedish newspaper headline": "Soviets can put a satellite in space, can't stop Garrincha." Widely cited in football literature; the specific Swedish newspaper is rarely identified.
- "*Garrincha: Alegria do Povo*": de Andrade, Joaquim Pedro. *Garrincha: Alegria do Povo.* (1962; Rio de Janeiro, Brazil: Globo Video).

## Chapter 4: The Vote

- "Mayor Chris Coleman praised the partnership in his State of the City address": Chris Coleman served as Mayor of St. Paul, Minnesota, from 2006 to 2018.
- "In 2004 and 2008, I studied in Brazil with Thadeu Goncalves at the Instituto Brasileiro de Futebol": Author attended coaching courses at the Instituto Brasileiro de Futebol in São Paulo in 2004 and 2008. Thadeu Goncalves trained under Julío Mazzei and Telê Santana.
- "Arthur Samuel was working on a checkers program": Samuel, A. L. "Some Studies in Machine Learning Using the Game of Checkers," IBM Journal of Research and Development 3, no. 3 (1959): 210–229. Samuel developed one of the first self-learning programs at IBM in the 1950s. His philosophy—teaching the computer to learn rather than programming it to win—is paraphrased from his published work.

## Chapter 5: The Search

- "Ecological Dynamics": Theoretical framework for understanding motor learning. See: Davids, Keith, Chris Button, and Simon Bennett, *Dynamics of Skill Acquisition: A Constraints-Led Approach.* Human Kinetics, 2008.
- "The most successful college soccer coach in American history… twenty-two national championships": Anson Dorrance, head coach of the University of North Carolina women's soccer team. As of the most recent season, Dorrance has won twenty-two NCAA Division I national championships. See: Dorrance, Anson, with Gloria Averbuch. *The Vision of a Champion.* Huron River Press, 2002.
- "Evolution runs on three ingredients: Variation, Replication, Differential Survival": A standard distillation of Darwinian evolution applied broadly. For its application

to learning and cultural evolution, see: Dennett, Daniel. *Darwin's Dangerous Idea.* Simon & Schuster, 1995.; and Lewontin, R. C., "The Units of Selection," *Annual Review of Ecology and Systematics,* no. 1 (1970): 1-18.

## Chapter 6: The Landscape

- "Anson Dorrance built twenty-two national championships on one simple philosophy": The Competitive Cauldron is Dorrance's term for UNC's data-driven, hyper-competitive training environment.
- "Geneticist Sewall Wright": Wright, Sewall, "The Roles of Mutation, Inbreeding, Crossbreeding, and Selection in Evolution," *Proceedings of the Sixth International Congress of Genetics,* no. 1 (1932): 356–366. Wright introduced the fitness landscape (or "adaptive landscape") as a visualization of how populations move through evolutionary space.
- "Leslie Orgel, a chemist at the Salk Institute": Leslie Orgel (1927–2007), chemist at the Salk Institute for Biological Studies, La Jolla, California. Orgel's First Rule, in his own phrasing, holds that "whenever a spontaneous process is too slow or too inefficient, a protein will evolve to speed it up or make it more efficient." See Orgel's published work on prebiotic chemistry and the origin of life.
- "In 2004, during coaching courses in São Paulo, my instructor Thadeu Goncalves gave me the Brazilian definition of skill": "An action completed successfully in the least amount of time with the least amount of effort." From Thadeu Goncalves, Instituto Brasileiro de Futebol. Author was present.
- "Valery Brumel, the Soviet world record holder": Valery Brumel (1942–2003), Soviet high jumper. Held the world record (2.28 m) from 1963 to 1971. Olympic gold medalist, Tokyo 1964.

- "Dick Fosbury showed up at the Olympics and went over backward": Dick Fosbury (1947–2023) won gold in the high jump at the 1968 Mexico City Olympics with a clearance of 2.24 m using his back-first technique, later universally adopted as the "Fosbury Flop."
- "Stuart Kauffman": see: Kauffman, Stuart. *The Origins of Order: Self-Organization and Selection in Evolution.* Oxford University Press, 1993. Kauffman's NK model demonstrated that on rugged fitness landscapes, local optimization leads to entrapment on suboptimal peaks.
- "Jannik Sinner… said it out loud after losing to Carlos Alcaraz in the 2025 US Open final": Sinner's post-match press conference, 2025 US Open final, September 7, 2025. Sinner lost to Alcaraz 6–2, 3–6, 6–1, and 6–4.
- "In 2010, photographer Dan McLaughlin quit his job": Dan McLaughlin's Dan Plan ran from 2010 until approximately 2016, when he abandoned the project due to a back injury. At roughly 5,100 hours of deliberate practice, he had reached a 3.3 handicap. The ten-thousand-hour theory derives from Ericsson, K. Anders, Ralf Th. Krampe, and Clemens Tesch-Römer, "The Role of Deliberate Practice in the Acquisition of Expert Performance," *Psychological Review* 100, no. 3 (1993): 363–406.
- "Gérard Houllier": Gérard Houllier (1947–2020), French football coach and administrator. Technical Director of French football from 1988 to 1998 and instrumental in the development of Clairefontaine, the French national football academy.
- "You can grow the lemon, or you can squeeze the lemon. You can't do both.": Author was present at Houllier's SoccerEx London presentation in 2008.

## Chapter 7: Invasion of the Body Snatchers

- "Noam Chomsky composed a famous sentence in 1957": Chomsky, Noam. *Syntactic Structures.* Mouton, 1957.
- "Wolfgang Schöllhorn… 'Too much repetition along with too much ambition leads to a sort of disease of the prefrontal cortex'": Wolfgang Schöllhorn, Professor of Training Science at Johannes Gutenberg University Mainz. The quotes are from *The Fosbury Flop* podcast, hosted by Martí Cañellas Trias, Episode 8, October 2023. Schöllhorn uses the Parkinson's comparison as an analogy for prefrontal cortex overactivation, not as a clinical claim. See also: Schöllhorn, Wolfgang I., et al., "Differential Learning in Sports," *Sportwissenschaft* no. 36 (2006): 274–291.
- "Leo would score seven free-kick goals that season … a thirty-three percent conversion rate": Author's records as Edison High School coach. For comparison, career direct free-kick conversion rates among elite professionals are far lower—Cristiano Ronaldo at approximately six to seven percent and Lionel Messi at approximately eight to ten percent, depending on the dataset and time period. Sources: FBref and Transfermarkt.
- "Nassim Taleb, in *Antifragile*": Taleb, Nassim Nicholas. *Antifragile: Things That Gain from Disorder.* Random House, 2012.

## Chapter 8: The Spandrels

- "Stephen Jay Gould and Richard Lewontin": Gould, Stephen Jay, and Richard C. Lewontin, "The Spandrels of San Marco and the Panglossian Paradigm: A Critique of the Adaptationist Programme," Proceedings of the Royal Society of London B 205, no. 1161 (1979): 581–598. The term exaptation was formally introduced three years later in: Gould, Stephen Jay, and Elisabeth S. Vrba, "Exaptation—A Missing Term in the Science of Form," *Paleobiology 8*, no. 1

(1982): 4–15. Strictly speaking, the spandrels paper critiqued adaptationism; exaptation came later.

- "McEnroe and Carillo went on to win the 1977 French Open mixed doubles title": McEnroe was eighteen. This was his first Grand Slam title of any kind. See McEnroe, John. *You Cannot Be Serious.* Putnam, 2002.
- "From Zlatan himself": Ibrahimović, Zlatan, with David Lagercrantz. *I Am Zlatan Ibrahimović.* Random House, 2013.
- "Orgel's second rule: 'Evolution is cleverer than you are'": Widely attributed to Leslie Orgel. See: Crick, Francis, *What Mad Pursuit.* Basic Books, 1988.
- "In his book *The Sports Gene,* David Epstein": Epstein, David. *The Sports Gene: Inside the Science of Extraordinary Athletic Performance.* Current/Penguin, 2013. The Stefan Holm–Donald Thomas comparison appears in Chapter 2.
- "In 2003, researchers at Queen's University": Soberlak, Peter, and Jean Côté, "The Developmental Activities of Elite Ice Hockey Players," *Journal of Applied Sport Psychology* 15, no. 1 (2003): 41–49.
- "Viktor Frankl said it plainly": Frankl, Viktor E. *Man's Search for Meaning.* Beacon Press, 1959. The widely cited quotation about pursuing happiness appears in the preface to the 1984 edition.

## Chapter 9: The Professor

- "His name was Stephen Krashen": Stephen Krashen, Professor Emeritus of Education at the University of Southern California. Key works include *Second Language Acquisition and Second Language Learning* (Pergamon, 1981) and *The Input Hypothesis: Issues and Implications* (Longman, 1985). Krashen was developing these ideas during the period the author attended his class (1977). The formal publication of the theory came in the early 1980s.

- "Krashen called the anxiety barrier the affective filter": The Affective Filter Hypothesis is one of Krashen's five hypotheses. See: Krashen, *The Input Hypothesis* (1985).
- "The most important challenge came from Merrill Swain": Swain, Merrill, "Communicative Competence: Some Roles of Comprehensible Input and Comprehensible Output in Its Development," in Susan Gass and Carolyn Madden, eds., *Input in Second Language Acquisition.* Newbury House, 1985.
- "The errors fossilized": The concept of *fossilization* in second-language acquisition was developed by Larry Selinker. See: Selinker, Larry, "Interlanguage," *International Review of Applied Linguistics in Language Teaching* 10, no. 3 (1972): 209–231. Swain's immersion data demonstrated fossilized grammatical errors despite years of meaningful exposure.
- "I pulled up the Soberlak and Côté study from 2003": The author's comparison of Soberlak and Côté's developmental curves with standard Peak Height Velocity growth charts is the author's own analysis and has not been independently replicated in peer-reviewed literature.
- "The failure rate isn't fifty percent. It's closer to ninety-five percent.": The author's informal characterization of high school Spanish outcomes in the United States. The American Council on the Teaching of Foreign Languages (ACTFL) reports that the vast majority of U.S. high school students do not reach functional fluency through classroom instruction alone. See ACTFL. *World-Readiness Standards for Learning Languages*. 4th ed., 2015. and ACTFL proficiency assessment data.

## Chapter 10: The Confession

- "Wittgenstein argued exactly this—there is no private language": Wittgenstein, Ludwig. *Philosophical Investigations*, translated by G. E. M. Anscombe. Blackwell, 1953.

Wittgenstein argued that language requires a community of users—a word only one person understands is not a word.

- "Richard Dawkins, writing about the evolution of communication": Dawkins, Richard, and John R. Krebs. "Animal Signals: Information or Manipulation?" in John R. Krebs and Nicholas B. Davies, eds., *Behavioural Ecology: An Evolutionary Approach.* Blackwell, 1978. The formulation "enter the muscles of others on your behalf" is the author's application of Dawkins and Krebs's signaling theory to Kinetic Linguistics.
- "A vervet monkey's alarm call": Seyfarth, Robert M., Dorothy L. Cheney, and Peter Marler, "Monkey Responses to Three Different Alarm Calls: Evidence of Predator Classification and Semantic Communication," *Science* 210, no. 4471 (1980): 801–803.
- "Movement—five hundred million years older than speech": Coordinated movement in animals predates vocal communication by hundreds of millions of years. The earliest animals with nervous systems capable of coordinated movement (Cambrian period, approximately 540 million years ago) predate the evolution of human speech by at least 500 million years. This figure is an approximation.
- "Messi walks more than any elite player in the world": Messi's low-intensity match movement has been widely reported and analyzed using GPS and tracking data. Various analyses have estimated he spends seventy to eighty-five percent of match time walking or standing, depending on the match and data source. See Tobias Escher's analysis at *Spielverlagerung*, and StatsBomb match-data publications.
- "Like Salieri hearing Mozart": The Salieri–Mozart archetype as dramatized in: *Amadeus,* script by Peter Shaffer, Royal National Theatre, 1979. The reference is to the dramatic figure of the craftsman who can recognize genius but cannot produce it.

- "Countersteering": A well-documented phenomenon in motorcycle and bicycle dynamics. At speed, a rider initiates a turn by briefly steering in the opposite direction. See: Cossalter, Vittore. *Motorcycle Dynamics.* Self-published, Lulu, 2nd ed., 2006.

## Chapter 11: The Discovery

- "Robert Axelrod ran a famous experiment in game theory": Axelrod, Robert. *The Evolution of Cooperation.* Basic Books, 1984. Axelrod's iterated Prisoner's Dilemma tournament found that the simplest strategy—Tit for Tat, submitted by Anatol Rapoport—won by cooperating first and then mirroring the opponent's previous move.
- "Raymond Verheijen… 'Power is overcompensation for lack of ability'": Raymond Verheijen, Dutch football coach and conditioning specialist. From a coaching course attended by the author, Split, Croatia, 2019. For background on Verheijen's broader periodization framework, see: Verheijen, Raymond. *Complete Handbook of Conditioning for Soccer.* Reedswain, 1998.
- "Johan Cruyff echoed this: 'If you see a player sprinting, it means he started too late'": Widely attributed to Johan Cruyff. See: Winner, David. *Brilliant Orange: The Neurotic Genius of Dutch Football,* Bloomsbury, 2000; and: Cruyff, Johan. *My Turn: A Life of Total Football.* Macmillan, 2016.
- "Robert Trivers proposed a disturbing idea": Trivers, Robert. *The Folly of Fools: The Logic of Deceit and Self-Deception in Human Life.* Basic Books, 2011. See also: Trivers's earlier theoretical groundwork in his foreword to Richard Dawkins, *The Selfish Gene.* Oxford University Press, 1976.
- "Andre Agassi couldn't beat Boris Becker": Agassi, Andre. *Open: An Autobiography.* Knopf, 2009. The Becker tongue-tell story appears in Agassi's memoir.
- "Mário Zagallo… part of all five World Cup wins": Mário

Jorge Lobo Zagallo (1931–2024) won the FIFA World Cup as a player (1958, 1962), as head coach (1970), and as assistant or technical coordinator across later Brazilian teams. The exact nature of his role in the 2002 World Cup-winning campaign is documented variously as "technical coordinator" and "special advisor."

- "Roberto Ayala": Roberto Ayala earned 115 caps for Argentina (1994–2007) and captained the team on numerous occasions. The conversation took place at the Copacabana Palace Hotel during SoccerEx Rio de Janeiro, 2012. Author was present.
- "At one presentation, Zico issued a warning": Arthur Antunes Coimbra, known as Zico, speaking at SoccerEx Rio de Janeiro, 2012. Author was present.
- "SoccerEx in Rio de Janeiro": Author attended SoccerEx Global, Rio de Janeiro, November 2012.

## Chapter 12: The Science

- "the first-ever Scientific Conference on Motor Skill Acquisition": Held at Kisakallio Sports Institute, approximately sixty kilometers outside Helsinki, Finland, late autumn 2015. Author was present.
- "Nikolai Bernstein": Bernstein, Nikolai A. *The Co-ordination and Regulation of Movements.* Pergamon, 1967. A Soviet neurophysiologist, Bernstein's "degrees of freedom problem" and his observation that expert performers never repeat the same movement exactly ("repetition without repetition") are foundational to modern motor control theory.
- "James Gibson": Gibson, James J. *The Ecological Approach to Visual Perception.* Houghton Mifflin, 1979. Gibson's theory of *affordances*—that organisms perceive the environment directly in terms of action possibilities—became a pillar of Ecological Dynamics in sports science.

- "Jia Yi Chow… Nonlinear Pedagogy": Chow, Jia Yi, Keith Davids, Chris Button, and Ian Renshaw. *Nonlinear Pedagogy in Skill Acquisition: An Introduction.* Routledge, 2016. (pg. )
- "Wolfgang Schöllhorn… Differential Learning": Schöllhorn quotes from the 2015 Kisakallio conference. Author was present.
- "Jean Côté": Côté, Jean, "The Influence of the Family in the Development of Talent in Sport," *The Sport Psychologist* 13, no. 4 (1999): 395–417. See also Côté, Jean, Joseph Baker, and Bruce Abernethy, "Practice and Play in the Development of Sport Expertise," in K. Anders Ericsson et al., eds., *The Cambridge Handbook of Expertise and Expert Performance.* Cambridge University Press, 2006, 184–202.
- "David Epstein picked up on this in his book Range": Epstein, David. *Range: Why Generalists Triumph in a Specialized World.* Riverhead, 2019.
- "Rob Gray, a baseball researcher": Gray, Rob, "Comparing Cueing and Constraints Interventions for Increasing Launch Angle in Baseball Batting," *Sport, Exercise, and Performance Psychology* 7, no. 3 (August 2018): 318–332. Gray is Professor of Human Systems Engineering at Arizona State University.
- "Keith Davids": Keith Davids, Professor of Motor Learning at Sheffield Hallam University. See: Davids, Keith and Chris Button, and Simon Bennett. *Dynamics of Skill Acquisition.* Human Kinetics, 2008.
- "Ginés Meléndez and Gérard Houllier on long-term development": Ginés Meléndez Sotos served as Technical Director of the Royal Spanish Football Federation (RFEF) from 2011 to 2018. Both quotes are from author's notes, SoccerEx Rio de Janeiro, 2012.

## Chapter 13: The Proof

- "Q1 (Jan–Mar): Forty percent. Q4 (Oct–Dec): Ten percent": The Relative Age Effect in youth soccer is well documented. See: Helsen, Werner F., Jan Van Winckel, and A. Mark Williams, "The Relative Age Effect in Youth Soccer Across Europe," *Journal of Sports Sciences* 23, no. 6 (2005): 629–636; and: Cobley, Stephen, et al., "Annual Age-Grouping and Athlete Development: A Meta-Analytical Review of Relative Age Effects in Sport," *Sports Medicine* 39, no. 3 (2009): 235–256. Figures are representative; exact percentages vary by country, sport, and age group.
- "A 2020 study of FC Barcelona's male football academy": Doncaster, Greg, Jorge Medina, Adam Drobnic, Brendan R. Gough, and Vasco Unnithan, "Appreciating Factors Beyond the Physical in Talent Identification and Development: Insights From the FC Barcelona Sporting Model," *Frontiers in Sports and Active Living* 2 (2020): 91. The cited distribution across Barcelona's academy youth groups (Q1 = fifty-three percent, Q2 = twenty-seven percent, Q3 = fourteen percent, Q4 = six percent) was statistically significant at $p < 0.001$.
- "A study of Canadian NHL players … Only seventeen percent of All-Stars were first-quarter births": On the Reverse Relative Age Effect among NHL elite players, see: Gibbs, Benjamin G., Jonathan A. Jarvis, and Mikaela J. Dufur, "The Rise of the Underdog? The Relative Age Effect Reversal Among Canadian-Born NHL Hockey Players: A Reply to Nolan and Howell," *International Review for the Sociology of Sport* 47, no. 5 (2012): 644–649. See also: Fumarco, Luca, et al., "The Relative Age Effect Reversal Among the National Hockey League Elite," *PLoS ONE* 12, no. 8 (2017), https://doi.org/10.1371/journal.pone.0182827.
- "The 2026 US roster … forty-three percent of the team was born in the last quarter of the year": Author's analysis of

the twenty-five player 2026 U.S. Olympic Men's Ice Hockey roster announced by USA Hockey on January 2, 2026. Birth dates retrieved from NHL.com player profiles. The United States defeated Canada two to one in overtime in the gold-medal game, February 22, 2026, at PalaItalia in Milan—the first U.S. men's Olympic ice hockey gold since 1980.

- "The 1962 World Cup rosters show no relative age effect": Author's analysis of birth dates of the rosters of the eight quarterfinalists at the 1962 FIFA World Cup in Chile. The historical-versus-modern comparison is offered as a directional finding. See: Helsen, Werner, Jan Van Winckel, and Andrew Mark Williams, "The relative age effect in youth soccer across Europe," *Journal of Sports Sciences* 23, no. 6 (2005): 629-636.
- "Mateo Kovačić": Based on the author's conversations with GNK Dinamo Zagreb academy coaches during their visit to Joy of the People, summer 2014. The 123-to-9 right-foot to left-foot count is the author's analysis of publicly available Kovačić highlight footage.
- "Ford and colleagues": Ford, Paul R., Paul Ward, Nicola J. Hodges, and A. Mark Williams, "The Role of Deliberate Practice and Play in Career Progression in Sport: The Early Engagement Hypothesis," *High Ability Studies* 20, no. 1 (2009): 65–75.
- "Güllich et al. found that self-directed play in childhood was the strongest single predictor": Güllich, Arne, Brooke N. Macnamara, and David Z. Hambrick, "What Makes a Champion? Early Multidisciplinary Practice, Not Early Specialization, Predicts World-Class Performance," *Perspectives on Psychological Science* 17, no. 1 (2022): 6–29. See also: Güllich, Arne, "International Medallists' and Non-Medallists' Developmental Sport Activities—A Matched-Pairs Analysis," *Journal of Sports Sciences* 35, no. 23 (2017): 2281–2288.

- "American girls playing year-round soccer have greater than a one-in-six chance of tearing their ACL": For more on ACL injury rates in female youth soccer, see: Prodromos, Chadwick C., et al., "A Meta-Analysis of the Incidence of Anterior Cruciate Ligament Tears as a Function of Gender, Sport, and a Knee Injury–Reduction Regimen," *Arthroscopy* 23, no. 12 (2007): 1320–1325. See also: LaBella, Cynthia R., et al., "Anterior Cruciate Ligament Injuries: Diagnosis, Treatment, and Prevention," *Pediatrics* 133, no. 5 (2014): e1437–e1450; and: Beck, Nicholas A., et al., "ACL Tears in School-Aged Children and Adolescents over 20 Years," *Pediatrics* 139, no. 3 (2017): e20161877.
- "the Constrained Action Hypothesis": See: Wulf, Gabriele, Nancy McNevin, and Charles H. Shea, "The Automaticity of Complex Motor Skill Learning as a Function of Attentional Focus," *Quarterly Journal of Experimental Psychology Section A* 54, no. 4 (2001): 1143–1154; and: Wulf, Gabriele, "Attentional Focus and Motor Learning: A Review of 15 Years," *International Review of Sport and Exercise Psychology* 6, no. 1 (2013): 77–104. The fifty to one hundred millisecond reactive movement window and three hundred to five hundred millisecond conscious processing window are standard estimates from the motor control literature; see also: Schmidt, Richard A., and Timothy D. Lee. *Motor Control and Learning: A Behavioral Emphasis*. Human Kinetics, 5th ed., 2011.
- "A meta-analysis in the American Journal of Sports Medicine found neuromuscular training before age fourteen reduced ACL injury risk by seventy-two percent": See: Sugimoto, Dai, et al., "Critical Components of Neuromuscular Training to Reduce Risk of Anterior Cruciate Ligament Injury in Female Athletes: Meta-Regression Analysis," *British Journal of Sports Medicine* 50, no. 20 (2016): 1259–1266; and related work by Myer, Gregory D., et al., "When

to Initiate Integrative Neuromuscular Training to Reduce Sports-Related Injuries and Enhance Health in Youth?" *Current Sports Medicine Reports* 10, no. 3 (2011): 155–166. The age fourteen window is well documented across the neuromuscular training literature.

- "Elinor Ostrom": Ostrom, Elinor. *Governing the Commons: The Evolution of Institutions for Collective Action.* Cambridge University Press, 1990. Ostrom was awarded the Nobel Memorial Prize in Economic Sciences in 2009 "for her analysis of economic governance, especially the commons."
- "England's EPPP delivers up to 10,000 contact hours": The Elite Player Performance Plan was introduced by the English Premier League in 2011 and implemented in 2012. The 10,000-hour figure represents the upper range of contact time across a Category One academy career. See: Premier League, *Elite Player Performance Plan,* 2011; and Calvin, Michael. *No Hunger in Paradise: How to Save Football.* (Century, 2017).
- "Ninety-one percent of the 12,000 boys inside England's academy system will be released": See Calvin, Michael. *No Hunger in Paradise: How to Save Football.* Century, 2017. Figures are widely cited in English football media.

## Chapter 14: The Underload Index

- "the United States covered more total distance per match than any other team in the tournament": FIFA Training Centre, "Setting the Benchmark, Part 1: Distances Teams Covered." Analysis of FIFA World Cup Qatar 2022, with data normalized for ninety or more minutes (excluding goalkeepers and extra time). Per FIFA's official analysis, the top five ranked teams for total distance per match were the United States, IR Iran, Australia, Canada, and Serbia; the United States ranked first in total distance, high-intensity distance, and sprint distance. Peer-reviewed publication of the same data appears in: Serner, Andreas, et al., "Time-loss Injuries and Illnesses at the FIFA World Cup 2022," *Science and Medicine in Football* 9, no. 3 (2025).

- "keepers dive left or right ninety-four percent of the time": Bar-Eli, Michael, Ofer H. Azar, Ilana Ritov, Yael Keidar-Levin, and Galit Schein, "Action Bias Among Elite Soccer Goalkeepers: The Case of Penalty Kicks," *Journal of Economic Psychology* 28, no. 5 (October 2007): 606–621. The 94 percent figure derives from the study's finding that goalkeepers stayed in the center in only 6.3 percent of penalty kicks.
- "Israeli researchers studied 286 penalty kicks": Bar-Eli et al., "Action Bias," (2007). The original sample comprised 311 penalty kicks; 286 were retained for the main analysis after excluding kicks that did not reach the goal frame. The chapter's figure refers to the analysed subsample.
- "Central shots convert at eighty-seven percent—higher than corners at eighty-three percent": Penalty kick conversion data drawn from ongoing analytics published by Opta and StatsBomb.
- "Zidane against Buffon, World Cup 2006": France vs. Italy, 2006 FIFA World Cup final, Olympiastadion, Berlin, July 9, 2006. Zinedine Zidane scored a Panenka chip past Italian goalkeeper Gianluigi Buffon in the seventh minute. The match ended 1–1; Italy won 5–3 on penalties.
- "UI = Goals - xGOT": The Underload Index is the author's original framework. It has not been independently validated or published in peer-reviewed literature. The formula is proposed as a testable hypothesis. The metric works most cleanly on penalty kicks because the variables are isolated; extension to open play requires further development. xGOT (Expected Goals on Target) is an established analytics metric; see Opta and StatsBomb published methodology.

- "Youth sports in America is a forty-billion-dollar industry": The $40 billion figure for the United States youth sports industry has been widely cited and refined across multiple sources. See: Aspen Institute, Project Play, *State of Play* annual reports (2018–2024); and Wintergreen Research market analyses. Estimates of the size of the youth-sports economy vary; the figure is intended as illustrative rather than precise.
- "KC Airbnb pricing during the World Cup": Author's personal experience renting short-term accommodations in Kansas City, comparing standard weekly rates to FIFA World Cup 2026 pricing. The 2026 FIFA World Cup, hosted across the United States, Mexico, and Canada, from June 11 to July 19, 2026; Kansas City's Arrowhead Stadium is one of eleven U.S. host venues.

## Chapter 15: The Monarch Rules

- "three thousand miles to Mexico": Eastern monarch migration distance is approximately two thousand to three thousand miles from the northern United States and southern Canada to overwintering sites in central Mexico. Three thousand miles is at the upper end for monarchs originating in Minnesota. See Xerces Society for Invertebrate Conservation publications on monarch migration ecology.
- "The philosopher Ludwig Wittgenstein argued that there is no private language": Wittgenstein. *Philosophical Investigations.* 1953.
- "Linguists talk about critical windows": The Critical Period Hypothesis was proposed by Eric Lenneberg in *Biological Foundations of Language*. Wiley, 1967. See also: Johnson, Jacqueline S., and Elissa L. Newport, "Critical Period Effects in Second Language Learning: The Influence of Maturational State on the Acquisition of English as a Second Language," *Cognitive Psychology* 21, no. 1 (1989): 60–99.

- "Roughly ages five to twelve seem to be the critical period for physical fluency": The application of the critical period concept to motor skill acquisition is the author's framework, drawing on parallels to language acquisition. A precisely defined critical period for motor fluency analogous to Lenneberg's linguistic window has not been established in the peer-reviewed motor learning literature. For background on motor skill development across childhood, see: Gallahue, David L., John C. Ozmun, and Jacqueline D. Goodway. *Understanding Motor Development: Infants, Children, Adolescents, Adults*, 8th ed. McGraw-Hill, 2019.; and: Branta, Crystal, John Haubenstricker, and Vern Seefeldt, "Age Changes in Motor Skills During Childhood and Adolescence," *Exercise and Sport Sciences Reviews* 12 (1984): 467–520.
- "Phil led Division II in scoring. Conference MVP. National Player of the Year finalist": Phil's collegiate statistics, St. Cloud State University, NCAA Division II men's soccer.

## Chapter 16: The Environment

- "Charles Goodhart was a British economist": Goodhart, Charles. "Problems of Monetary Management: The U.K. Experience." In Anthony S. Courakis, ed., *Inflation, Depression, and Economic Policy in the West.* Rowman & Littlefield, 1981. The popular formulation—"When a measure becomes a target, it ceases to be a good measure"—is Marilyn Strathern's generalization of Goodhart's original, more technical observation about monetary indicators.
- "Montessori said play is the work of the child": Widely attributed to Maria Montessori (1870–1952). See: Montessori, Maria. *The Absorbent Mind.* translated by Claude A. Claremont. Holt, 1967. Montessori's published works emphasize self-directed activity as the child's primary developmental work.

- "Researchers studying play in rats found something interesting": Pellis, Sergio M., and Vivien C. Pellis. *The Playful Brain: Venturing to the Limits of Neuroscience.* Oneworld, 2009. Research on play fighting in rats shows that dominant animals self-handicap, allowing subordinate partners to win approximately thirty percent of encounters.
- "Vanuatu is the most language-dense nation on Earth": Vanuatu is recognized by linguists as having the highest language density per capita in the world, with approximately 110 to 130 indigenous languages spoken among a population of roughly three hundred thousand. The exact count varies by classification methodology. See: Crowley, Terry. *An Introduction to Historical Linguistics.* Oxford University Press, 1997.
- "They have a cultural practice called Kastom": *Kastom* (from English "custom") refers to the traditional governance and social practices of ni-Vanuatu communities. See: Lindstrom, Lamont. *Knowledge and Power in a South Pacific Society.* Smithsonian Institution Press, 1990.; and: Bolton, Lissant. *Unfolding the Moon: Enacting Women's Kastom in Vanuatu.* University of Hawai'i Press, 2003.
- "'He skates like a Ranger, eh'": *Ranger* is Iron Range vernacular for someone from northern Minnesota's Iron Range—the iron-mining region encompassing the Mesabi, Vermilion, and Cuyuna ranges. The Iron Range's Scandinavian and Canadian linguistic influence (including the characteristic "eh") gives the area a distinct local vocabulary. The region has produced a disproportionate number of NHL and Olympic hockey players relative to its population.

## Chapter 17: The Game

- "Henry Boucha—a tall, powerfully built Ojibwe forward": Henry Boucha (born 1951), member of the White Earth

Nation (Ojibwe), hockey player from Warroad, Minnesota. Won silver with Team USA at the 1972 Sapporo Winter Olympics; played in the National Hockey League. Inducted into the United States Hockey Hall of Fame in 1995. See: Boucha, Henry, with Tony Pluta. *Boucha: Star on Ice.* Beaver's Pond Press, 2013.

- "Herb Brooks was asked, 'What can Boucha do with the puck?' 'He can make it talk'": Attributed to Herb Brooks. Part of Minnesota hockey lore. See: Gilbert, John. *Herb Brooks: The Inside Story of a Hockey Mastermind.* MVP Books, 2008.
- "In overtime, Edina finally wore them down. They won 5–4": 1969 Minnesota State High School League Boys Ice Hockey Tournament championship game. Edina High School defeated Warroad High School 5–4 in overtime. See MSHSL historical records.
- "Edina has won fourteen state titles": As of the 2024 season, Edina has won fourteen Minnesota State High School League boys hockey championships (eleven as Edina, three as Edina East), the most in state history. See MSHSL historical records.
- "Warroad—population 1,500—has produced seven Olympians": Warroad, Minnesota, has produced a remarkable number of Olympic hockey players relative to its population, earning the city the informal designation "Hockeytown USA." Olympians associated with Warroad include Henry Boucha (1972 silver), Dave Christian (1980 gold), Gigi Marvin (multiple Olympic appearances for the U.S. women's team), and others. The chapter's population figure is consistent with Warroad's population across recent decades; the 2020 Census recorded approximately 1,800 residents.
- "Pep Guardiola said it best": Widely attributed to Pep Guardiola. See: Perarnau, Martí. *Pep Confidential: Inside*

*Pep Guardiola's First Season at Bayern Munich.* Arena Sport, 2014.; and: Balagué, Guillem. *Pep Guardiola: Another Way of Winning.* Orion, 2012.

- "Z was first team all-state and a Mr. Soccer finalist": Minnesota high school boys soccer records.
- "'My dad was never disappointed in me,' he told them": Zinedine Kroeten, in an interview with the *Minnesota Star Tribune*, October 8, 2018.
- "The number one ranked team in the National Premier Soccer League. Undefeated, 11–0": River City FC's 2021 NPSL season record at the time of the match against Joy AC. NPSL standings, July 2021.

# About the Author

Ted Kroeten is the co-founder and Artistic Director of Joy of the People, a play-based soccer and futsal program in St. Paul, Minnesota that has served thousands of children since 2009. Co-founded with Glenn Kroeten, Raffi Tanachian, Franklin Tawah, Victor Kasanezky, Haris Handzija and Colleen Kroeten, the program has produced two national futsal championships, professional players, and a community of kids who love the game. A former Director of Coaching in the Minnesota youth soccer system, Kroeten captained the Minnesota state select team and played for the Minnesota Thunder. He has spent two decades investigating talent development, visiting elite academies in Porto, Split, Belgrade and Asunción, futsal courts in Colombia and Brazil, and research conferences in Finland, England and Germany. Kroeten studied under linguist Stephen Krashen at USC in the late 1970s—an experience that would later transform his understanding of how skills are acquired. He also coaches high school soccer at Minneapolis Edison. He lives in St. Louis Park, Minnesota, with his wife Colleen and their two dogs. Their daughter Dare represented the United States on the Youth National Futsal team in Buenos Aires and Madrid. Their son Z's journey from dandelion-picker to game-winner is at the heart of *The Talent Thief*.

www.ingramcontent.com/pod-product-compliance
Lightning Source LLC
LaVergne TN
LVHW010641110826
845149LV00014B/2915